THE ARMENIANS
THEIR HISTORY & CULTURE

THE ARMENIANS
THEIR HISTORY & CULTURE
ARA BALIOZIAN

AGBU ARARAT PRESS

THE ARMENIANS. Copyright © 1980 by Ara Baliozian. All rights reserved. Printed in the United States of America. No part of this book may be used or reproduced in any manner whatsoever without written permission of the publisher, except for brief quotations embodied in articles and reviews. Published by AGBU Ararat Press, 585 Saddle River Rd., Saddle Brook, N.J.07662
1/201/797/7600
Reprinted, 1985
Library of Congress Cataloging in Publication Data

Baliozian, Ara.
The Armenians.
Includes index.
1. Armenians. I. Title.
DS165. B27 1980 956.6'2 80-19619
ISBN 0-933706-21-9
ISBN 0-933706-22-7 (pbk.)

To My Mother

The world is an immense groping,
an immense search,
an immense attack;
it can only progress
at the cost of many failures
and many casualties.
The sufferers,
whatever the nature of their suffering,
are the reflection of this austere
but noble condition.
They are not useless
and diminished elements.
They are merely those
who pay the price of universal
progress and triumph.
They are the ones who have fallen
on the field of honor.

Teilhard de Chardin

Contents

Introduction — xi

Preface to the Second Edition — xv

HISTORY — 3

RELIGION — 29

LANGUAGE — 37

LITERATURE — 43

MUSIC — 134

ART & ARCHITECTURE — 144

CINEMA — 159

SCIENCE & TECHNOLOGY — 165

CUISINE — 171

NATIONAL CHARACTERISTICS — 174

Index — 179

Introduction

Eskimos, it has been said, are better known to the world at large than Armenians. Every Armenian will tell you that at one time or another he has been mistaken for an Aramaean or Roumanian. "Armenian?" a well-known Canadian writer said to me recently. "To be frank I don't know much about them. But I do remember as a child my mother telling me that I should think of the hungry Armenians." *I am as hungry as an Armenian!* a *salaud* once declared in my presence pretending ignorance of my background.

This simplistic cliche of Armenians as victims of the Turkish massacres and deportations of 1915 has been no doubt reinforced by many books, reminiscences, and eyewitness accounts published during and after World War I. In point of fact, the majority of books about Armenians, certainly the most widely read and admired—from Franz Werfel's *Forty Days of Musa Dagh* (1933) to Michael J. Arlen's *Passage to Ararat* (1975)—emphasize the Genocide. As Puzant Granian, an Armenian author of the diaspora put it recently, Armenians, it seems, are destined to go down in history as a nation whose sole contribution consists of a million and a half victims to the holocaust of 1915.

In 1916, the eminent Italian Marxist philosopher and political activist Antonio Gramsci (1891-1937), expressed an awareness of this when he urged Armenians to make themselves better known by speaking and writing more about their culture, poetry, and language. Everyone, said Gramsci, has heard about the massacres, but very few know anything about Armenians as living people, and it is difficult to concern oneself with individuals that "fail to conjure up images of real human beings."

The process whereby understanding and sympathy are preceded by some form of human contact is illustrated beautifully though somewhat perversely by the British historian Arnold J. Toynbee. In one of his autobiographical books, Toynbee tells us that after writing a number of books on the Armenian massacres he "was not only haunted by the victims' sufferings" but also "by the criminals' deeds"; and that in order to answer the question: "How it could be possible for human beings to do what those perpetrators of genocide had done?" he began to study the Turkish language and in the process acquired Turkish friends. Toynbee goes on to say that he was surprised to discover that Turks were human beings after all and that Armenians themselves had not been as blameless as he had, in his ignorance and youthful zeal, portrayed them to be in his books.[1]

If it is true that well-adjusted, happy people have a natural tendency to ignore the anguished cry of victims out of a need to defend a comforting view of life, it must also be true that historians and philosophers have an analogous need to *understand* and *explain* evil; and if, in the process, they *explain* it *away,* and to some extent perhaps even justify it, so much the better. Who likes to see anyone getting away with murder—unless of course his victim deserved everything he got. This is how history is revised and victims are held responsible for atrocities committed against them.[2]

Toynbee's case however is far from unique. The Genocide has found apologists not only among Turcophile historians but among Armenians as well. A familiar phenomenon of the diaspora is the Armenian who out of a morbid, self-destructive impulse will "explain" the Genocide by placing part or all of the blame on Armenian extremists and political activists.[3] Such an Armenian, as a rule, has no interest in his own past, in the history and culture of his people; he has more often than not changed his name to hide his ethnic background as if it were a dark secret. In his *Passage to Ararat*, Michael J. Arlen writes that until he reached manhood, he knew little or nothing about Armenians, and that as a child he was warned by his father, the best-selling novelist Michael Arlen (Kouyoumdjian), to stay away from them because they dwell too much on unpleasant events of the past (in Arlen's words: "Armenian problems. ... starving Armenians... distant and repellent events"). "They are sweet people, but you can't let them get too close," Arlen *fils* quotes Arlen *pere*. "They end up boring you to death."

But as Arlen himself demonstrates in his *Passage*, a genocide is a national trauma that cannot be forgotten or ignored forever. Sooner or later it must be remembered, relived, and shared. And most Armenians were indeed grateful to Arlen for sharing their trauma and for reminding the world of a genocide that has variously been called "unremembered" (Housepian), "almost forgotten" (Manvell/Fraenkel) and "forgotten" (Boyajian). But many Armenians were also disappointed, even offended, by the final pages of *Passage* where, after questioning the existence of an "Armenian culture" (in his own words: "One hears of 'Armenian culture'—at least, from Armenians—but it is surely not that"), Arlen urges his compatriots to transcend their narrow nationalism because it was from that type of "madness and pride" that Armenians themselves "have suffered as much as any people." He then goes on to speak about what he dismissed as the "dreadful tangle" of Armenian dreams.

Gostan Zarian, a contemporary of Arlen *pere*, was another writer who spoke about Armenian dreams. Like Arlen *fils*, Zarian discovered his Armenian identity only after he reached manhood. But unlike Arlen, Zarian went on to study the Armenian language and eventually produced some of the most masterful prose and verse in recent Armenian literature (*see* LITERATURE). "An empty dream? An illusion?" Zarian writes in a famous passage. "Then let it be a dream so long as it's *our* dream. Let it be a mistake, so long as it's *our* mistake. Because you must always consider the possibility that tomorrow you may suddenly wake up with the certainty that yours too was a dream and *someone else's* dream; yours too was a mistake and *someone else's* mistake."

Like any other nation on earth, Armenians have had their share of dreams, defeats, and tragedies; but having "paid the price" in Teilhard de Chardin's words, they have made and continue to make contributions to "universal progress and triumph." In the book that follows I propose to discuss some of these contributions.

[1] See Arnold J. Toynbee, "Some Turkish Friends," in *Acquaintances* (London, 1967). The relevant passages read: "When one becomes personally acquainted with a fellow human being, of whatever religion, nationality, or race, one cannot fail to recognize that he is human like oneself." And: "Since the Russo-Turkish War of 1877-8, the Armenian diaspora in the northeastern territories of the Ottoman Empire had been nursing political ambitions. Like the Greek diaspora farther to the west in Anatolia, the Armenians had been hoping to be able, one day, to carve out a successor-state. These Greek and Armenian political aspirations had not been legitimate."

[2] In this connection see Richard G. Hovannisian, "Rewriting History: Revisionism and Beyond in the Study of Armenian-Turkish Relations," in *Ararat* (Summer 1978).

[3] It is often forgotten not only by laymen but by historians who have followed developments in the Middle East from a ringside seat that in the Ottoman context, Armenian nationalism meant much more than vague aspirations for national autonomy. It meant a struggle for fundamental human rights and social justice—concepts so alien to the Ottoman bureaucracy that it could respond only by wholesale massacres.

Preface to the Second Edition

Conceived and written in the winter of 1974/75 and published on the occasion of the 60th anniversary of the Genocide, the first edition of this book was more or less an improvised piece of work written in a little over two months. Though it contained separate chapters on literature, music, language, art and architecture, it emphasized history rather than culture. In the present revised edition the emphasis is on culture. The original 32 pages devoted to literature, for instance, have now been expanded to nearly a hundred. Even so, this chapter, like the others, is far from comprehensive. I have refrained from dwelling on (and sometimes even mentioning) not only peripheral figures but important ones as well. Those selected for discussion and evaluation however may claim to be the most representative.

Nearly all the books listed at the end of each chapter are in English and may be obtained from the Diocese of the Armenian Church of America, 630 Second Ave., New York, N.Y. 10016; the National Association for Armenian Studies and Research, Book Department, 175 Mt. Auburn St., Cambridge, Mass. 02138; or wherever Armenian-interest books are sold.

The transliteration of Armenian names follows no particular system except that of common sense and practicality. Established variants are sometimes given in brackets. The use of the Julian calendar in some reference works may explain the discrepancy of certain dates.

Of the various libraries I have used I want particularly to thank the Kitchener Public Library and the University of Waterloo Library. Thanks are also due to the Canada Council for its financial support of the initial work.

Ara Baliozian
Kitchener, Ontario
May 5, 1980

THE ARMENIANS
THEIR HISTORY & CULTURE

History

Armenian history goes back 5000 years—a historical span about, twenty-five times that of the United States of America. Movses Khorenatsi,[1] a 5th-century historian, traces Armenian origins back to Noah, and even Adam. One traditional site of the Garden of Eden[2] is in Armenia, and the four rivers mentioned in Genesis as rising in the Garden still flow through the Armenian land.

Armenians call themselves Hai (pronounced *high*) and their country Hayastan after Haik, a legendary archer, grandson of Japhet who was son of Noah (Genesis 10:1) whose Ark came to rest on Mount Ararat (Massis) at the end of the Flood (Genesis 8:4)[3]. It was Haik, according to Khorenatsi, who led his people from the tyranny of Pel (Belus) in the plain of Shinar (Mesopotamia), to the cold but free mountains of Armenia. And when Pel invaded Armenia, threatening to bury under the arrows of his multitudes Haik's small but brave army, Haik marched forth to meet him halfway. The first shock was so terrible and costly in men that Pel, confused and frightened, began to withdraw. But Haik's unerring arrow pierced his breast and killed him. Whereupon Pel's mighty forces fled in disorder.[4]

For many years, scholars believed that Khorenatsi, in an effort to preserve all he could, may have included in his *History* many legends which have little or nothing to do with historical reality. Recent archaeological discoveries on the plains of Ararat however, have enhanced his credibility. An impressive piece of evidence turned up in 1956. Bronze arrowheads of a peculiar design—three-winged, with rhomboid cuts in the arms—at first thought to have been of Scythian origin, are now believed to have belonged to the local population. Their location, quantity, and concentration are proof of the accuracy of this conclusion, another being a description supplied by Khorenatsi who tells us it was with this type of arrowhead that Haik killed Pel.[5]

"The Armenians are perhaps the oldest established of the civilized races in Western Asia," writes Arnold J. Toynbee. N. Mikhailov, a contemporary Soviet scholar, calls Armenia "the oldest state to have existed on the territory of the Soviet Union and one of the most ancient in the world."

It is now known that since time immemorial man has been present in the mountainous region between the Caspian, the Mediterranean, and the Black Seas, which during the first millenium B.C. came to be known as the Empire of Urartu (Ararat in Hebrew). Urartians themselves are sometimes identified as descendants of the Hurrians, who had a powerful kingdom in the second millenium B.C. and exerted considerable influence on the Hittites of Anatolia. It was from Hurrians that the Hittites took over most of their mythology and transmitted some stories to Greece.

A Persian legend refers to Mount Ararat (which, with Lake Van, is now within the eastern borders of Turkey, but was for a very long time in the heart of Armenia) as the cradle of the human race. According to another legend, Armenians were the first race of men to appear in the world after the Deluge. In the *Aeneid,* Virgil locates the cradle of Rome in Asia Minor.

Archaeological discoveries are still being made in Armenia—many remains going to a very ancient civilization, and some as far back as Early Stone Age. The country is rich in ancient megalithic structures: dolmens (tombs), great upright monoliths, cyclopean walls, and labyrinths.

It was here that 8,000 years ago man learned to cultivate food-plants, including grapevines (Genesis 9:20-21), and to domesticate animals—activities that changed his mode of living from that of a hunter/brigand to a farmer/craftsman, which in its turn allowed him to develop a civilization. It is also here that man first discovered metals and worked them into tools and weapons. The region is rich in mineral resources, especially metal ores—a fact well known to the Sumerians, the Greeks, and the Assyrians. Both Mesopotamia and Greece are seriously deficient in copper and tin (for weapons and tools), and the precious metals (for jewelry and as mediums of exchange). Sumerian tablets of the 3rd millenium B.C. speak of many military expeditions to Armenia the purpose of which was to provide these metals rather than to acquire territory. The Greek legend of the Golden Fleece echoes these Sumerian raids. Scholars now agree that the legendary quest of the Golden Fleece by Jason and his band of Argonauts reflects historical and economic reality, namely the search for mineral wealth in the Caucasian isthmus by Greek pirates. Likewise, the emphasis on bronze and iron in the booty lists of the Assyrian emperors suggests that the main purpose of Assyrian warfare was to acquire these metals.

Techniques of metalworking were probably introduced into Egypt by migrant groups from the Caucasus. Writes Carl Roebuck:

> *The early settlers of Egypt were short, slender people, fine-boned and delicate-featured, who are identified as native to Africa and who are called Hamites. Their physical characteristics appear still among the Berbers and in southern Egypt. About 3600 B.C. people of a different physical type appeared in Egypt, stockier, broad-faced and heavy in appearance. These were probably Armenoids who came in small groups from Syria and Palestine. Possibly they brought the knowledge of metal-*

working with them, for after 3600 B.C. the static agricultural communities began to grow and Egypt moved towards civilization.[6]

It is still not clear why they are called Armenians. The name first occurs in the Behistun inscription, which dates from the 6th century B.C. Cut on an almost inaccessible rock 500 feet above the road at Behistun, in Iran, and thus designed to impress the passerby by its setting, this great cuneiform inscription has been described as a combination of official autobiography and imperial manifesto. In it, Darius the Great (reigned 521-486 B.C.) defends in three languages (Old Persian, Assyrian, and Elamite) the murder of a rival claimant to the Achaemenid throne, recounts his genealogy, and enumerates his many wars and victories in which Armenia ("Armina" or Armaniya") is mentioned for the first time. Some have suggested that it may be a confusion with Aramaea—a kingdom in northern Syria. But since, after a difficult and bloody war that lasted more than a year, Darius did in fact annex Armenia to the Persian Empire, it may refer to the country of the Armens.

Who were these Armens that by the 6th century B.C. had already dominated and assimilated the native Urartians?

Hittite records end abruptly soon after 1200 B.C. But Egyptian records from this period speak of a mysterious "People of the Sea" from the west, probably the Balkans, who overwhelmed and destroyed the Hittite Empire, Cilicia, the Syrian coasts and the approaches of Egypt. Pharaoh Rameses III (1198-1167 B.C.) records: "But no country resisted them, beginning with the Hittites" —who had been Egypt's most formidable enemies. Some scholars now agree that these "People of the Sea" were probably the Armens who advanced as far as Armenia and settled there, eventually assimilating the native population. The racial term Armenoid coined by the German physical anthropologist Felix von Luschan (1854-1924) is sometimes used to describe a type that extends from the Alps to the Caucasus, and includes among its ancient representatives Hurrians, Hittites, and Assyrians, and among its modern representatives Jews and Kurds.

Assyrian cuneiform inscriptions of the second and first millenium B.C. speak of many conflicts with the kings of Urartu. "They [the

Urartians] fled to the impregnable mountains," reads one such inscription,

> so that I might not be able to get at them, for the mighty summits were like drawn swords pointing to the skies. Only the birds of heaven soaring on their wings could reach them. In three days I was there, spreading terror in places where they had taken refuge. Their corpses, like autumn leaves, filled the clefts. The rest escaped to distant inaccessible heights.

The word "enigmatic" is often used by historians in reference to Urartu. For, compared with their Assyrian colleagues, Urartian scribes were the soul of brevity. The records they left often consist of bare catalogues with little or no narrative. Consequently, our knowledge of Urartian history is based mainly on Assyrian records, which admit of no defeats. "Assyrian scribes," remarks Will Durant, "were more royalist than the king." More likely their work was closely supervised and censored. It would be safe therefore to assume that the status of an Assyrian scribe was similar to that of a modern typist in the Ministry of Information (i.e. Propaganda) of a totalitarian regime. The boastful account above, translated into a more objective language, would probably read something like this:

> As a result of minor skirmishes, one or two key mountain villages held by Urartu were taken, and the Urartian forces dislodged from the area in which they menaced Assyrian security.[7]

"Militarily," writes Toynbee, "Urartu was the most effective as well as the most resolute, of all Assyria's opponents in the last millenium B.C." And: "The Assyrian Empire never succeeded in conquering the rival Empire of Urartu."[8]

According to Khorenatsi, one of Haik's descendants, King Aram (9th century B.C.), collected an army of 50,000 and subdued Barsham, King of Assyria. Corresponding Assyrian records speak of the Assyrian King Shalmaneser III (reigned 858-824 B.C.) who fought and overcame an Urartian king named Arramu.

Aram's successor was King Ara ("the Beautiful") (who may be the legendary King Er, son of Armenius in Plato's *Republic*) with whom Semiramis (also Shamiram or Sammu-ramat)—"that wanton and lustful woman" (Khorenatsi)—fell so violently in love that she conducted a military campaign against him in order to satisfy her lust. Semiramis sent messages, writes Khorenatsi, "with gifts and offerings, with many prayers and promises, begging Ara to come to her and to either wed her or fulfill her desires." When diplomacy failed to work, she resorted to military action:

> *Whereupon she arose and took all the multitude of her hosts and hastened to the land of Armenia, not so much to kill him as to subdue him and bring him by force to satisfy the desires of her passion . . . . After the battle the Queen sent out to the battlefield to search for the body of her beloved amongst those who had died. And they found the body of Ara amongst the brave ones that had fallen, and she commanded them to place it in an upper chamber in her castle.*

This may indeed be a mythical episode, for the evidence unearthed and deciphered so far indicates that Assyrian military power during Semiramis's regency (810-806 B.C.) was in decline, and Assyrian foreign policy isolationist. While the Urartians under the dynasty founded by Sarduri I (reigned ca. 840-830 B.C.), which was to last 2½ centuries, extended their frontiers reaching within 20 miles of Halap (Aleppo) in Syria. This wave of expansion was somewhat slowed down by Tiglathpileser III of Assyria (reigned 744-727 B.C.), the real founder of the Assyrian Empire, and finally checked by his successor Sargon II (reigned 725-705 B.C.).[9]

In 707 B.C. Urartu was overrun by a horde of nomads from southern Russia, the Cimmerians. King Rusas I is reported to have killed himself in despair when his capital fell. Intent on plunder and destruction rather than settlement, the warlike Cimmerians went on to ravage the neighboring kingdom of Phrygia whose ruler, Midas by name (a foolish and greedy man whose touch, according to a Greek legend, turned objects to gold—the fulfillment of a wish that nearly starved him to death) is also said to have committed suicide by drinking bull's blood (696 B.C.). Finally, with Assyrian help, the Lydians put an end to the Cimmerian orgy. The encounter must have been so costly that both Lydians and Cimmerians dropped from history shortly thereafter.[10]

After the Cimmerian devastation, Urartu seems to have gone through a period of renascence. Urartian inscriptions of this period have been found near the Black and Caspian Seas, also in present-day Iran—evidence that Urartu may have even extended its borders. After Rusas I, we have the names of several Urartian kings who reigned during this peaceful interlude that lasted a century: Argishti II (712-685), Rusas II (685-645), Sarduri III (644-640), then Sarduri IV, Erimena, and Rusas III.

Between 612 and 609 B.C. the empire was attacked on three fronts by Babylonians, Medes, and Scythians. Like the Cimmerians, the Scythians came from the north. They were ferocious, bearded giants who rode bareback on wild horses, drank the blood of their enemies, destroyed and killed everything and everyone in their path. They advanced as far as Egypt where they were suddenly decimated by a mysterious disease, after which they were overcome by the Medes and driven back to Russia. There is some evidence suggesting that Urartu may have survived even this second catastrophe and continued to exist as an independent state as late as 593 B.C. (Jeremiah 51:27).

As we have seen in the Behistun inscription, in the 6th century B.C., Armenia with a few other countries—among them Egypt, Palestine, Assyria, Babylonia, and Ionia—became a satrapy of Persia—two satrapies to be exact: Armenia Major and Armenia Minor, one east and the other west of the Euphrates (Yeprad).

Throughout the 5th century B.C., Armenians enjoyed a semi-independent status. With the exception of Xerxes (reigned 486-465 B.C.), whose fleet was destroyed at the battle of Salamis (480 B.C.), the successors of Darius the Great did not share his imperialist ambitions and preferred to eat, drink, intrigue, poison, and assassinate one another. "The decline of Persia," writes Will Durant, "anticipates almost in detail the decline of Rome: immorality and degeneration among the people accompanied violence and negligence on the throne." The culinary arts and related subjects were developed to the detriment of the martial arts. They ate once a day—one meal prolonged from noon to night. The king's harem contained hundreds of concubines. A concubine was not allowed to share the royal couch twice unless she was exceptionally attractive. Although the *Zend Avesta*, the sacred scriptures of the Persians, excoriates sodomy, the Persians, writes Herodotus, had learned from the Greeks "a passion for boys."

When, in 334 B.C., Alexander the Great appeared on the scene with a negligible force of 35,000 troops, Darius III, the last Achaemenid king of Persia, confronted him with two hordes, the first of which numbered 600,000, and the second 1,000,000 men. Both these improvised mobs failed to delay the Macedonian's advance to India and the introduction of Hellenism in Asia Minor. For his incompetence and cowardice, Darius III was murdered by his own men. All Persian territories were annexed to the Macedonian Empire, which proved to be as ephemeral as its successor, the Seleucid Empire.

Even during Alexander's lifetime, the Macedonian Empire began to disintegrate through the maladministration and greed of his officials, some of whom had to be removed and put to death. When in 323 B.C., at the age of 33, Alexander contracted a fever in Babylon and died, he left no successor, only a pregnant wife and a mentally defective half-brother, both of whom were to perish in the so-called Wars of Successors, lasting 50 years. Egypt fell to Ptolemy, whose descendants, the Ptolemies, were to rule the land until the suicide of Cleopatra in 31 B.C., and the Persian Empire fell to Seleucus I, founder of the Seleucid dynasty. The Seleucids were weak and incompetent rulers, given to endless palace intrigues and territorial quarrels. Soon, their hold on the empire relaxed and many subject provinces, Armenia with them, split away and became independent states.

In the 1st century B.C., Armenia under Tigran II the Great (reigned 94-56 B.C.) supplanted the Seleucids as the great power of the Middle East. It is recorded that under Tigran,

> *all men and women wore fine garments of divers colors, richly embroidered, which made the ill-favored to look fair and the beautiful to look like demi-gods. Tigran, the bringer of peace and prosperity, caused all men to grow fat with butter and honey. The splendor of his arms and equipments was enough of itself to drive back the enemy.*

He pacified and annexed Syria, Persia, Mesopotamia, and nearly all of Asia Minor. "He made the Republic of Rome tremble before the prowess of his arms," writes Cicero. When he saw the Roman legions under Lucullus, Tigran is quoted as having said: "If they come as ambassadors, they are too many. If they come as soldiers, they are too few."[11]

After Tigran, Armenia entered again its fatal cycle of invasion, collapse, and renascence. The periods of relative calm were the exception rather than the rule and they occurred whenever, through diplomatic skill, territorial concessions, political compromises, and the payment of bribes and tributes, the Armenians were able to establish a *modus vivendi* with their powerful neighbors—Persians, Parthians, Romans, Byzantines, Arabs, and later Ottomans and Russians. But again and again they had to meet with attacks on all fronts by roaming nomadic tribes like the Turks, the Mongols, and the ubiquitous Kurds. In his *Outline of History*, H.G. Wells maintains that the aim of these Asiatic nomads was to stamp out civilization itself, since they not only burned and massacred, but also destroyed irrigation systems that had endured for thousands of years. It is more likely that they destroyed for the sake of destruction without any consistent policy or long-range plan in mind because, as we shall see, they often slaughtered one another with equal savagery. Remnants of these and many other warlike tribes (Circassians, Chechens, Avars, Dagestanis, Kalmuks, Khevsurs, Lesghians, Mingrelians, Ossets, Svans, Abkhazians) still survive in isolated mountain fastnesses in the Caucasus. Their efforts to subdue and assimilate the fiercely individualistic Armenians lasted as long as their occupying forces did—seldom more than a few ephemeral decades.

Before it became an Arab province in the second half of the 7th century A.D., Armenia was annexed to the Roman Empire, then partitioned between Byzantium and Persia. As a buffer zone between these powerful nations, Armenia became one vast military encampment, often a battleground, and sometimes a slaughterhouse.

In the 6th century, Armenia became the recruiting ground of the Byzantine Empire and "supplied the best warriors," writes Merry Ottin. "Individual Armenians played a particularly significant role in the internal life of Byzantium," says J.M. Hussey. In addition to the famous Narses, who conquered Italy, Procopius mentions 16 Armenian generals in the armies of Justinian. Byzantium owed its victorious campaigns against the Arabs primarily to the skill of such Armenian generals as Petronas, John Curcuas (Ohan Kourken) and

Melias (Mleh) called Melik-al-Armeni by Arab historians. Curcuas and Melias are moreover two prototypes of the great Byzantine epic hero Digenis Akritas (from *akritai*—border fighters, because they waged unceasing war against the Arabs and later the Turks). Extant in several versions, this celebrated Greek epic influenced not only Old Russian and Modern Greek literatures, but also French medieval epic and provided many motifs for Western literature and folklore.[12]

It was also from Armenia that Constantinople drew the sources of its wealth and many of its finest intellects. Writes Steven Runciman: "Armenian influence on Byzantium was probably greater than Byzantine influence on Armenia"; and: "The Armenians provided not only many of Byzantium's most vigorous rulers, but also a large proportion of its best business brains; and they had a large, but still disputed, influence on Byzantine art and craftsmanship."

From the 7th to the 11th century, in addition to many military leaders and diplomats, Armenians provided three powerful imperial dynasties: the Heraclians, the Isaurians, and the Macedonians. Heraclius, founder of the Heraclian dynasty (610-717), Leo III (the Isaurian), founder of the Isaurian dynasty (717-867), and Basil I (the Macedonian), founder of the Macedonian dynasty (867-1081), were all Armenians. Even the usurpers of this period—Romanus I Lecapenus (919-944), Nicephorus Phocas (963-969), and John Tzimisces (969-976)—were Armenians. The so-called Macedonian dynasty—also known as the Sword dynasty, because generals instead of emperors mostly ruled—was in point of fact Armenian. Basil I (the Macedonian), founder of the dynasty, was the descendant of an Armenian family whose home was in Macedonia. From this the dynasty receives its accepted but inexact title.

Byzantine scholars are unanimous in calling Basil I one of the greatest emperors of Byzantium. Oswald Spengler calls him "a Napoleonic figure." Writes Will Durant:

> *He established the longest of all Byzantine dynasties, and began a 19-year reign of excellent administration, legislating wisely, judging justly, replenishing the treasury, and building new churches and palaces.*

Elsewhere we read: "His reign initiated what was probably the most glorious period of Byzantine history."

Named after him, the *Basilica*, a collection of all the laws of the Empire in 60 books, remains, in the words of Hazeltine, "the one really great codification of Graeco-Roman law in the Later Roman Empire after the time of Justinian."

Edward Gibbon, who was out of sympathy with Byzantine civilization, says of him:

> *The evils which had been sanctified by time and example were corrected by his master-hand; and he revived, if not the national spirit, at least the order and majesty of the Roman Empire. His application was indefatigable, his temper was cool, his understanding vigorous and decisive . . . . In the character of a judge he was assiduous and imperial, desirous to save, but not afraid to strike: the oppressors of the people were severely chastised . . . .*

Basil's many achievements have been praised by the two "most cultivated and learned of all Emperors" (Gregoire), his son and successor Leo VI (the Wise) and his grandson Constantine VII Porphyrogenitus, in a biography which is famous. We read here that Basil was a man of herculean strength with a talent for taming unruly horses and that he could trace his descent to the first great Armenian royal dynasty, the Arsacids or Arshakunis—which may explain why, upon ascending the imperial throne Basil adopted the Arshakuni emblem, the double-headed eagle that was later adopted by the Russian czars and a number of other European dynasties.

Leo VI was named the Wise because of his diplomatic skill as well as enthusiasm for scholarship and men of learning. He wrote poetry, treatises on theology, administration, and war. He reorganized the provincial and ecclesiastical government, and regulated the industrial system.

Constantine VII Porphyrogenitus was himself proficient in mathematics, astronomy, architecture, sculpture, painting, and music. Writes Toynbee:

> *Constantine was a natural-born scholar and a competent self-taught painter, and he had enough practical knowledge of sculpture, architecture, goldsmiths' and silversmiths' and blacksmiths' work, shipbuilding, and*

music, to be an effective critic, as well as an active patron, in all these fields.[13]

Byzantinists are likewise unanimous in their praise of the three "Macedonian" usurpers: Romanus I Lecapenus, Nicephorus II Phocas, and John I Tzimisces. "He was the embodiment of prudent moderation," Ostrogorsky writes of Lecapenus, and:

> *He possessed one of the most important qualities in a ruler, the ability to choose his colleagues wisely.... Energetic and strong willed in character, though entirely averse from any form of radicalism, he pursued his plans with cold-blooded perseverance without undue haste but also, without any lowering of his aim.*

The diplomatic skill with which he averted a military confrontation with the Bulgars "justifies the opinion of those who regard Romanus Lecapenus as perhaps the nearest to genius of all the Byzantine sovereigns," writes Gregoire.[14]

It was Nicephorus II Phocas ("the Terror of the Saracens") who, by storming and capturing Crete in 961 from the hands of Arab pirates, restored at one stroke the Byzantine supremacy at sea which had been lost for 150 years. He went on to conquer Aleppo (961), Adana (964), Tarsus (965), Cyprus (965), Antioch (968)—victories that shattered the Abbasid Caliphate. Nicephorus Phocas united, in the popular opinion, the double merit of a hero and a saint. "In the former character," writes Gibbon,

> *his qualifications were genuine and splendid: the descendant of a race illustrious by their military exploits, he had displayed in every station and in every province the courage of a soldier and the conduct of a chief.*

As an ascetic, he founded the Holy Mountain of Athos, the famous center of monastic life active to this day, and as a warrior, he wrote a brilliant manual providing an introduction to guerrilla warfare.[15]

A great-nephew of the outstanding Armenian general John Curcuas mentioned above, John Tzimisces (also Zimiskes and Chemeskig) has been called "one of the greatest and most powerful" of the Byzantine emperors, and "a general of great genius" (Ostrogorsky). Writes Gibbon:

> *His diminutive body was endowed with strength, beauty, and the soul of a hero. His gentle and generous behaviour delighted all who ap-*

proached his person . . . . By his double triumph over the Russians and the Saracens he deserved the title of saviour of the empire and conqueror of the East.

His campaign against the Russians ranks "among the most splendid achievements in the annals of Byzantine military history" (Ostrogorsky); and the Russian defeat was brought about by the personal intervention of the Emperor, and "by the valour of the Armenian infantry" (Gregoire).

The period of the Armenian emperors and usurpers (867-1081) has been called the Golden Age of the Byzantine Empire. "In terms of general civilization, it was one of the most brilliant in the history of Byzantium" (Lemerle). The empire extended from Italy to Mesopotamia and its influence radiated much farther. Constantinople, with a population of at least a million, became a fabulous city, and the economic and artistic center of the Mediterranean world. Its reputation penetrated to China. To the Russians it was "Czarigrad," the supreme imperial city, ". . . the queen of cities," writes Diehl,

> that held within her walls all the grace, all the refinements of art and luxury, and the subtle pleasures of the mind. There were to be found masterpieces of cunning craftsmanship and of architecture, as well as the entertainments of circus and theater. This was "the Paris of the Middle Ages," whose wealth and splendour aroused the greedy admiration of the barbarian world.[16]

Another country in which Armenians played a significant role is Bulgaria. Armenian presence in Bulgaria dates back to well over a thousand years. Initially, Armenians were resettled in Thrace, near Macedonia, in the 6th century A.D. by Emperor Justinian (527-565) as part of a deliberate Byzantine policy of divide and rule. Several such transfers of population took place in the 7th and 8th centuries. Many of these colonists were seized by Khan Krum (803-814) and carried away into northern Bulgaria. This may explain how one of the greatest Bulgarian rulers came to be a man who was of wholly or partly Armenian descent. Czar Samuel (976-1014), the builder of a great empire that extended from the Adriatic to the Black Sea and from the Danube to the Peloponnesus, was one of the four Cometopuli brothers whose mother's name was Ripsimia or Hripsime, a common and exclusively Armenian name taken from that of one of the holiest martyrs of the early Armenian Church. According to the 11th-century historian Stephen of Taron (Stepanos Taronetsi), called Asolik (Asoghik), the author of an important *Universal History*, Czar Samuel and his family were natives of the Armenian province of Derjan, west of Erzerum (Garin). It is to be noted that Czar Samuel's hard-won empire, which lasted from 993 to 1014, was lost to Basil II Bulgaroktonus, who was himself the descendant of Armenian captives deported to Bulgaria by that same ferocious Khan Krum.[17]

When in the 9th century Armenia threw off the Muslim yoke and entered the Byzantine sphere of influence, the Caliph of Baghdad sent a force of 200,000 warriors who razed cities and villages and exterminated a great number of the nobility, except for the Bagratunis. Ashot Bagratuni fought so skillfully that the Caliph appointed him King of Armenia in 885. In this way was founded the dynasty of the Bagratunis (or Bagratids) whose kings kept Armenia independent of both the Byzantine Empire and the Abbasid Caliphate for three centuries.[18]

Like the Mamikonians and the Ardzrunis, two other powerful clans, the Bagratunis were competent military leaders: the very cognomens by which some of them were known—"the Iron," "the Carnivorous," "the Valiant," "the Great," "the Conqueror"—sound ominous. But unlike the Mamikonians and the Ardzrunis, they were also shrewd diplomats. Contemporary chroniclers recount many fascinating anecdotes that illustrate the Bagratuni brand of cunning and courage. It is said of Sempat Bagratuni (6th century) for instance that when he offered armed resistance to Byzantium, he was taken prisoner and thrown to the beasts of the arena in Constantinople. His strength was such, however, that he was able to overpower a bear and a lion, whereupon he was pardoned by the circus mob. The 12th-century chronicler Matthew of Edessa recounts that a Bagratuni king once caused a scandal throughout the Middle East when he invited a Greek bishop to dinner and murdered him by tying him up in a sack with his dog whom he (the bishop) had named "Armenian."

Ruthless and Machiavellian, the Bagratunis reigned for a full thousand years, sometimes in Armenia, sometimes Georgia, and sometimes both countries at once. They reigned in Georgia right up to the accession of the Russian czar Alexander I in 1801—surely a world record for continuous rule by any one dynastic family. Even after they lost their throne, the Bagratunis refused to fade into oblivion. Prince Bagration (1765-1812), the general who distinguished himself during the Napoleonic wars, was a member of this dynasty.[19]

In 952 Ani became the new capital of the Bagratunis. The city formed a huge triangle bordered on the one side by the River Akhourian (Arpa-Chai), the other by a deep ravine, and the third by a magnificently constructed rampart, flanked with towers and gates with drawbridges. The royal palace was built with mosaic-covered walls. The churches—a thousand it was said—were decorated with superb sculptures, their interiors embellished with wall paintings. Ani became "the boulevard of Western civilization leading to Asia." Industry and commerce flourished. "And in those days," writes Asoghik,

> the Lord showed benevolence to our Land of Armenia. He defended her and favored her in all good undertakings. At that time all dwelt in their inherited possessions and having appropriated the land, they set out vineyards and planted olive trees and gardens, they ploughed up fields among the thorns and gathered a harvest a hundred fold. The barns were filled with wheat after the harvest and the cellars were filled with wine after the gathering of the grapes. The mountains rejoiced since the herds of cattle and of sheep multiplied on them.

Aristakes Lastivertsi, another chronicler, writes:

> Princes with joyous countenances sat on the princely thrones; they were clad in brilliant colors and looked like spring gardens. One heard only gay words and songs. The sound of flutes, of cymbals, and of other instruments filled one's heart with the comfort of great joy.

Merchants from distant lands came to sell their products and buy Armenian fabrics and textiles, metal work, armor, jewelry, horses and cattle, salt, cereals, wine, honey, timber, leather, and furs.

In 1045, Ani, the city of forty gates, a hundred palaces, and a thousand churches was seized by the Byzantine Emperor Constantine Monomachus, and shortly thereafter (1064) destroyed by Alp Arslan the Turk. The plundering was so terrible that thirty years later, a detachment of Crusaders reconnoitring in the neighborhood, is said to have nearly starved to death.[20]

Armenians emigrated to Georgia, Iran, Poland, Hungary, Rumania, sometimes reaching as far as Indonesia and Ireland. A considerable number took refuge in the mountain ranges of Taurus and Antitaurus overhanging the Cilician plain (Armenia Minor), and it was there that they welcomed the Crusaders as liberators. Contemporary Armenian manuscripts speak of the "valiant nation from the West" whose arrival shows that "God has visited His people according to His promise." In his bull *Romana Ecclesia,* Pope Gregory XIII states: "No nation and no people came to the Crusaders' aid more promptly and zealously than the Armenians, with men, horses, supplies, counsel; with all their forces and with the greatest courage and fidelity."

The Armenians descended from their mountain strongholds into the arable lands of the plain and into the large coastal cities which were situated on the trade routes. The port of Lajazzo (also Laiassus and Ayas) became one of the principal emporiums of the Near East and a major outlet in the Mediterranean for goods brought from Central Asia. With Leo II the Great (1186-1219) and his successor Hetum I (1226-1269), two monarchs of "administrative genius, military prowess, diplomatic skill, and above all grandiose political vision" (Toumanoff), Armenia Minor reached the summit of power and played a decisive role in world politics and international commerce. Extensive privileges, such as reduction of customs-dues, were granted to the Genoese and the Venetians. The judicial system was organized on the Western pattern. Next to Armenian, Latin and French became the official languages of the realm. "The king of Armenia rules his dominions with strict regard to justice," wrote Marco Polo in his celebrated book of *Travels,* which opens with a chapter on Armenia Minor. "The towns, fortified places, and castles are numerous here. There is also abundance of all necessaries of life, as well as of those things which contribute to its comfort."

Even after the Crusaders lost their last continental bridgehead in

1291 to a counterattack by Egyptian Mamelukes, Armenians in Cilicia continued to hold out for almost a century before they too lost their political independence when the Mamelukes captured Sis, the capital city.

Sis fell on April 13, 1375, after a heroic defense. Leo VI de Lusignan, the last king of Armenia, was taken as a prisoner to Cairo. After seven years of captivity, he was released and died in Paris. Armenia Minor had ceased to exist. Local Armenian communities survived in their highland fastnesses until the holocaust of 1915.[21]

In the meantime, Armenia Major had been successively overrun by Mongols, Tartars, Persians, Russians, and Osmanli and Ottoman Turks.

Warlike nomads from Asia, the Turks first appeared on the scene in the 11th century. But it was only after they had reached and conquered Greece—that is, nearly four centuries later—that they were able to subdue the fiercely independent Armenians and absorb a large section of Armenia into the Ottoman Empire which was to last six centuries. Though they suffered under Turkish rule, and in many places were not even allowed to speak their mother tongue, Armenians kept their faith, their culture, and their strong family unity. Warriors by choice, Turks considered peaceful pursuits degrading. Armenians became their manufacturers, teachers, architects, lawyers, doctors, bankers, translators, and were generally regarded as the most loyal ethnic group in the Ottoman mosaic of nations.[22]

But when, as a result of mismanagement and corruption, the Ottoman Empire began to disintegrate in the 19th century, both Russia and Great Britain became interested in the fate of Armenia. To the Russians, Armenia was the road to India and Egypt; to the British, it was the shield guarding their colonies from Russian expansion. Consequently, both powers became actively involved in "saving" Armenia from Turkish tyranny. Hence "the Armenian question" became a much discussed factor in international politics. The loss of some Armenian territory to the Russians following the Russo-Turkish war of 1878, and Armenian demands for much needed reforms, turned Turkish suspicion of the Armenians into active elimination. In the words of Sultan Abdul-Hamid II (1876-1909), also called Abdul the Damned and the Red Sultan: "The way to get rid of the Armenian question is to get rid of the Armenians."

The policy of suppression, which until then had been entrusted to tax collectors, the police, the judges, and to armed Kurdish bands, was now carried out through massacres. Between 1894 and 1896 alone, it is estimated that over 200,000 Armenians were slain. But even these massacres were to be overshadowed by the far more systematic and extensive genocide of the Armenian population in 1915.

In 1914, the Turks entered World War I on the side of Germany and shortly thereafter decided to settle the Armenian question once and for all by exterminating the entire Armenian population in Turkey. It has been said that the massacre of 2,000,000 Armenians in World War I was probably the greatest organized crime in history before the Nazis beat the record by killing 6,000,000 Jews in World War II.

First, Armenians living along railway lines were forced out of their homes. It was feared that they might attempt to engage in sabotage. All men of military age were rounded up, taken outside the towns and villages, and bayoneted, sabred, or shot. In Istanbul, intellectuals and leaders among the Armenians were hanged or assassinated in the streets. The rest were driven into the mountains and deserts to die of hunger and exposure.

In some places, after witnessing murder and massacre, Armenians decided to resist. They took all the antiquated guns and scanty ammunition they could find, expelled the murderers, and stood siege against far superior forces of regular Turkish soldiers equipped with machine guns and cannon, and reinforced as always by Kurdish bandits. Van and Musa Dagh, two such pockets of resistance, after standing siege that lasted over a month, were relieved by Russian and French forces respectively.[23] But the heroic Armenians of Moush, Zeitun, and Sassoun were not so lucky. They held the assassins at bay for as long as their provisions and ammunition lasted, after which they were overwhelmed and annihilated.

When the United States invited Germany to exercise its good offices on behalf of the Armenians, the German ambassador in Washington denied that there had been any massacres, adding that what was happening in Turkey was perfectly justifiable suppression of Armenian riots, and that individual Armenians had been deservedly shot as spies and traitors, and that these isolated incidents had been blown into massacres by Allied propaganda.

Out of 3,000,000 Armenians living within the boundary of Turkey, only 1,000,000 escaped into the newly-formed but short-lived Republic of Armenia, and into such neighboring countries as Bulgaria, Greece, Egypt, Syria, and Lebanon.[24]

The collapse of the Ottoman Empire and the outbreak of the Russian Revolution in May 1918, allowed the Armenians a breathing space during which they declared their independence which was to last from May 28, 1918 to November 29, 1920. These were extremely difficult years for the Republic. The economy was at a standstill, the country in the grip of famine and epidemic. And yet, a hurriedly organized Armenian force of 35,000 men was successful in arresting the advance of a vastly superior Turkish army in Sardarabad, Bash Abaran, and Kharakilisse.[25]

In the treaty of Sevres between the Turks and the Entente (1920), Armenia was recognized as a free and independent state and allotted 55,000 square miles of territory.[26] The fate of Armenia, however, was decided not by treaties which the Allies were unwilling to enforce, but by the armed forces of Communist Russia and Kemalist Turkey, both signatories of a friendship treaty in 1918.

As Fridtjof Nansen (1861-1930), the great Norwegian Arctic explorer, scientist and Nobel prize-winning statesman said:

> *They [the Allies] allowed Armenian blood to be shed on their behalf and then, after 1918, they repaid them with worthless paper . . . . They have lost interest in the Armenian nation as completely as they have forgotten their own promises. Woe to the Armenian people for allowing themselves to become involved in European politics. Better by far if the name of their country had never come to the lips of a European diplomat . . . .*
>
> *The very name of Armenia awakens memories of a tragic chain of broken promises for the fulfillment of which they [the Allies] have not raised a*

finger. After all it was only a culturally gifted nation, possessing no oil wells or gold mines....[27]

The plan to make Armenia a protectorate of the United States and the League of Nations failed—neither was willing to accept the responsibility. On September 29, 1920, the nationalist soldiers of Kemal Ataturk invaded Armenia slaughtering 30,000 more Armenian civilians in their advance.[28] When Armenia's appeals to the Allies remained unanswered, Armenia had no other choice but to turn to Communist Russia.

The Russians responded by nationalizing all lands, forests, and waters; confiscating food, cattle, and clothing; silencing opposition by mass arrests; and deporting all officers of the Armenian army (about 560 men, some say 1500) to Baku. Writes Oliver Baldwin in his eyewitness account: "The road to Baku was littered with the bodies of poor officers, dead and hungry and cold in the midst of the terrible Caucasian winter."[29]

This led to revolt during which many commissars and Communist sympathizers were summarily executed. Russian counter-attack was swift. Again Armenian appeals for help were ignored by the West. Early in 1921, units of the Red army entered Yerevan and shortly thereafter the free and independent Republic of Armenia ceased to exist. Armenians who had opposed Communist takeover withdrew into Iranian territory. Those who chose to stay behind became outcasts in their own homeland, deprived of their civil rights, or were liquidated or deported.[30]

Soviet persecution of Armenian nationalists was resumed with even more severity during Stalin's Great Terror of 1936-37 which claimed the lives of many important political and intellectual figures (see LITERATURE).[31] Notwithstanding these setbacks, however, Armenia under the Soviets has made spectacular advances and is generally regarded as one of the most industrially developed and progressive republics in the Union.[32]

The fate of Armenians in territories that fell to the Turks is unknown. The tragic reality is that the genocidal policy adopted by the Young Turks in 1915 continues to this day. Armenians in the interior of present-day Turkey are coerced into accepting Islam and their churches are desecrated. Only recently a Turkish paper reported that an Armenian village in the Sassoun region had renounced Christianity and accepted Islam.[33]

Of the estimated six million Armenians today (1980), four million live in Soviet Armenia and the neighboring republics of Georgia and Azerbaijan; and two million in the diaspora, which extends from Australia to the Americas, with large concentrations in the Middle East and the United States.

Until very recently two of the most prosperous and important Armenian communities in the diaspora were those of Lebanon and Iran.[34] As a result of recent political upheavals however, Armenians of these countries and of the Middle East in general (Egypt, Syria, Iraq), have begun to emigrate to Canada and the United States. The number of Armenians on the North American continent is now estimated to be well over 500,000—with large concentrations in such urban areas as Los Angeles, Fresno, New York, Boston, Detroit, Montreal, and Toronto. Armenians in these cities have their own community centers, schools, churches, charitable institutions, and Armenian, as well as English, language periodicals and newspapers.[35]

Though their educational level and economic status are above average, as an ethnic group and political force, Armenians in the diaspora remain hopelessly fragmented and divided. There are two main political organizations: those who are more or less resigned to the Soviet presence in Armenia (or rather what remains of historic Armenia—about 11,500 square miles, one tenth of the national territories); and the nationalists who are unwilling to give up their dream of a free and independent homeland.[36] There are, in addition, two fairly large contingents, one of which may be described as non-partisan, and the other assimilationist.[37] Despite a number of recent attempts to unite these disparate groups, a consensus has so far failed to emerge.[38]

[1]Armenian names and words are accented on the last syllable. Vowels are pronounced as in Italian or Latin; consonants as in English, except that "g" is always hard.

[2]For a thorough investigation of its location, see "Prelude" of Thomas Mann's tetralogy *Joseph and His Brothers* (New York, 1948).

[3] During the last few years Mount Ararat and Noah's Ark have been the focus of world wide attention as a result of a number of books and a widely advertised and televised documentary film. The most scholarly and authoritative book on the subject is an anthology titled *The Quest of Noah's Ark* (Minneapolis, 1972), introduced, edited, and annotated by the American explorer and theologian John Warwick Montgomery. See also my *Armenia Observed* (New York, 1979).

[4] For more details, see Mardiros Ananikian, "Armenian Mythology" in *The Mythology of All Races*, volume 7 (Boston, 1925).

[5] See Margaret Israelian, *History of the Erebuni Acropolis* (Yerevan, 1971).

[6] See Carl Roebuck, *The World of Ancient Times* (New York, 1966).

[7] See Francois Thureau-Dangin, *Une Relation de la huitieme campagne de Sargon (714 avant Jesus Christ)* (Paris, 1912); Georges Contenau, *Everyday Life in Babylon and Assyria* (London, 1954).

[8] See Arnold J. Toynbee, *A Study of History*, vol. 10 (London, 1961), and *Mankind and Mother Earth* (New York, 1976).

[9] The best source on Queen Semiramis is Diodorus Siculus, *Library of History* (Loeb Classical Library) (New York, 1933). See also A. J. Bedronis, *Semiramis et Ara le Bel* (Avignon, 1947).

[10] See Will Durant, *The Story of Civilization: Our Oriental Heritage* (New York, 1935).

[11] See H. A. Manandian, *Tigrane II et Rome* (Lisbon, 1963); Hrant Armen, *Tigranes the Great* (Detroit, 1940).

[12] N. Adonts, *Les fonds historique de l'epopee byzantine Digenis Akritas* (Lisbon, 1965); H. Gregoire *Digenis Akritas: The Byzantine Epic in History and Poetry* (New York, 1942); Jack Lindsay, *Byzantium into Europe* (London, 1952).

[13] Arnold J. Toynbee, *Constantine Porphyrogenitus and His World* (London, 1973).

[14] See Steven Runciman, *The Emperor Lecapenus and His Reign* (London, 1929).

[15] See G. Schlumberger, *Un empereur byzantin au Xe siecle: Nicephor Phocas* (Paris, 1890).

[16] Armenian presence in the Byzantine Commonwealth has been amply documented by Henri Gregoire, "The Amorians and the Macedonians: 842-1025" in *The Cambridge Medieval History*, edited by J. M. Hussey (Cambridge, 1966); Sirarpie Der Nersessian, *Armenia and the Byzantine Empire* (Harvard, 1945); Peter Charanis, *The Armenians in the Byzantine Empire* (Lisbon, 1963); Nicholas Adonts, *Etudes Armeno-Byzantines* (Lisbon, 1965). See also Paul Lemerle, *A History of Byzantium* (New York, 1960); George Ostrogorsky, *History of the Byzantine State* (New Brunswick, 1955); Edward Gibbon, *The Decline and Fall of the Roman Empire* (London, 1776-78); Enno Franzius, *A Short History of the Byzantine Empire* (New York, 1967); Merry Ottin, *Land of Emperors and Sultans: The Forgotten Cultures of Asia Minor* (London, 1962); Charles Diehl, *Byzantium: Greatness and Decline* (New Brunswick, 1957).

[17] David Marshall Lang, *The Bulgarians: From Pagan Times to the Ottoman Conquest* (London, 1976).

[18] See Aram Ter-Ghewondian, *The Arab Emirates in Bagratid Armenia*, translated by Nina G. Garsoian (Lisbon, 1976).

[19] Cyril Toumanoff, "Armenia and Georgia," in *The Cambridge Medieval History*, edited by J. M. Hussey (1966); D. M. Lang, *The Georgians* (London, 1966).

[20] H. F. B. Lynch, *Armenia: Travels and Studies*, 2 volumes (London, 1901), contains an excellent chapter on Ani with separate sections on its history and architecture. See also M. F. Brosset, *Ruines d'Ani* (St. Petersburg, 1860).

[21] T. S. R. Boase (editor), *The Cilician Kingdom of Armenia* (London, 1978); N. Iorga, *Breve histoire de la Petite Armenie* (Paris, 1930); Sirarpie Der Nersessian, "The Kingdom of Cilician Armenia," in *A History of the Crusades*, volume 2, edited by Wolff and Hazard (Philadelphia, 1962); Paul Bedoukian, *Coinage of Cilician Armenia* (New York, 1962); Leo Alishan, *Sissouan ou l'Armeno-Cilicie* (Venice, 1899).

[22] For an exhaustive and scholarly study of the Armenian contribution to the administration and welfare of the Ottoman Empire, see Mesrob K. Krikorian, *Armenians in the Service of the Ottoman Empire: 1860-1908* (Boston, 1978).

[23] For more details on the siege of Van, see Rafael de Nogales, *Four Years Beneath the Crescent* (New York, 1926); and on the siege of Musa Dagh, see Franz Werfel, *Forty Days of Musa Dagh* (New York, 1934)—Werfel shortened the actual ordeal by 13 days. De Nogales writes from the Turkish side, Werfel from the Armenian.

[24] As already noted (*see INTRODUCTION*) no aspect of Armenian history has been more amply documented than the Genocide. The bibliography on this topic is vast and for the sake of convenience it may be divided into three headings: general background, specialized works, and personal testimony.
General background:
M. S. Anderson, *The Eastern Question: 1774-1923* (London, 1966); E. Driault, *La question d'Orient depuis ses origines jusqu'a nos jours* (Paris, 1912); M. Leart, *La question armenienne a la lumiere des documents* (Paris, 1913); A. O. Sarkissian, *History of the Armenian Question up to 1885* (Illinois, 1938). Hratch Dasnabedian, *The Armenian Question* (Jerusalem, 1978).
Specialized works:
J. Guttmann, *The Beginnings of Genocide: A Brief Account of the Armenian Massacres in World War I* (New York, 1948); Peter Lanne, *Armenia: The First Genocide of the 20th Century*, translated from the German by Krikor Balekdjian (Boston, 1977); Dickran Boyajian *The Case for a Forgotten Genocide* (New Jersey, 1972); Henry Morgenthau, *The Murder of a Nation* (New York, 1975); Arnold J. Toynbee, *Armenian Atrocities: The Murder of a Nation* (London, 1915); H. A. Gibbons, *The Blackest Page of Modern History: Events in Armenia in 1915* (New York, 1916); James Nazer, *The Armenian Massacres* (New York, 1975); Fa'is El Hussein, *Martyred Armenia* (New York, 1975); Jean-Marie Carzou, *Armenie 1915: Un genocide exemplaire* (Paris, 1975); Yves Ternon, *Les Armeniens: Histoire d'un genocide* (Paris, 1977); P. du Veou, *La passion de la Cilicie: 1919-1922* (Paris, 1954); Orietta Avenati and Kevork Orfalian, *Destinazione: Morte* (Rome,

1976); Michael J. Arlen, *Passage to Ararat* (New York, 1975); *The Memoirs of Naim Bey: Turkish official documents relating to the deportations and massacres of Armenians,* compiled by Aram Andonian (London, 1920); Johannes Lepsius, *Deutschland und Armenien: 1914-1918* (Potsdam, 1919); Viscount Bryce, *The Treatment of Armenians in the Ottoman Empire (1915-1916)* (Beirut, 1972; originally published in 1916); Arnold J. Toynbee, *The Murderous Tyranny of the Turks* (New York, 1975; originally published in 1917); Arnold J. Toynbee, *Documents Relating to the Treatment of Armenians and Assyrian Christians in the Ottoman Empire and Northwest Persia* (London, 1916).

Personal Testimony:

Leon Surmelian, *I Ask You Ladies and Gentlemen* (New York, 1945); David Kherdian, *The Road from Home* (New York, 1979); John Aroian, *Mountains Stand Firm* (New York, 1977); James Sutherland, *Adventures of an Armenian Boy* (Ann Arbor, 1964); Aramais Hovsepian, *Conversations with My Memory* (Calif., 1978); Kerop Bedoukian, *Some of Us Survived* (New York, 1979), American edition of *The Urchin* (London, 1978); Elizabeth C. Payne, *Daughter of the Euphrates* (New Jersey, 1979; originally published in 1939); Marie Sarrafian Banker, *My Beloved Armenia* (Chicago, 1936); Abraham H. Hartunian, *Neither to Laugh Nor to Weep* (Boston, 1976).

[25]This thorny chapter of Armenian history is examined with admirable impartiality by Richard G. Hovannisian, *Armenia on the Road to Independence, 1918* (Los Angeles, 1967), and *The Republic of Armenia, 1918-1919* (Los Angeles, 1971); a third volume is promised to carry the story to the Soviet conquest of 1920. See also Jacques Kayaloff, *The Battle of Sardarabad* (The Hague, 1973).

[26]See J. A. S. Grenville, *The Major International Treaties 1914-1973; A History and Guide with Texts* (New York, 1975).

[27]See Fridtjof Nansen, *Armenia and the Near East* (New York, 1928).

[28]See James B. Gidney, *A Mandate for Armenia* (Kent, Ohio, 1966); George Scott, *The Rise and Fall of the League of Nations* (New York, 1974); Elmer Bendiner, *A Time for Angels; The Tragicomic History of the League of Nations* (New York, 1975).

[29]Oliver Baldwin, *Six Prisons and Two Revolutions* (London, 1925).

[30]There are several works that examine Soviet policy in Armenia following the 1921 takeover. The most competent and thorough is by M. K. Matossian, *The Impact of Soviet Policies in Armenia* (Leyden, 1962). See also M. E. Elliot, *Beginning Again at Ararat* (New York, 1924); Aghavnie Yeghenian, *The Red Flag at Ararat* (New York, 1932); Manuel Sarkisyanz, *A Modern History of Transcaucasian Armenia* (Leyden, 1975).

[31]Suppression of Armenian nationalists or advocates of self-determination continues to this day. In this connection see Andrei Sakharov, *My Country and the World* (New York, 1975).

[32]For a superlative photographic album on present-day Armenia, see Arthur Tcholakian, *Armenia: State/People/Life* (New York, 1976). Other works in which Armenia is observed and described in some detail: Nane Carzou, *Voyage en Armenie*

(Paris, 1974); Puzant Granian, *My Land, My People* (Los Angeles, 1978); see also my *Armenia Observed* (New York, 1979). Nearly all guides and travelogues of the Soviet Union contain sections dealing exclusively with Armenia, with particular emphasis on Yerevan and its environs. The following is a short list of representative works: Eugene and Jeffrey Gross, *The Soviet Union: A Guide for Travellers* (New York, 1977); Victor and Jennifer Louis, *The Complete Guide to the Soviet Union* (London, 1976); *Fodor's Soviet Union 1977/78*, edited by Eugene Fodor and Robert G. Fisher (New York, 1978); Lee and Barb Williams, *On the Road Through the Soviet Union* (New York, 1975); George St. George, *Russia* (London, 1973); N. Mikhailov, *Discovering the Soviet Union* (Moscow, 1965); Vlasta Ludvikova, *The Soviet Union: A Guide and Information Handbook* (New York, 1978).

[33] See Shavarsh Toriguian, *The Armenian Question and International Law* (Beirut, 1973).

[34] A special supplement of *Ararat* (Summer 1978) is devoted to the Armenian presence in Lebanon, and another (Summer 1979) to Armenians in Iran. See also D. M. Lang and C. Walker, *The Armenians* (London, 1976), which contains some valuable information on the Armenian diaspora.

[35] There are many works dealing with Armenian presence in America. The most thorough, competent, and up to date is *Ararat, Special Issue: Armenians in America,* edited by Jack Antreassian (Winter 1977), which contains separate sections on the history, demography, contributions to arts and sciences, the Church, etc. Also a valuable bibliography by Linda Hamalian. See also Vladimir Wertsman, *Armenians in America: A Chronology and Fact Book* (New York, 1978); Arra Avakian, *The Armenians in America* (Minneapolis, 1978); M. Vartan Malcom, *Armenians of the United States* (Boston, 1919); James H. Tashjian, *The Armenians of the United States and Canada* (Boston, 1947); Aram S. Yeretzian, *A History of Armenian Immigration to America* (Calif., 1974); Charles Mahakian, *History of Armenians in California* (Calif., 1974); G. A. Kulhanjian, *The Historical and Sociological Aspects of Armenian Immigration to the United States, 1890-1930* (Calif., 1975); Sheila Henry, *Cultural Persistence and Socio-Economic Mobility: A Comparative Study of Assimilation Among Armenians and Japanese in Los Angeles* (Calif., 1978); *Armenians in Massachusetts,* Federal Writers' Project (New York, 1975; originally published in 1937); Rouben Gavoor, "Armenian Americans," in *One America,* edited by Francis J. Brown and Josef S. Roucek (New Jersey, 1962; originally published in 1952); Louis Adamic, *From Many Lands* (New York, 1940).

[36] For a better understanding of the origins and character of Armenian political parties, see Sarkis Atamian, *The Armenian Community* (New York, 1955), and Louise Nalbandian, *The Armenian Revolutionary Movement* (Calif., 1967).

[37] In the final pages of *Passage to Ararat* (New York, 1975), Michael J. Arlen espouses the assimilationist cause.

[38] The present political fragmentation of the Armenian diaspora is described by J. Karnusian, *Return to the Ararat Plateau* (New York, 1979).

Further Reading:

Some of the best Western works on Armenian history are in French: Rene Grousset, *Histoire de l'Armenie* (Paris, 1947); H. Pasdermadjian, *Histoire de l'Armenie depuis les origines jusqu'au traite de Lauzanne* (Paris, 1949); Jacques de Morgan, *Histoire du peuple armenien* (Paris, 1919); H. Thorossian, *Histoire de l'Armenie et du peuple armenien* (Paris, 1957); F. Tournebize, *Histoire politique et religieuse de l'Armenie depuis les origines des armeniens jusqu'a la mort de leur dernier roi: l'an 1393* (Paris, 1900); and in English: David M. Lang, *Armenia: Cradle of Civilization* (London, 1978: revised edition); Sirarpie Der Nersessian, *The Armenians* (New York, 1969); Vahan Kurkjian, *A History of Armenia* (New York, 1958); Stephen Svajian, *A Trip Through Historic Armenia* (New York, 1977).

Religion

At the world's edge you stood,
Swallowing your tears,
And with shame and pain turned away
From the bearded cites of the East.

Osip Mandelstam

Peculiarly admirable is their fidelity to Christianity, for few races have produced more martyrs in ancient as well as modern times, or come in contact with more persecutors.

Sir Charles Eliot

When, in 1453, Sultan Mehmed II (the Conqueror) entered Constantinople in triumph and galloped into the basilica of Haghia Sophia to proclaim the victory of Allah, the whole of the East was submerged in Islam. Armenia became a Christian island in a Muslim sea.

But a full thousand years before Mehmed II's triumph, Armenians had already fought a religious war against the Persians. Known as *Vartanants,* after Vartan Mamikonian, the *sparabed* or commander in chief of the Armenian forces, this war was fought in 451.

Armenians were the first people to adopt Christianity as the state religion. Tertullian and Eusebius of Caesaria suggest that Christianity was practiced in Armenia as early as the 2nd century. Eusebius also mentions an exchange of letters between Jesus Christ and the Armenian king of Edessa Abkar V (the Black) (9-46 A.D.). Legend claims for Armenia the graves of four apostles: Bartholomew, Simon, Thaddaeus, and Jude.

It was sometime between 288 and 301 that St. Gregory the Illuminator (Grigor Loussavorich: ca. 240-332), who had been subjected to cruel tortures and incarcerated in a grave (Khor Virab) for 13 years for refusing to participate in pagan rites, converted King Tiridates III (238-314). In 302, St. Gregory was ordained bishop, and in 303 he founded the Cathedral of Etchmiadzin, near Mount Ararat, which, to this day, is the seat of the supreme patriarch or catholicos, the head of the Armenian Church. St. Gregory went on to evangelize several other Caucasian nations and baptized the kings of Iberia (Georgia), Lazes, and Albania. Sometime before his death he retired to a solitary life in the wilderness. The patron saint of Armenia, he is now venerated in both the Eastern and Latin Church.

Soon after Christianity became the official religion of the Armenian state, the Byzantines and the Sassanid Persians clashed over the possession of Armenia. In 438, several Armenian provinces came under the control of the Persians, who watched with alarm the rapid expansion of Christianity ("which extinguishes Fires, pollutes the Waters, and corrupts the Earth" according to a Persian spokesman), and the concurrent expansion of the Byzantine sphere of influence. Christians in Persian territories were massacred. When entire villages began to disappear, the massacre was restricted to priests, monks, and nuns. Next an effort was made to introduce Mazdaism (Zoroastrianism or the worship of Ahura Mazda) into Armenia. This led to revolt, and in 451 the Persians invaded Armenian territory. At the cost of heavy losses, the

Persians won the battle of Avarayr. Vartan Mamikonian was among the slain; but his heroic resistance against a much more powerful army (66,000 Armenians against 220,000 Persians reinforced by squadrons of armored elephants), followed by guerrilla warfare by Hmayak and Vahan Mamikonian, convinced the Persians of the impossibility of uprooting Christianity from the hearts of the people. A Persian observer reported back to the Sassanid King Yezdegird (Yazdgard): "Even if the immortals themselves came to our aid, it would be impossible to establish Mazdaism in Armenia." At this, Yezdegird was obliged to give up his religious policy in Armenia.

Vartan Mamikonian died the death of a hero; his daughter, Shushanik Mamikonian, that of a martyr. Both have been canonized by the Church. The Martyrdom of St. Shushanik is the first original work of Georgian literature, and was written between 476 and 483 by her father-confessor Jacob of Tsurtavi.

Shushanik married a Georgian prince named Vazken, who abandoned Christianity for Mazdaism to ingratiate himself with the Persians. Her refusal to renounce Christianity infuriated her opportunistic husband who, after shouting foul-mouthed insults,

> kicked her with his foot; picking up a poker,... crashed it down on her head and split it open and injured one of her eyes; and ... struck her face unmercifully with his fist and dragged her to and fro by her hair, bellowing like a wild beast and roaring like a madman.

After seven years of such humiliations and tortures, eaten up by ulcers and vermin, Shushanik finally succumbed. Her tormentor was ultimately put to death by the Georgian King Vakhtang I Gorgaslan (446-510).[1]

Persian persecution of Christians was soon replaced by Byzantine persecution of heretics under Justinian (reigned 527-565). Byzantine theological disputes generally concealed deep national and political rivalries. Consequently heretics were treated as dangerous subversives and deprived of their civil rights.

At the Council of Chalcedon in 451 (the year of Vartanants, which is also the year in which the Armenian translation of the Bible was completed), Armenians were branded as Monophysites—a heresy that maintains Christ did not have two distinct natures, the human and the divine, but one composite divine-human (both natures having coalesced in the womb of Mary, producing Jesus who was neither God nor man, but God-man). The Armenian Church responded to this charge of heresy by anathematizing Chalcedon.[2]

Byzantine persecution of Monophysites (a designation Armenians never accepted) was somewhat mitigated by Justinian's wife Empress Theodora, very probably an Armenian, who took an active part in ecclesiastical politics. Emotionally deeply committed to the Monophysite cause, she spent most of her reign trying to neutralize the laws against the Monophysites.

Among the heretics who arose in Armenia about this time none excited more fear and persecution than the Paulicians. According to Gibbon, they shook the East and enlightened the West; they are now viewed by many scholars as early Protestants against "Catholic" abuses.

Probably influenced by Mazdaism and mainly a popular manifestation of feudal and clerical oppression, Paulicians preached absolute equality of all men and cast aside all the hierarchy and machinery of the Church—though they gradually developed a hierarchy of their own, and inevitably doctrinal differences and sub-heresies. They further distinguished between the good God, ruler of heaven, and the evil God, or Satan, ruler of the material and temporal universe. Identifying Jehovah with Satan, they rejected the Old Testament; along with the cult of images, saints, the doctrine of incarnation, the cross, and the sacraments—since water, oil, bread and wine could not possibly be the instruments of supernatural grace, belonging as they did to the realm of Satan. Regarding themselves as the true Christians (the designation Paulicians was given them by their enemies, Paulicians themselves referred contemptuously to adherents of the official Church as "anti-Christians" and "Romanists") they hated priests and monks, and believed that only a pious life and rigid asceticism were pleasing to God, not external observances and prayers. But since they regarded material things and physical activity as absolutely insignificant and bodily sin as inculpable, their life is said to have degenerated into licentious living little in accord with traditional Christian virtues.

In his tract against the Paulicians, Hovannes Otznetsi (see LITERATURE) calls them "obscene men." Stubborn, courageous, and warlike, the Paulicians nevertheless made excellent soldiers, and were sometimes employed as border fighters by Iconoclastic Byzantine emperors sympathetic to their cause. More often than not, however, they allied themselves with the Arabs and aided them in their attacks on the Empire. In the 9th century their military power became so great that they were able to reach as far as the Aegean coasts and demand the surrender of the whole of Asia Minor.

The first Paulician community was founded in the 7th century in southern Armenia by an Armenian called Constantine, who took the additional name of Silvanus (after Silas, one of St. Paul's companions). Excommunicated, relentlessly persecuted, deported *en masse*, even martyred (after a ministry of 27 years, Constantine-Silvanus was stoned to death, and his successor, Simeon, was burned alive), the Paulicians spread rapidly throughout the Byzantine Empire reaching Bulgaria (where they became known as the Bogomils), Italy and France (the Cathari or Albigenses). Derivative sects continue to exist to this day in Armenia.[3]

The following are some of the minor points of doctrine on which the creed of the Armenian Church (sometimes called Gregorian or Apostolic) differs from that of other Christian communities: Armenians deny purgatory, but they pray for the dead like the Catholics; they baptize by triple immersion; confirmation follows very soon after baptism; they make use of unleavened bread and of wine unmixed with water as elements for the Eucharist; in addition to the saints of the Greek and Latin Church, they have their national saints—among them St. Hripsime and St. Gayane, who fled Rome to avoid the carnal desires of the Emperor and took refuge in Armenia, where their blood was shed for the cause of the gospel; the above-mentioned St. Gregory the Illuminator and St. Vartan Mamikonian; also St. Grigor Narekatsi and St. Nerses Shnorhali (see LITERATURE).

They have two classes of priests: the *vartabeds* or doctors, who are unmarried, and the parish priests, who must be married before ordination to the diaconate. Only *vartabeds* can become bishops.

The present situation of the Armenian Church is somewhat complicated. Political influences have caused a division in the Armenian Church in recent years. The separation is largely administrative—not affecting the rituals and teachings of the Church itself—with one part linking itself to the Catholicate of Antelias rather than to the Mother See of Etchmiadzin. There is a continuing effort for the reunification of the Church. In addition, there are Armenian Evangelicals (Protestants) and Catholics. The Catholics conform with Rome in doctrinal points, but in all other respects agree with the Gregorian Church. The history of Catholic Armenians, however, antedates recent troubles.

Throughout their history, there have always been some Armenians who recognized the supremacy of Rome. At the time of the Crusades, Armenians of Cilicia (Armenia Minor) were in constant contact with the Roman Curia and an uneasy union was achieved under Pope Innocent III in 1198. The Council of Sis in 1307 attempted to consolidate dogmatic unity with Rome and to enforce several liturgical uses; but a number of groups resisted.

In 1330 a Dominican called Bartholomew the Small and an Armenian John of Kerna, founded an Order of "Brothers of Unity," later called Uniates, to promote closer union with Rome. At the Genoese colony of Caffa in the Crimea, this Order, which within 30 years was 700 strong, established a house of studies, where various theologians were translated into Armenian, among them St. Thomas Aquinas. Other orders followed—Augustinians, Jesuits, French Lazarists. An occasional catholicos was likewise united with Rome. The Mekhitarists of Venice and Vienna, active since the 18th century and highly influential as scholars and educators (*see* LITERATURE) are Catholics. An outstanding recent Catholic patriarch was Gregory Peter XV Aghajanian (1895-1971), who was made a cardinal in 1945. Active mainly at the Vatican, where he rose to be head of the Sacred Congregation for the Propagation of the Faith, Aghajanian was regarded by many "brilliantly suited for the papacy."[4] There are about 100,000 Armenian Catholics today throughout the world.[5]

Armenian Protestantism dates back to the early part of the 19th century. Following the mutual friendship agreement in 1831 between the United States and the Ottoman Empire, American missionaries established many schools, colleges, and theological seminaries throughout the Armenian provinces of the Empire. By 1914, these mission schools and colleges numbered 426, including 8 colleges, 3 theological seminaries, 46 secondary schools, and 371 other schools. A translation of the Bible into modern Armenian was published in 1852, and another translation into Turkish written with Armenian letters for Armenians who had lost their own language and spoke only Turkish. In addition, Protestant missionaries published many religious books, school texts, hymnals, commentaries, and a family newspaper in two separate editions, one in Armenian, the other in Turkish. The number of Protestant Armenians (actually the Armenian Evangelical Church) is somewhat larger than that of Catholic Armenians.[6]

---

[1] See David M. Lang, *The Georgians* (London, 1966).

[2] See Karekin Sarkissian, *The Council of Chalcedon and the Armenian Church* (New York, 1975).

[3] For a sympathetic view of Paulicianism, see Edward Gibbon, *The Decline and Fall of the Roman Empire*. The definitive work on the subject, however, is by Nina Garsoian, *The Paulician Heresy: A Study of the Origins and Development of Paulicianism in Armenia and the Eastern Provinces of the Byzantine Empire* (New York, 1967). See also *The Key of Truth: A Manual of the Paulician Church of Armenia*, translated, edited and with an introduction (of nearly 200 closely printed pages) by F. C. Conybeare (Oxford, 1898). Works in which Paulician influence on the heresies of the West is examined: D. Obolensky, *The Bogomils* (Cambridge, 1948); S. Runciman, *The Medieval Manichee* (Cambridge, 1955); E. G. A. Holmes, *The Albigensian or Catharist Heresy* (London, 1925).

[4] See Lawrence Elliott, *I Will Be Called John: A Biography of Pope John XXII* (New York, 1973).

[5] See D. Vernier, *Histoire du patriarchat armenien catholique* (Paris, 1890); *New Catholic Encyclopedia*, editor in chief, William J. McDonald (New York, 1967).

[6] Three of the best texts on the Armenian Church and its history are: Leon Arpee, *A*

History of Armenian Christianity from the Beginning to Our Own Times (New York, 1946); Hagop Nersoyan, *A History of the Armenian Church* (New York, 1963); Malachia Ormanian, *The Church of Armenia,* English translation by M. Marcar Gregory (London, 1955). For recent developments, see M. K. Matossian, *The Impact of Soviet Policies in Armenia* (Leiden, 1962); K. V. Sarkissian, "The Armenian Church," in *Religion in the Middle East,* edited by A. J. Arberry (London, 1969).

Language

The Armenian language cannot be worn out; its boots are made of stone. And of course its word is thick-walled, its semivowels seamed with air. But is that all its charm? No! Then where does one's craving for it come from? How to explain it? Make sense of it?

Osip Mandelstam

The Armenian language is of great interest to philologists because it is the only modern representative of a distinct branch of the Indo-European language family—probably a superimposition of the Thracian branch on the language spoken by the Urartians. Of the 70 different languages spoken in the Caucasus—"though others, who care nothing for the facts, actually say 300," remarks

Strabo, a Greek geographer and historian writing in the first century B.C.—Armenian is one of the few languages that have survived. 19th-century philologists like Cirbied and Vater have asserted that it is so distinct from all other languages in its fundamental character that it cannot be classified with any of the great families of languages. It was mainly through the efforts of the German linguist H. Huebschmann, author of an *Armenische Grammatik*, 2 volumes (1895-97), that scholars agreed in 1875 to include Armenian in the Indo-European family of languages. So far only 2,000 words have been supplied with reasonably tenable etymologies. Borrowings from Caucasian languages are negligible.

The alphabet of 36 letters (two more signs were added later) was devised by St. Mesrob Mashtots in about 400 A.D., and bears no relation to the hieroglyphs of the invading Armens, or to Vannic, the rare form of cuneiform that was in use in Urartu and which was deciphered by A.H. Sayce in 1882. Mesrob also invented the Georgian and the Caucasian Albanian alphabets. (One reason Georgian is still spoken, writes David M. Lang in his book *The Georgians*, is their alphabet, which is still in use today under the Soviet regime).

From Koriun's admirable biographical sketch, Mesrob Mashtots (ca. 361-440) emerges as one of those rare individuals who combined the resoluteness and energy of a man of action with the wisdom of a man of contemplation. As a young man, Koriun writes, "he was esteemed by his men for his mastery of the martial arts." Later he subjected himself to all types of spiritual disciplines—"solitude, mountain dwelling, hunger, thirst, and living on herbs, in dark cells, clad in sackcloth, with the floor as his bed."

At the age of forty, as he began his preaching in different parts of Armenia, Mesrob Mashtots conceived the idea of inventing Armenian characters. This was done after much research and experimentation. "The Armenian alphabet," writes Antoine Meillet, a French philologist and comparative linguist, and author of an *Esquisse d'une grammaire comparee de l'armenien classique* (1936),

> *is a masterpiece . . . . It is so well founded that it has provided the Armenian nation with a definitive system of phonetics which has been main-*

tained to this day without undergoing any alteration, or needing to receive any improvement for it was perfect from the beginning.

After devising the alphabet, Mashtots proceeded to open schools, to teach, to translate, and to write sermons and epistles making difficult doctrines intelligible "even to fools and those distracted by secular things." He also established "countless monastic orders in inhabited as well as in uninhabited places, in lowlands, in mountains, and in caves." The monasteries became centers of learning and were soon "filled with incomparable scribes, scholars, doctors, skillful painters, and philosophers as profound as the sea. . . ." In 438, Mashtots assumed government of the Church in Armenia until his death. He was buried in Oshagan near Yerevan, where a sanctuary was erected over his remains.[1]

The Armenian language has a unique, independent character all its own. It has a rich vocabulary and is amazingly versatile. Translations of Greek and Latin classics are so accurate that if the original versions were lost, one could translate them back from Armenian into Greek or Latin without losing any of the accuracy of the originals. The art of translating was thought of as a highly respected scholarly discipline, and translators were known as *sourp tarkmanichk* (holy translators). The incandescent beauty, the almost miraculous simplicity of the Armenian translation of the Bible, has led scholars to call it "the Queen of Translations."

Armenian can sing, boom, caress, thunder—depending on the subject and the speaker. It has an orchestral quality with percussive, brass, string, and woodwind words. In the mouth of a compelling orator, it can turn into a formidable instrument.

Both French and German philologists have pointed out the astonishing ability of the Armenian language to coin new terms by compounding several linguistic elements of independent meaning into a single word. The invention of the telephone, for example, created the need of a new word, which was coined by combining the Armenian words *herou* (far) and *tsain* (sound) into *heratsain*. In English, as well as Italian, French, Spanish, and a few other languages, the same challenge was met by adopting two Greek words: *tele* (far) and *phone* (sound).

There are two main dialects: Eastern Armenian (Soviet Armenia, Iran), and Western Armenian (Middle East, Europe, and America). Despite some fundamental differences in grammar and pronunciation, they are mutually intelligible.

Some foreign scholars, imperfectly acquainted with the language, have called it harsh in sound—"Armenian words are wildcats," Osip Mandelstam writes in his cycle of poems dedicated to Armenia, "harassing, scratching my ear . . . ." It is not. In the following examples I have avoided transcribing words that would look as bad as, say, "strength" (an eight-letter word seven of which are consonants) but, when pronounced, sound less menacing:

cov (կով) cow
catou (կատու) cat
akrav (ագռաւ) crow
toun (դուն) thou
loussin (լուսին) moon

amar (ամառ) summer
atel (ատել) to hate
baits (բայց) but
doustre (դուստր) daughter

It is a precise language—in the words of a contemporary poet, "its aim is as unerring as Haik's arrow." Armenian grammar and syntax demand a style that leaves the reader and listener no doubt about the logical connection between words and phrases, between main and subordinate clauses.

Mandelstam believed that the Armenian language would be studied long after the phonetic ores of the West are exhausted. More recently, the distinguished American anthropologist Margaret Mead proposed Armenian as a living language suitable for international use—a proposal that has so far been ignored perhaps because it is not an easy language to master. When Lord Byron found that his "mind wanted something craggy to break upon," he decided to study Armenian. However, after a few lessons with a Mekhitarist scholar on the Island of San Lazzaro in Venice, he wrote to a friend that he had managed to master only "30 of the 38 cursed scratches of Mesrob and some words of one syllable."

Armenians love their language with a passion. Armenian poets have probably dedicated more odes to their mother tongue than to feminine charms. In a poem titled *Advice to My Son*, Sylva

Gaboudikian writes of the "one thousand and one treasures of the Armenian language," and after comparing its splendors to the eternal snows of Mt. Ararat, says:

Wherever you are,
Wherever you go,
Defend your mother tongue
As you would defend your mother
Against an assassin's drawn dagger.

"Our language is music, poetry, a mighty medium of expression," writes Puzant Granian in his *My Land, My People*. "It is a work of art, an architectural masterpiece with large interior spaces. Its taste can be relished with all one's senses. It was to the earth, to space, to God, that the first Armenian directed his speech. He then transferred its spirit to stones and parchments . . . . It is a priceless treasure that we entrust to our children. We conquer immortality. We arrest the passing moment and we make of it something durable, everlasting. We recreate the past and foresee the future." And here is how Shavarsh Nartuni, an author who spent most of his life in Paris (*see* LITERATURE) expressed his longing to speak his mother tongue:

This morning more than ever
I am seized by an irresistible longing
to speak my mother tongue.
I search for an Armenian, any Armenian,
with whom I can speak. If you understand
this strange, irresistible longing,
please help me.

I would like to meet an Armenian,
any Armenian, even an alienated one
who has completely forgotten his mother tongue.
Let him remember a single word only;
and let our paths cross
in order that I may say to him:
"Are you Armenian?"
And if he were to nod "yes" with his head,
I would immediately cry out the word
taught to me by my father and mother:
"PARI LOUYS!" (Good morning).
In the name of everything that is sacred,

*I swear to you there can be nothing sweeter,
nothing more heart-rending.*

*How much meaning have our ancestors
placed in that expression!...
Oh, my lovely Armenian language:
as fresh as the morn
and as deep as the night;
as frolicsome as a child
and as wise as an old man;
as consoling as a prayer
and as beautiful as spring.*

*Oh, my sweet Armenian language:
fit for a king as well as a laborer,
suitable for townspeople as well as villagers,
ever youthful, ever mighty,
may you live forever!*

[1]See Koriun, *The Life of Mashtots*, English translation by Bedros Norehad (New York, 1964). Vahan Kurkjian, *Sahak and Mesrob* (New York, 1958).

Further Reading
There are many texts on Classical *(Krapar)*, Western and Eastern Armenian. Three of the best are: R. W. Thomson, *An Introduction to Classical Armenian* (New York, 1975); Kevork Bardakjian and R. W. Thomson, *A Textbook of Modern Western Armenian* (New York, 1977); G. Fairbanks and E. Stevick, *Spoken East Armenian* (Moscow, 1975), with cassettes. See also Stella Malkasian and Hagop Atamian, *Functional Armenian* (New York, 1977); Zareh Melkonian, *Armenian Made Easy* (Detroit, 1976); See also Adour Yacoubian, *English-Armenian and Armenian-English Dictionary* (with Armenian words spelled in Latin) (Los Angeles, 1944); Mardiros Koushakdjian and Dicran Khantrouni, *English-Armenian and Armenian-English Modern Dictionary* (Beirut, 1970).

Literature

It has been the destiny of the Armenian people to wage a struggle against foreign nations for the protection of their physical and spiritual life. The inner meaning of our history lies principally in that struggle, and it is also that struggle of which our literature has generally been the expression.
                              Manoog Abeghian

Of Armenian oral literature, which goes back at least 4000 years, only short fragments and random passages have come down to us. Judged by the texture of the language and the sophisticated use of such stylistic devices as similes, metaphors, alliteration, assonance, and repetition, these fragments reveal a highly developed tradition. In the following passage for instance we read of the birth of the mythical god Vahagn (keep in mind that these poems were intended to be sung or recited aloud):

Earth and heaven
Were in labor,
The purple sea itself
Was in labor.
A red reed
Came forth from the sea
And from this reed
Came forth smoke
And from this smoke, fire
And from this fire
A child sprang forth—
A boy whose hair
Was in flames
And his eyes
Were like suns . . . .

The 5th-century historian who quotes this passage in his chronicle, comments: "I heard these words sung to the accompaniment of the harp with my own ears. They sing, moreover, that he [Vahagn] fought with dragons and overcame them; and some say that his deeds of valor were like unto those of Hercules."

Another Herculean personage whose many heroic deeds have been handed down to us by word of mouth is David of Sassoun. Forgotten by educated Armenians but remembered by illiterate peasants, the poem known in Armenian as *Sassna Dzerer* was not committed to writing until the 19th century. In this great epic we read about legendary heroes who domesticated lions and tigers, slew tyrants and delivered the people from oppression. Written in a kind of rhythmic prose, interspersed with lyric passages, songs, prayers, and invocations, it speaks of the exploits of Sanasar and Balthasar, the builders of Sassoun; of Sanasar's sons Ohan-the-Thunder-Voiced (whose voice could be heard throughout seven cities—"he wrapped himself up in seven buffalo hides not to burst wide open when he shouted") and Mher (a giant who could pull up trees by their roots, and break a man's arm in seven places by giving him a hearty handshake); of Mher's son, David (who has the strength of Hercules, the cunning of Ulysses, the humor of Till

Eulenspiegel, and the philanthropy of Robin Hood); and of David's son, Little Mher.

Little Mher is a complex, mysterious, fascinating character who speaks some of the best lines in the epic. Here he is, crying out in anguish at his father's grave:

> *Blessed is our Lord God, great is his mercy.*
> *Rise up father dear from your dreamless sleep!*
> *I am frozen numb on this wintry peak.*
> *Tell me what to do, where to dwell*
> *On this ancient earth crumbling under my feet . . . .*
> *Expelled from our house by mine own kin*
> *I wander aimlessly with no place to rest*
> *Longing for your words, your fatherly scent,*
> *Living in exile, homeless everywhere.*

Solitary, arrogant, dispossessed, Little Mher is the strongest of all the Sassoun strong men. On his horse he looks like "a mountain on a mountain"; when he slaps a face, the head flies off; when he touches a tombstone, he leaves marks that are visible to this day. Doomed to live in exile, yet immortal, Little Mher speaks with the voice of Armenians throughout the world.

The language of *Sassna Dzerer* is unsophisticated and simple enough to be understood by a large audience. The story moves rapidly, abruptly. The style is staccato, the sentences short, descriptive passages almost absent, the dialogue laconic—ideal reading matter for the impatient reader of a restless age. When a woman desires a man, she simply says: "I want you to sleep with me." "Impossible!" replies the man. "That's an unheard of thing in my country. I am a Christian and you are nothing but a lawless pagan. I can't go to bed with you." A short scene of seduction follows, after which we are told: "They spent the night together."

When Misra Melik, the mighty king of Egypt, sends emissaries to Sassoun and demands:

> *Forty measures of gold*
> *Forty measures of silver*
> *Forty heifers, forty cows, forty oxen*
> *Forty women tall in stature to load camels*
> *Forty women short in stature to grind the grain*

Forty women of middle size to play and sing
Forty virgins as personal gifts to me as King

David of Sassoun replies: "Forty virgins! My horse is too good for his wife." In the ensuing battle, David defeats single-handed the armies of Misra Melik and his seven powerful allies—

The bodies of the slain piled up on both sides of him as he swept across the plain, and his horse killed as many more, striking them down with his tail, biting off their legs and arms, cracking their skulls under his hooves, trampling them to death like so many ants.

Although none of these epic heroes of Sassoun has been identified with historic personages, the poem itself has been dated back to the 9th century A.D. But there are elements in it that suggest a much older tradition.

The actual writing of *Sassountsi David* or *Mher's Door* (as the first version of the epic came to be known) by Karekin Servantsediants (1840-1892) could be the subject of another epic. Servantsediants came upon the story by chance, and for three years, he tells us, he went from village to village trying to find someone who knew the entire story. Finally, in a village on the plain of Moush, he met a fractious character by the name of Gurbo, who had not recited it for so long that he had forgotten a good deal of it. "Nevertheless I kept him with me for three days," writes Servantsediants; "I begged him, cajoled him, honored him, rewarded him, and when he felt better and was in the proper mood he recited the tale for me in his own village dialect, and I wrote it all down in his own words."

Sassountsi David was first published in Istanbul,[1] in 1874. In addition to fulfilling a longing for an epic of Homeric dimensions in the vernacular, it caused an awakening of interest in the national past. It has been translated into many languages, including Byelorussian and Chinese. "It holds its own in comparison with the greatest works," wrote Simone de Beauvoir after reading the French translation. David of Sassoun is now the Armenian national hero.[2]

Armenian kings and princes of the pre-Christian period were great patrons of the arts. Plutarch mentions that Euripides's *Bacchae* was performed at the Armenian court, and that King Ardavast II (reigned 53-34 B.C.), son of Tigran the Great, was himself the author of many tragedies, histories, and orations in Greek—Greek being the literary as well as commercial and legal medium of exchange in all of Asia Minor. Of these works, however, and in general of pre-Christian written literature, very little has survived: after Armenians were converted to Christianity, pagan books were burned and destroyed.

The alphabet was invented by St. Mesrob Mashtots and a school of translators established by St. Sahak with the financial support of King Vramshapuh (reigned 392-414 A.D.) in the 5th century, the Golden Age *(Vosketar)* of Armenian literature. One hundred scholars were sent abroad to such cultural centers as Athens, Constantinople, Alexandria, and Rome. They were assigned to learn foreign languages and to collect all current literary, philosophical, scientific, religious, and historical works. The Bible, works of Greek (Plato, Aristotle, Euclid), Latin, and Assyrian literatures were translated. The ferment created by this school of translators *(Sourp Tarkmanichk)* inspired a new generation of writers who went on to compile anthologies and write original works—universal histories, chronicles, biographies, polemics, commentaries, sermons, religious and secular poems. Most of these manuscripts were lost, destroyed or burned during the numberless invasions and conquests by barbarians; but a sufficient number survive—12,000 scrolls and 200,000 incunabula and manuscripts in the Matenadaran library (Yerevan) alone, and several other valuable collections in Venice, Jerusalem, Vienna, Leningrad, Tiflis, Ispahan, and a number of art galleries in the United States—to give us a fairly accurate idea of the heights attained by Armenian men of letters. The celebrated French philologist Antoine Meillet once remarked that, at a time when the French spoke a dialect of Latin and had no literature to speak of, the Armenians had already produced a body of important literary works.[3]

Of the 5th century works that have survived, sometimes in mutilated form, particular mentioned should be made of the polemic *Refutation of the Sects* by Yeznik Goghpatsi (Eznik of Kolb), in which we find valuable information about Armenian, Iranian, Greek, and other religious practices of the time;[4] the already mentioned biography of Mashtots by Koriun (see LANGUAGE); a collection of moral discourses by Hovan Mantaguni; an account of the Armeno-

Persian War of 451-454 *(see RELIGION)* and an *Interpretation of Creation* by Yeghishe (Eliseus); and historical works by Paustos Piuzantatsi (Faustus of Byzantium), Ghazar Parbetsi (Lazarus of Pharpi), and Movses Khorenatsi (Moses of Khoren).[5]

A disciple of St. Sahak and St. Mesrob, Khorenatsi (sometimes referred to as "the Armenian Herodotus") belonged to that group of one hundred scholars who were sent abroad to develop their knowledge of foreign languages. Educated at the universities of Edessa and Alexandria, widely travelled in Italy, Greece, and the Middle East, conversant with the languages and literatures of his time, Khorenatsi was a man of wide interests and encyclopedic knowledge. Although commissioned by the governor Sahak Bagratuni (481-484), his *History of the Armenians* has all the earmarks of a labor of love. It is "a work of the first importance for the primitive history of Armenia, not least through its incorporation of many literary remains of the pre-Christian period" *(Oxford Dictionary of the Christian Church)*. The literary remains consist of popular songs, fragments, and summaries of epics that were still sung in Khorenatsi's day in the province of Goghtan, a region known for the excellence of its wines and singers.

It is through Khorenatsi that we first learn of Vahagn (see above), whose parents were Earth and Heaven, and whose eyes were like suns (he has been identified as the god of war or courage); of Ara's rejection of Shamiram (which may be an echo of Gilgamesh's rejection of Ishtar, the goddess of love); of King Yervant, who had so powerful an evil eye that he could break stones in pieces merely by gazing fixedly at them; and of the giant Dork-Ankegh, a descendant of Haik. Ugly and of tremendous strength, Dork-Ankegh was able to break great stones with his hands, and sink ships by hurling rocks at them. But unlike Polyphemus, the cyclop in Homer's *Odyssey,* Dork-Ankegh had the soul of an artist: he smoothed stones and covered them with drawings of eagles and other pictures.

If at times, Khorenatsi sounds more like Homer rather than Herodotus, that is because he did not aim at producing an objective account, but at resurrecting the past of his nation. The age was not one to encourage detached judgment. The works of 5th-century Byzantine historians, like Socrates, Sozomen, and Zosimus of Constantinople, are filled with superstitions, legends, and miracles. Procopius himself, the one great Byzantine historian of the 6th century, shared the superstitions of his age and darkened his pages with portents, oracles, miracles, and dreams.

Written from a patriotic, nationalistic viewpoint, corrected in many details, probably touched up by later hands, Khorenatsi's *History* has lost none of its fascination. It has been translated into many languages, including Latin, French, German, Russian, Italian, Hungarian, and English.

Modern scholars, whose knowledge of ancient history has increased conspicuously by the study of inscriptions and archaeological diggings, have pointed out some inaccuracies and anachronisms in Khorenatsi's work. Some have suggested that he did not live in the 5th century but somewhat later, probably in the 8th century.

Generally speaking however Armenian literary historians like Aram Raffi and Nikol Aghbalian among others, do not doubt Khorenatsi's authenticity. They explain the anachronistic references to events of the 8th century as additions by later copyists. Foreign scholars on the other hand are more skeptical and tend to view Khorenatsi as a propagandist of the Bagratuni dynasty who distorted facts, invented tales, plagiarized, and devised imaginary archives to buttress orally transmitted accounts and his own inventions, in short "an audacious and mendacious faker"—in the words of Robert W. Thomson, an American Armenologist and author of a recent translation of Khorenatsi's book.[6]

Be that as it may, the final and most persuasive argument against Khorenatsi's detractors is to be found in the book itself. Writes Aram Raffi: "In descriptive passages Khorenatsi is unrivalled not only among Armenians, but even as compared with Greek and Roman historians. His statements are concise; what others would take pages to express, he conveys in a few words . . . . His graphic pictures of people and places, together with his remarks and reflections and his frequent quotations from national epics, prove his historical skill and literary taste. As one reads him, one feels him to be a genius of the first magnitude."[7]

"His style is brief, precise, and beautiful," writes Nikol Aghbalian. "Khorenatsi can condense an entire page into one sentence and to summarize an event in a single word . . . . He is a poet whose style is not mere form but the instrument of a cultured and disciplined intellect . . . . His book is composed of 400 medium size pages but contains descriptions of over 1600 individuals, places, mountains, and rivers."[8]

David Anhaght (the Invincible), so called because no one could overcome him in argument, is another great literary figure of the Golden Age. He studied Greek in Byzantium, Alexandria, and Athens (where he was offered the Chair of Philosophy), and spent his last years in an Armenian monastery. Three of his philosophical works have survived: *A Definition of Philosophy,* wherein he criticizes skeptics and pessimists and asserts the cognitive ability of man; *An Interpretation of Aristotle's Analytics,* wherein he supports Christian theology with Greek philosophy; and *An Analysis of the Introduction by Porphyrius,* a Neoplatonist critic of Christianity and biographer of Plotinus and Pythagoras. The world of learning is indebted to the Armenians for preserving and transmitting the works of this philosopher as well as those of many other ancient scholars whose works have perished in their original form—among them, Zeno of Citium (335-263 B.C.), the founder of the Stoic school; Dionysius Thrax (b. 166 B.C.), a Greek grammarian; Theon of Alexandria, the rhetorician; Hermes Trismegistus, the fictitious "divine" author of a large collection of religious writings; Evagrius Ponticus (346-399 A.D.), a desert monk suprisingly active in the literary field; the *Homilies* of St. John Chrysostom; the *Chronicle* of Eusebius; and the Biblical commentaries of Philo.

The enigmatic figure of Agathangelos, a historian who has left a widely translated eyewitness account of the conversion of Armenia by St. Gregory the Illuminator in the 3rd century (*see RELIGION*) may also belong to the 5th century.[9]

The 7th century produced the important *History of Heraclius* of Sebeos—its importance enhanced by the fact that Byzantine historiographical works of this period have been destroyed or have survived only in mutilated form. Little is known about Sebeos, except that he was an ordained bishop and that he wrote his *History* at the request of an unidentified person.

The central theme of Sebeos's book is the conflict between the Byzantine Emperor of Armenian descent Heraclius (610-641) and the Persian King of Kings Khosrov II Parvez (the Victorious: 590-641). It also contains a brief account of the preceding period, besides dealing in some detail with ecclesiastical affairs in Armenia.[10]

Another eminent figure of this period is Hovannes Otznetsi (John of Otzun: ca. 650-729). Esteemed for holiness and learning, Otznetsi was chosen Catholicos in 718. His chief writings consist of pastoral letters, a treatise on the Incarnation, a work against the Paulicians (*see RELIGION*), and many canonical works.

Literary works of the next three centuries consist primarily of historical and military accounts. Ghevont Vartabed's *History of the Caliphs*; Tovma Ardzruni's *History of the House of Ardzruni* which, despite its family bias, is the main source of information on the history of Armenia down to 936—an anonymous historian updated the work to 1121; Stepanos Taronetsi's (Asoghik) *Universal History*; Hovannes Trashkhanakertsi's *History of Armenia*, which at times, reads like a memoir, and contains an unforgettable account of the famine caused by the Arab invasions, during the reign of Ashot Bagratuni (the Iron); and Aristakes Lastivertsi's *History of Armenia*, which centers on the Seljuk invasions in the 11th-century, the fall of the Bagratunis (1045) and the destruction of Ani (1064)—it has been called "as much a prose elegy as a history."

These are learned and able historians, well acquainted with the events they narrate. Most of them were men of high position and had access to information that would ordinarily never have been known.[11]

Another well-known figure of the 11th century is Gregory Magistros, one of the few lay authors in medieval Armenia. A man of vast erudition, Magistros (ca. 990-1059) wrote about astronomy, grammar, medicine, mathematics, philosophy, theology, and history. He was a great admirer of Greek culture and translated many works into Armenian. He writes in a letter: "I have translated numerous writings which I did not find in our language: two dialogues of Plato, the *Timaeus* and the *Phaedo*, and many other writings of the philosophers . . . . I have also begun to translate Euclid's geometry. And if the Lord is willing to protect our life, I shall continue to translate, giving to it my entire care, what remains of the Greeks and the Syrians." Magistros went to Constantinople in 1045 and was received by emperor Constantine Monomachus with marked honor, and welcomed by the Byzantine scholars as one of the great minds of the century. It was said of him that he could "write poetry like Homer and speak like Plato."

From the Golden Age to the 11th century, the Armenian intellectual elite remained faithful to Hellenistic culture. With Grigor Narekatsi (Gregory of Narek: ca. 950-1003) we note a break with this tradition. Little is known about Narekatsi except that his father was a famous bishop and he himself spent most of his life in a monastery not far from Lake Van, praying, studying, teaching, and writing. His works include a *Commentary on the Song of Songs*, which is a prose masterpiece, many panegyrics, hymns, prayers, and chants that are still sung in Armenian churches. His best-known work however is the strikingly original *Book of Lamentations*, also known as *Narek*, a tragic, devotional monologue in 95 chapters. In it, the author portrays himself as one of the vilest creatures ("a wicked and slothful servant; an abusive contradicter; an ass's foal, intractable, wild, and uncouth; the broken lock on a door; the useless coin buried beneath the soil; ever active in satanic inventions; slow in mine observance of promises; diligent in malignant acts of ribaldry"), saying that if he were to transform the waters of some sea into ink and cut into pens a groveful of reeds from the forest, he would not be able to enumerate all his sins. But that God in his infinite mercy, power and glory ("bestower of life unto the dead; reviver of the universe; unclouded wisdom; unerring vision; cup of enchantment; inviolable garment; inexhaustible treasure; irrevocable command") will bleach these sins as snow. The purpose of *Narek* is to produce completeness in the expression of grief and to bring about a cleansing of the conscience through a total confession of sin.

A visionary and a mystic, yet an acute observer, Narekatsi writes in a precise, muscular style and at times attains rhapsodic heights in which divine intoxication is never without a homey common sense. The device of dramatic contrast is constantly used. Biblical quotations abound. His mania for repetition has an irresistible, almost incantatory quality. Writes Aram Raffi: "Narek was formerly regarded with veneration little short of that accorded to the Bible itself. Within recent times superstitious people ascribed to it miraculous medical qualities, believing that if certain chapters were read over a patient he would be cured." Elsewhere we read that "pious people for long centuries have put it—and still do put it—under their pillows as a guard against the power of evil."[12]

After the 11th-century Seljuk invasions, Armenian literature was divided into a Western (Armenia Minor) and an Eastern (Armenia Major) branch. The Silver Age occurred in Cilicia (Armenia Minor), in the 12th century. Here, protected against north and west by high mountains, impregnable forts, and dense forests, Armenians were able to develop once more a literary culture "on a higher artistic level than anything yet achieved in the West" (Jack Lindsay).

Nerses Shnorhali (the Gracious: 1098-1172) is celebrated for his elegant style, his erudition, his unerring judgment. In the total range of his talents he was unequaled by any other man of his time. Sincerely interested in reconciling the Greek and Armenian churches, Shnorhali also reveals himself, in his correspondence with Emperor Manuel Comnenus of Byzantium, to be a skillful diplomat.

The author of an astonishing number of works, ranging from encyclicals to riddles, Shnorhali's most important writings include a verse history of the Armenian nation, an elegy on the fall of the city of Edessa to the Saracens, a panegyric of the True Cross, a vast poem on the life of Christ titled *Jesus, Only-Begotten of the Father,* and some of the most beautiful sacred poems, prayers, and hymns in the language. Collections of his prayers and poems have been translated into 36 languages. Like Narekatsi, Shnorhali was an accomplished composer and often set his poems and prayers to melodies of his own composition. Some of these chants or *sharagans* (literally "rows of gems") have been incorporated in the traditional liturgy and are still sung in Armenian churches.[13]

This is also the epoch of outstanding chroniclers whose first-hand accounts of a critical period in the history of Armenia, Iran, and Byzantium, are indispensable even if at times partisan: Matthew of Edessa; Samuel of Ani, author of a famous *Chronology* (Jamanagakroutiun), which enumerates important events up to 1179; Vartan the Great (*History of the Archers*), Vahram Rapuni, Constable Sempat (13th century); Stephen Orbelian of Siunia (14th century); Thomas Metsop (*History of Timur*—15th century). Most of these writers participated in the events they describe. Verbatim quotations of important letters and conversations are many. In Matthew of Edessa's *Chronicle* for instance we find Emperor John Tzimisces of Byzantium (*see* HISTORY) describing the purpose of his military operations in Syria:

> The aim of our campaign was to chasten the pride and arrogance of the Amir al-Mumenin, ruler of the Africans, called the Baghrid Arabs, who have attacked us with considerable forces. First they placed our army in danger, but then we conquered them thanks to our irresistible strength and the help of God, and they retreated in disgrace like our other enemies. We then attacked the interior of the country and put to the sword the peoples of many provinces; and finally we made a prompt withdrawal to our winter quarters.

New literary forms also began to appear at this time. Mekhitar Gosh (1133-1213) compiled a *Lawbook* (Tadastanakirk Hayots) which became the basis of Armenian Law, and wrote fables, 190 of which have survived.[14]

Vartan Aykegtsi (ca. 1180-1255) is another fabulist who satirized social types in the guise of beasts. A wandering preacher by avocation, Aykegtsi liked to illustrate his sermons with anecdotes and fables, forty of which are now regarded as original, the rest going back to the legendary figure of Aesop, himself more of a collector and adapter than an original story-teller. After undergoing many changes, Aykegtsi's fables were gathered in collections variously titled *Vartan's Fables* and *The Book of the Fox*.

A typical Armenian beast fable tells the story of an ambitious owl who proposes marriage to a foolish eagle with the words: "You are the ruler of the day, and I am the ruler of the night. It will be in our interest to form an alliance by marriage." The eagle accepts the proposal, but the marriage is a complete failure because the bridegroom cannot see by day, and the bride cannot see by night. This fable was meant as a warning against marriages between Christians and pagans.

Some of these stories or apologues speak in examples and lack a story line. To illustrate the futility of misguided action, Aykegtsi tells of three men, one of whom climbed mountains trying to catch a wind and take it home with him: "But though he tried a hundred years, he never caught a wind that was as big as a drop of rain." The other man sat down by the side of a river, trying to use its waters as a tablet on which to inscribe an elegy: "But though he labored for a hundred years, he could not trace a single letter." The third man surpassed the other two by undertaking two impossible enterprises at once: during the day, he tried to catch his own shadow, and at night, he shot arrows at the stars in order to bring them home that he alone might have light.

Armenian folktales have a charm and flavor of their own. They invariably begin and end with the words: "There was and there was not . . ." and, "Three apples fell from heaven: the first for the one who told the tale, the second for the one who listened, and the third for the one who understood."[15]

In this connection let us also mention Armenian proverbial sayings which reflect the longings and trials, the joys and sorrows, and above all the warmth, wisdom, and indomitable humor of a people that maintained its identity through millennia of persecution and massacre.

Here are some typical examples:

"Teaching consists in opening the mind; the mouth will open by itself."

"A wise man needs few words; a fool needs many."

"A wealthy man is nothing but a thief who has not yet been caught."

"Cat-play is mouse-death.

"His cunning is such that he even knows where the devil sleeps."

"To the poor, everyone is generous with advice."
"Crime for the rich, punishment for the poor."
"When the price of bread goes up, the price of life comes down."
"When God wants to make a poor man happy, He makes him lose his donkey and then find it again."
"Better an ant's head than a lion's tail."
"Give flowers to a donkey and he will eat them."[16]

Krikor Datevatsi (Gregory of Datev: 1346-1410) is the foremost theologian and philosopher of the Armenian Church. He was active mainly in the monastery of Datev which in its heyday contained over 500 monks, scribes, scholars, painters, and musicians. His massive, encyclopaedic outline of theology, titled *The Book of Questions* (Kirk Hartsmants), is a masterful synthesis of the works and teachings of St. Augustine, Albertus Magnus, St. Thomas Aquinas (whose *Summa Theologica* had been translated into Armenian in 1347) and other Church Fathers of both East and West. Datevatsi was also an accomplished painter and musician.

His nephew, Arakel Siunetsi (ca. 1350-1425) was likewise an able philosopher, theologian, musician, and poet whose *Book of Adam* (Adamkirk) has been called "the oriental *Paradise Lost.*" Speaking of Adam, Siunetsi writes: "He deserted God, but not the woman. Without her, half of his body was dead, and with the other half it was impossible to live."

Following Timur's invasion in the 15th century, Western Armenian culture moved from Cilicia to Constantinople. Thereafter Western literature came under the influence of European masters, while Eastern literature acquired a more Russian character.

The invention of the printing press in 1476 and the revival of nationalism in the 19th century, ushered in two additional periods of intense literary activity. The first Armenian book, titled *Parzatumar* (Explanatory Calendar) was published in Venice in 1512. The first Armenian magazine, *Azdarar* (Herald) was issued in 1794 in Madras (India). The first Armenian newspaper, the weekly *Arevelian Tsanutsmants* (Eastern News) was published in 1815 in

Astrakhan. By 1920, more than 460 printing houses had been in operation at various times throughout the world, publishing books, magazines, and newspapers in the Armenian language.

In 1717, following the Turkish conquest of Morea (Peloponnesus), a Catholic Armenian monk by the name of Mekhitar Petrossian (1676-1749) chose the Island of San Lazzaro in Venice as the site of his new monastery. Mekhitar was not the first Armenian to settle in Venice. The Armenians were already firmly established there at the beginning of the 12th century, their position consolidated by the financial assistance of a Doge who had made a fortune in Armenia Minor.

A man of untiring energy, Mekhitar founded a religious community known as the Mekhitarists, in addition he collected many manuscripts, built a school and a printing press, compiled a monumental dictionary and two grammars of the Armenian language, one of *krapar*, the other of *ashkharapar*. The Mekhitarists are active to this day, publishing complete editions of classic and modern authors, translations from foreign literatures—from Homer, Plato, Virgil, Dante, Shakespeare and Milton to Goethe, Dickens, Chateaubriand, Leopardi, Turgenev, Paul Valery and many others—and making original contributions of their own. Some of the most prolific and influential men of letters of recent times have been Mekhitarist monks—historian Mikael Chamichian (1738-1823); philologist and theologian Gabriel Avedikian (1790-1827); grammarian and poet Arsen Bagratuni (1790-1860), author of an epic poem of gigantic dimensions titled *Haik, the Hero* (Haik Tiutsazn), whose central character is Haik, the forefather of the Armenian nation; ethnographer and romantic poet Leo Alishan (1820-1901); and more recently literary historian Mesrob Janashian (1908-1974), author of an important *History of Modern Armenian Literature: 1701-1920* (Venice, 1956).[17]

Among these the most celebrated and prolific figure is Leo Alishan. Born in Istanbul, Alishan was educated in a number of universities in Europe and spent most of his life in Venice teaching, editing *Pazmaveb* (a literary periodical still published to this day), and producing an enormous quantity of prose and verse of a more or less patriotic cast. His poetry (*Songs of a Patriarch, The Nightingale of Avarair*, which is based on the 5th-century historian Yeghishe, recorder of Vartanants, *Shoushan of Shavarshan*, and many others) was widely read, and influenced the younger generation of poets, among them Daniel Varoujan (see below) who called Alishan "an eagle with a sun in his heart."

Alishan also produced voluminous studies on the philology, history, ethnography, geography, and botany of several Armenian provinces *(Shirak, Ayrarat, Sissakan,* and others), some of which, like the one devoted to Armenia Minor, *Sissouan ou l'Armeno-Cilicie* (Venice, 1889), have been translated into French.

Alishan was the first major writer of his time to abandon *krapar* for *ashkharapar*. He did this independently of Abovian, who is generally regarded as the father of modern Armenian literature.

Though often out of touch with real political conditions and literary currents, the Mekhitarists' activities as educators, writers and publishers (activities that were supported by wealthy Armenian merchants from India) were instrumental in awakening interest in the national past and introducing European influences in Armenian culture.

The Mekhitarists of Venice and their splinter group in Vienna are now two important Armenian intellectual centers of the diaspora. The Library of San Lazzaro in Venice contains one of the greatest collections of rare manuscripts in the world; also paintings by Tiepolo, Aivazovsky, and many others, relics of Byron—who spent some time there—and a visitors' book which includes the signatures of Browning, Longfellow, Marcel Proust, William Dean Howells, and an endless array of diplomats, statesmen, and kings.

Mkrtich Khrimian (1820-1907), better known as Khrimian Hairik (Little Father), was a contemporary of Alishan and one of the most important figures of the East-Armenian literary and political revival. A devoted champion of the Armenian national liberation movement, Khrimian was a powerful author of both prose and verse, also founder and editor of the influential periodicals *Eagle of Vaspuragan* and *Eagle of Taron*. Writes Henry F.B. Lynch:

> *His labors were directed to the education of his countrymen; "educate, educate"—the girls no less than the boys—may be said to have been his*

watchword.... Schools sprang up in abundance beneath the magic of his individuality, and teachers were imbued with that enthusiasm for their high calling without which their profession savors of drudgery and tends to produce a similar impression upon their pupils ....

In 1892, at the age of 71, Khrimian was unanimously elected Catholicos or Supreme Patriarch of all Armenians; and when, in 1905, the Czar issued a decree appropriating all properties of the Armenian Church, Khrimian temporarily dismissed all the abbots, primates, and diocesan leaders so that he alone could be held responsible for his policy of non-violent non-cooperation.

One of Khrimian's pupils and devoted admirers was Karekin Servantsediants, author, editor, teacher, and compiler of *Sassountsi David* (discussed above). Another admirer was the lyric poet Bedros Tourian.

Another major literary figure of the East-Armenian literary and political revival is Abovian. Regarded by literary historians as the father of modern Armenian literature, Khachatur Abovian (1805-1848) authored the first Armenian novel in *ashkharapar*, or the spoken idiom, *The Wounds of Armenia* (Verk Hayastani) which, after *Narek*, is probably the most critically acclaimed and *widely* discussed and admired work in Armenian literature.

Abovian's life reads like a novel with an adventure-story beginning and a mysterious as well as tragic ending. Of peasant stock, he was brought up in the village of Kanaker, not far from Yerevan. At the age of eighteen he entered the service of the Catholicos at Etchmiadzin. The turning point in his life was the arrival there of Dr. Friedrich Parrot, a professor of natural philosophy from the University of Dorpat (Tartu) in Estonia. With Abovian's help Dr. Parrot became the first explorer in modern times to reach the summit of Ararat in 1829. The two men became fast friends. From 1830 to 1836 Abovian studied philosophy, languages (German, French, English, Latin), music, history, and the sciences at the University of Dorpat. From 1836 to 1848 he devoted his life to writing, translating (among others Homer, Goethe, Schiller, Karamzin), and teaching.

Shortly after he began to teach in Tiflis, Abovian observed that his pupils preferred to read Russian, because Armenian books (mostly about kings, princes, saints, or biblical personages) were written in a nearly incomprehensible *krapar* or classical Armenian. The idea of writing a novel that could be read and enjoyed by anyone familiar with the Armenian alphabet excited him so much that he spent many feverish, sleepless nights buried in books and papers studying the language of the *ashughs* (minstrels) together with the most recent technical innovations in the art of fiction. Abovian's merit however goes beyond matters concerning technique and the use of the spoken idiom. Abovian wrote about heroes with whom the people could easily identify—Aghasi, the protagonist of his novel, is a common peasant—stressing not so much obedience to authority (the predominant "message" in the literature of all authoritarian regimes) but love for parents, friends, and country (subversive themes and ultimately, in the eyes of the establishment, revolutionary concepts).

Abovian was an intensely committed writer—and committed in the Sartrian sense—a writer who saw the "angularity" of his time and the options that the historic moment presented: obedience to the Asiatic tyrant and eventual assimilation on the one hand, and on the other, self-determination and the adoption of the best ideological and technological elements of the West. Writes Rouben Zarian, the author of an excellent biography: "Abovian was a man of great culture, a profoundly erudite man with a wide range of interests. Fluent in seven or eight languages, he was interested in everything —philosophy, psychology, economy, history, pedagogy . . . ." As a pedagogue, Abovian was greatly influenced by the doctrines of Rousseau and Pestalozzi and believed that every person, even the lowest, has inherent powers capable of development. These liberal views, together with his persistent efforts to reform the educational system, alienated him from the Armenian establishment—the clergy and the wealthy merchants: an alliance that has always been on the side of reaction rather than progress. As a result, he may have committed suicide, or, as a thinker impossible to muzzle, he may have been secretly assassinated by agents of the Czar.

Abovian was a revolutionary with the temperament of a martyr. "All I want," he once declared, "is to give my life to my beloved country; to serve her as long as there is breath in my mouth." He had none of the ruthless cunning of first-rate revolutionaries like Marx and Lenin. Perhaps for that reason, as a man, he is a much more attractive figure. It is impossible not to be touched by his youthful enthusiasm, energy, and idealism, even when he went to extremes. As a student in Dorpat (Estonia) for instance, in addition to mastering a wide range of disciplines within the university walls, he also tried to learn how to bake bread and manufacture glass. He already saw himself as the educator of an entire subcontinent, a man through whom not only the culture of the West, but its technology as well would be introduced into the Caucasus. Abovian's intense dedication to his people thus transcended all forms of narrow nationalism; it was instead an expression of humanism at its purest and best.[18]

Following Abovian's example, Berj Broshian (Perch Proshiants, Hovannes Der-Arakelian: 1837-1907), wrote short stories and a number of novels which give a realistic picture of Armenian village life of the late 19th century. His first novel, *Sos and Varditer* (1860), may be regarded as an Armenian village variant of Romeo and Juliet. In *The Problem of Bread* (1880), Broshian writes about a corrupt district chief whose abuse of power oppresses the helpless peasants and ruins an honorable family. *Apple of Contention* (1878), another one of his better-known novels, centers on the heroic self-defense of the villagers of Ashtarak under Persian domination. Broshian himself was born in Ashtarak, a village (now a city) twenty kilometers northwest of Yerevan. By profession a teacher, he was greatly influenced by the ideas of Tolstoy and the novels of Dickens, both of whom he translated into Armenian. But the decisive event in his life was a reading of Abovian's *Wounds of Armenia*. Immediately after reading it, Broshian writes in his *Autobiography*, "I bought paper and ink at the nearest stationery shop, five kopecks worth of bread at the bakery, and locked myself up in my room. With my knee for a desk I wrote. I was writing *Sos and Varditer*."

Another great regionalist and contemporary of Broshian was Ghazaros Aghayan (1840-1911), one of the founders of the autobiographical novel in Armenian literature. Most of his work appeared in the last century, but his influence extends to the twentieth. Mainly self-taught, Aghayan was also an editor and educator whose political activities made him a target of the Czarist secret police. His novels and poems—*Haroutiun and Manuel* (1867), *Two Sisters* (1872), *Anahid* (1881), *Dork Ankegh* (1888)—enjoyed wide popularity. He also authored translations (Krylov, Schiller, Heine, Tolstoy, Shakespeare, Pushkin), some of the most widely used school texts of his time, important essays on a large variety of topics, and an autobiography titled *The Main Events of My Life* (1893).

Though he was a radical critic of social conditions, Aghayan had no definite political views. "His worldview," writes Avedik Issahakian in his reminiscences, "was a peculiar combination of socialism, Christianity, democratic-humanism, nationalism, and cosmopolitanism. He was an optimist for whom sorrow and misfortune were interludes of very short duration. Throughout his life, Aghayan remained an enthusiastic believer and dreamer who dreamt with the intensity of an adolescent and never ran out of dreams."

The greatest novelist of the 19th century, however, is Raffi (Hagop Melik-Hagopian: 1835-1888). Born in a small village in Persian Armenia, but active mainly in Tiflis (Georgia), Raffi was a prolific writer who, in addition to many historical novels, produced scholarly works, short stories, and translations. He had all the satisfactions of being widely read in his own time, but his popularity brought him small financial yield. To support nine sisters and a growing family of his own, he wrote furiously all day, and sometimes deep into the night. His novels—*Jalaleddin* (1878), *The Fool* (1880), *David Beg* (1881), *The Golden Cockerel* (1882), *Sparks* (1883), *Samuel* (1896), and others—are a treasure-house of ethnographical information.

Like Abovian, Raffi aimed at uniting the Armenians of Persia, Turkey, and Russia in a common struggle against foreign domination. A gentle, soft-spoken man, he became unusually pugnacious when the subject turned to politics. He was convinced that words, action, and if necessary, force had to be used to combat tyranny. "Patriotism and nationalism," he said, "are holy duties for every individual and the war for freedom and protection of the fatherland is a holy war." Raffi blamed Christianity for the defenselessness of the Armenian people, regretting that the Armenians had built monasteries instead of fortresses, and had emphasized church implements instead of weapons. Foreseeing the indifference of European powers, Raffi wanted Armenians to be self-reliant and to expect no assistance from foreigners.

Raffi has been criticized for the shallow psychology of his characters—a criticism that he would have dismissed as irrelevant. What interested him was not the subterranean motivations of his characters, but their purpose in life, their awareness of history. In that sense, all his fictional heroes incarnate his ideals and political programs. The vision which concludes *The Fool* epitomizes Raffi's dreams of a future independent Armenia. Vartan, the protagonist, returning home from the Russo-Turkish wars (1877-78), finds the village of Alashkert destroyed and his beloved Lala dead. At her grave he falls unconscious with grief and exhaustion, and has a vision in which Eden has been reinstated in Armenia—but an Eden that has been brought about by hard, honest, skillful labor. Innocence, ignorance, and fear of a vengeful Jehovah have been replaced with awareness and wisdom. Vartan sees a completely rebuilt Alashkert, where even Armenia's perennial enemies, the Kurds, have been civilized and assimilated. "Kurds? What Kurds?" says an astonished villager when Vartan broaches the subject. "I remember reading about them in books of ancient history, but they no longer exist."[19] Vartan takes a walk through the village and everywhere he sees peace and harmony. Instead of uninviting, dreary shacks, he sees elegant stone houses with flowering gardens. The dusty roads have been transformed into tree-lined avenues.[20] Only one thing has not changed, Raffi hastens to add, and that is the Armenian language.

As a "bourgeois nationalist," Raffi's works were banned in the Soviet Union. But at the outbreak of World War II, when the Soviet regime wanted to propagate a militant patriotic spirit by recalling the courage and steadfastness which Armenians had shown in the past in their struggle against foreign invaders, Raffi was "rehabilitated" and his works were reprinted. The first edition sold out within a few hours. It is reported that such excited crowds gathered around Yerevan's principal bookstore that shop windows were broken and the militia had to be called to establish order.

Mikael Nalbandian (1829-1866) shared Raffi's intense nationalism and anticlericalism. He is generally regarded as one of the founders of modern literary criticism and esthetics. "When the Promethean fire of enlightenment flares before the eyes of the people," he said, "those they had previously admired will be revealed as no more than stubborn ignoramuses, children of darkness, and servants of lies." He was equally concerned with the subject of nationalism. "A people may want to rid themselves of nationalism and egoism, but they must not destroy their nationhood in the process. On the contrary, all nationalities should be recognized, all of them organized, since the universal organism of humanity may emerge from their unification."

Born in New Nakhitchevan, Nalbandian travelled widely in India, England, and Italy, where he witnessed Garibaldi's revolution. He became a close associate of such progressive Russian thinkers as Herzen, and Chernishevsky, with whom he was arrested and imprisoned. His works include patriotic verse, social, political, and philosophical essays, a posthumously published novel (*One's Word*), literary criticism, letters, polemics, and translations from German and Russian literatures.[21]

Of Yeghia Demirjibashian (1851-1908), one of the most brilliant figures of the literary revival in Istanbul, it is extremely difficult to say much in a little space. A potent but uneven intellect, he might have been a great poet, a great philosopher, or a great novelist; but he so dispersed his energies that he never attained the highest rank in any field. As a student, Demirjibashian became a convert to Schopenhauer's ethic of renunciation and pessimism. But in his reformist zeal and seething temperament, he reminds one of Nietzsche rather than Schopenhauer. His private life was a series of violent passions. After the early death of his parents and brother, he led a solitary, secluded existence. Emotionally unstable and subject to frequent fits of depression and persecution mania, he spent a few years in an asylum and took his own life at the age of forty-seven.

Demirjibashian's production includes novels, short stories,

essays, letters, funeral orations, dictionaries, philosophical and political works, and autobiographical writings, in addition to a corpus of brilliant journalistic commentary. A superlative stylist, he has been called "the Narekatsi of *ashkharapar*." He was an advocate of art for art's sake and maintained that "A true work of art is more moral than any book or sermon on morality."

Hagop Baronian (1842-1891) is the foremost satirist in the Armenian language. He was born and educated in Edirne (Adrianople), in that corner of Turkey which adjoins Greece and Bulgaria, but was active mainly in Istanbul. His family was extremely poor, his health precarious (he was to die of tuberculosis at the age of fifty), his education minimal. But being a brilliant child, he mastered several languages and read all the classics in Greek, French, and Italian. He began to work at an early age and held a variety of jobs in Istanbul, then one of the most important cultural centers of the Armenian diaspora. This gave him an excellent opportunity to study the marketplace with its many colorful occupations and types. After contributing sketches to several periodicals he became the editor of a periodical himself. He authored plays (among which *Brother Balthazar* enjoyed enormous popularity and is still widely performed today) and several novels, the most widely admired of which is *The Honorable Beggars*—a delightful and enduring little masterpiece about human greed and vanity wherein every character without exception is either an imbecile or a liar, and sometimes both at once.

The plot of *Honorable Beggars* (which is available in English) is simplicity itself. Apissoghom Agha, a wealthy merchant from Trebizond, comes to Istanbul in search for a wife. This search, however, is obstructed by a wide and colorful assortment of charlatans (editors, journalists, poets, priests, marriage brokers, lawyers, barbers . . .) who approach him one by one and insist on helping him in order that in the process they may help themselves. Of particular interest is Apissoghom Agha's encounter with a young, ambitious poet who asks him to be his patron and to subsidize the publication of one of his fiery patriotic speeches. Apissoghom Agha who, like Moliere's *bourgeois gentilhomme*, doesn't even know whether or not he speaks prose, gives him the money just to get rid of him. But immediately after, he has second thoughts. As a good merchant he can't see why he should give something and get nothing in return. He therefore asks the poet if it would be possible to list on the cover of the booklet his "cattle, sheep, donkeys, and farms in Trebizond." The poet, who seems to have dealt with this type before, replies: "Those things belong to the pastoral side of poetry." Understandably enough Apissoghom Agha says: "I don't understand you." The poet then explains that he could write a poem about his menagerie but since his muse visits him only once every two months, he cannot produce such a poem on short notice. Whereupon Apissoghom Agha, who is beginning to acquire a fairly accurate understanding of all matters regarding literary creation, makes the following inquiry:

"If we give her two or three pounds, would she come quickly?" "Well of course," the poet replies, "if you were to give two pounds, it would make things easier, and my muse would come running this week."[22]

Baronian's dialogue is authentic, his satire sharp. He rarely strikes a false note and his choice of situations that will project typical behavior in bold relief is always unerring. Notwithstanding his wide popularity however, Baronian was throughout his life overworked and underpaid.

Yervant Odian (1869-1926) is another brilliant satirist whose work has lost none of its relevance. Born in Istanbul into a wealthy family of diplomats and intellectuals, Odian began to write early. "First thing I did after I learned how to read and write was to publish a hand-written newspaper," he tells us in one of his autobiographical essays. "In it I recorded the fights between the maid and the cook, the day's menu, the people who came to see my father, and miscellaneous other occurrences." He goes on to say that the paper had only three subscribers: his father, his mother, and an aunt who happened to be staying with them at the time.

A lifelong bachelor and a heavy drinker, Odian was also an indefatigable traveller who at one time or another lived and worked in virtually all the major population centers between London and Bombay. Once, when asked why he drank so much, he said: "To drown my sorrows." Was he successful in drowning them? "No," he replied, "the rascals are excellent swimmers."

Reserved in emotion, a stoic, Odian was a pleasant mild-mannered man who had a Chekhovian distaste for all ideas and ideologies and by extension political parties, committees, and organizations. But I think it would be more accurate to say that what Odian detested most was the individual who by joining a group, any group, behaved according to its tenets and in the process shed part of his humanity.

Odian's satire may lack Baronian's bite, but his style is more polished, literate, and his outlook more cosmopolitan. He drew inspiration from models as diverse as Zola, Tolstoy, and Dostoevsky (all of whom he translated into Armenian). His plots are filled with screamingly amusing incidents. He generally withholds authorial comment, but he is never disinterested. All his works were written with intense moral passion in response to some specific event or character that had aroused his anger and scorn.

In addition to a series of autobiographical books (*Twelve Years Outside Constantinople, The Cursed Years, Literary Reminiscences, Blood-Stained Memories, Recollections of My Childhood,* and others), Odian wrote many novels, the most widely admired of which are: *The Revolutionary Parasites* (1899), *Family, Honor, Morality* (1910), *War and Peace* (1911), *The Art of Being Perfect* (1913), and *Comrade Panchoonie* (1914).

In *The Revolutionary Parasites,* Odian excoriates pettybourgeois intellectuals who pose as revolutionaries but are in fact social parasites, informers, spies, reactionaries, and incompetent meddlers.

The protagonist of *Family, Honor, Morality* is a "pillar of society," a vulgar and unscrupulous character, infinitely inconsiderate and selfish, who dies a horribly slow death of a knife-wound received in a bordello scuffle. His hypocrisy is such that in his will he stipulates that the words *Family, Honor, Morality* be engraved on his tombstone.

War and Peace is an epistolary novel in which two brothers, Hovan and Simon, exchange notes about life and describe their daily existence. Hovan has chosen a military career; Simon a family life with a wife and a nagging mother-in-law. Life at home turns out to be more lethal than actual combat.

The Art of Being Perfect is a collection of letters written by a merchant named Kosma, who preaches an oriental brand of American pragmatism and amoralism, in which financial success and the acquisition of wealth are represented as the noblest goals in life.

Comrade Panchoonie[23] is a savage attack on the misuse of language and more specifically political rhetoric. "With all his passion for talking," Odian writes in the short biographical sketch of Panchoonie that introduces the novel,

> little Panchoonie misused words repeatedly, often corrupting their meaning altogether. One day he picked up a valuable vase from the table and slammed it to the floor, shattering it into a hundred pieces.

Scolded by his father, Panchoonie justifies his act of vandalism by saying, "I fixed it."

> "What do you mean you fixed it? You broke it, you little devil." "No, father, I fixed it," the boy insisted.

From a foolish meddler, Panchoonie develops into a dangerous zealot convinced that his cause will change the course of human affairs for the better and that he himself is absolutely vital to the success of that cause. Panchoonie (literally "Hasnothing") is a character *sui generis*. He bears no resemblance to Don Quixote or Sancho Panza—he lacks Panza's horse sense and the Don's noble innocence (confronted with a windmill he would probably "fix it" as an instrument of bourgeois exploitation even if that meant starving the neighboring villages). Panchoonie moreover lives on a strict diet of black-and-white extremes and contradictions. In one of his seething letters to the Central Committee (which invariably end with the by now legendary words *Mi kich pogh oughargetsek*— Send a little money) he writes:

> "We are all Armenians, we are brothers. Why can't we live together? Why must we fight?" that filthy bourgeois kept repeating, not being able to comprehend that conflict is the basic condition of life, that class conflict is essential to socialist victory, and that it is impossible to do any good at all without at least a little bloodshed . . . .

In vain did I repeat that violent class conflict must be waged between us, that they had to use against us every evil means at their command—betrayal, false accusation, force; without these it would not be possible to have a dirty bourgeois class, the existence of which was essential if we were to wage our noble revolutionary struggle against it.

Odian wrote with unbelievable speed. Many of his works still lie buried in the files of old periodicals; nonetheless, what has been collected and published so far is staggering. The mere listing of the titles of his books would fill several pages. He seems to have been at ease in many genres—novels, short stories, plays, travelogues, biographical works, political journalism, literary essays, and translations.

Among Armenian dramatists, Gabriel Sundukian (1825-1912) is without a rival. Born in Tiflis, he studied Eastern languages at the University of St. Petersburg. An avid reader, his favorite writers were Shakespeare, Moliere, and above all Gogol. "I owe more to Gogol than to anyone else," he has said. Some of his better known plays —*Sneezing at Night Is a Good Omen* (1863), *Embarrassment (Khatabala*—1866), *Oskan Petrovich in the Next World* (1866), *Yet Another Victim* (1870), *Pepo* (1871), *The Husbands* (1890), *Love and Freedom* (1909)—are still widely performed today in Armenia and Georgia (where he is regarded as a Georgian playwright because the action of his plays is set in Tiflis and because Sundukian himself translated most of them into Georgian).

Sundukian was the first Armenian dramatist of commanding genius to deal with the middle and lower classes. His common people are profoundly human and his merciless attacks on greed and mendacity reveal a mind preoccupied more with moral and ethical questions than class conflict. His plays were admired by among others Alexandre Dumas *fils* and Maxim Gorky, who edited one of the three extant Russian translations of *Pepo*.

Bedros Tourian (1852-1872) was the first poet to free the language from its classical formalism and speak in a vernacular that was both pure and noble. Born and educated in Istanbul (Hagop Baronian was one of his teachers), Tourian died of tuberculosis at the age of twenty. His entire *oeuvre* consists of about ten plays on historic themes, thirteen letters, and forty poems, where he speaks of death and ruin, unrequited love, helpless anger at social injustice, and hatred of all despotism. Tourian is also said to have left an unfinished autobiographical novel titled *Nights of Bosphorus,* which, like some of his plays, perished in a fire shortly after his death. His influence on succeeding generations of poets was huge. "Tourian's tears touched my frozen soul and opened it like a flower in spring," one of them wrote. "It was through his poetry that I began to understand the language of flowers and the sweetness of sorrow . . . . I was inebriated with life's lyric song and the sun's wine." (Vahan Totovents.)

Another celebrated poet who, like Tourian, died of tuberculosis in his twenties, was Missak Medzarents (Medzadourian: 1886-1908). Medzarents began writing and publishing in his teens. His poems—mainly nature and love lyrics of a mystical cast—convey subtle sensations in musically expressive language. In addition to Tourian, Medzarents admired and studied closely Narekatsi and Armenian folk songs which even as a boy he loved to collect and sing. His entire output consists of two collections of verse—*Rainbow* (1906), and *New Songs* (1907).

The founder of East-Armenian realism in both fiction and drama, Shirvanzadeh (Alexander Movsessian: 1858-1935) was born in Shamakh, Azerbaijan or Shirvan (his pen name means "son of Shirvan"), and was mainly self-taught. He spent his formative years as an accountant in Baku—one of his greatest novels, *Chaos* (1898), contains an unforgettable picture of early days in the Baku oil industry. He also lived in Paris (1905-1910), the United States (1919-1926), and the USSR (1926-1935) where he died as an alcoholic.

In his fiction, Shirvanzadeh exposes a society dominated by greed, superstition, fierce puritanism, and its inevitable offspring, gossip—"How can it be slander," a character of his exclaims, "if the whole town knows and speaks about it?" Like Dostoevsky, Shirvanzadeh seems to have found some of his prototypes (the murderous old woman in his novel *The Evil Spirit,* for instance, and her victim, a saintly young woman who is also her daughter-in-law and a tormented epileptic) in gothic novels rather than real life. Even at its most sensational, however, his work is animated by a deep concern for truth and social justice. Though he has been criticized for consistently avoiding the major events that affected his people during his lifetime, in a series of short stories ("The Liar," "The Man of Principle," and others), Shirvanzadeh offered astute analyses of the Armenian temperament. His plays, which are mostly adaptations from his novels—the already-mentioned *Chaos, Namus* (1885), *For the Sake of Honor* (1914) [24]—are still widely performed today and they have been made into successful films and operas. He has also authored an insightful and amusing autobiography titled *From My Life* (1938). His complete works in ten volumes appeared in Yerevan in 1958-62.

Equally many-sided and prolific was the East-Armenian Hovannes Toumanian (1869-1923). The son of a clergyman, Toumanian was born in Loree (Armenia), educated in Tiflis, was active mainly in Yerevan, and died in Moscow. A deeply committed writer whose youthful, pre-Revolutionary political activities caused him great trouble, including prison sentences and exile, Toumanian is generally regarded as the national poet of Armenia. "Poetry for him wasn't simply a literary genre," writes the Soviet-Armenian critic Edward Topchian, "but a form of struggle for the survival of his people. Toumanian and the Armenian people, Toumanian and the destiny of the Armenian people, are indivisible concepts."

Toumanian's poetry began to appear in Tiflis in 1890. His work of this period bears the unmistakable influence of Alishan, Pushkin, and Lermontov. Gradually however he emerged as a writer of commanding genius and great popular appeal, who went on to produce an endless stream of social, patriotic, love, and nature lyrics, satirical verses, philosophical quatrains, short stories, fables for children, adaptations of national epics, masterful essays on, among others, Shakespeare, Tolstoy, Pushkin, Lermontov, Sayat-Nova, and Abovian, as well as criticism, legends, ballads, and narrative poems. He provided the poetic themes for two of Armenia's most popular operas: *Anoush* by Armen Tigranian and *Almast* by Alexander Spendiarian (*see* MUSIC). His language is rich in local dialect and other vernacular elements, and gives a faithful impression both of the background and of the mentality of his characters.

"A restless, complex, Faustian spirit," according to Avedik Issahakian, "Toumanian had so many projects that to carry them all out he would have to live for centuries. He wanted to be a millionaire, to own palaces and all kinds of luxuries; to host banquets . . . . He wanted to surround himself with beautiful things—antiques, precious stones, ornaments, works of art, horses, libraries, museums. He wanted to be wise. He wanted to read everything, to write, to produce comedies, dramas, especially dramas, essays . . . . He wanted to be everywhere, preside over meetings, win elections, manage activities and organize groups . . . . He loved nature like a peasant, he loved animals, he loved the earth, he loved stories and legends . . . ."

Toumanian has been translated into Russian (by Bryusov, Balmont, Khodasevich and others), English, French, German, Italian, Spanish, Arabic, Greek, Japanese, Chinese, and many other languages. He was himself a prolific translator of Pushkin, Lermontov, Nekrasov, Gorky, Byron, Schiller, Heine, Goethe, and others. There is a museum dedicated to him in Yerevan.[25]

Before we consider contemporary trends, let us examine three literary genres that have had long and brilliant careers in the history of Armenian literature: the poetry of minstrels, travelogues, and translations.

The poetry of *gusans* and *ashughs* (professional poets, composers, singers), who are mentioned in Armenian literary records as early as the 5th century, and the songs of the *bantukht*, the wandering exile driven from his native land by enemy invasions, occupy a special place in the genius of Armenian song creativity.

Ashughs (from the Arabic *ashiq*=lover) were active in palaces, towns, and villages throughout the Caucasus and the Middle East. They sang, accompanying themselves on a stringed instrument, in private homes and public squares, at fairs, weddings, banquets, tournaments, and feast days. Their lyrics were always accessible, even colloquial in tone, the topics ranging from feminine charms to social protest. *Ashughs* who acquired some degree of notoriety and eventually passed into literature number in the hundreds. Like their 12th-century French counterparts, the troubadours, however, some of these *ashughs* were not professional entertainers at all, but scholarly imitators, sometimes even members of the clergy. It is said of Sayat-Nova (Haroutiun Sayatian: 1712-1795)—one of the most famous *ashughs* of his time whose exquisite lyrics are still sung in Armenian, Georgian, and Azerbaijani—that even after he withdrew into a monastery and became a bishop, he would continue to participate incognito in public poetry tournaments. When Tiflis (where he was born and lived) was conquered by the Persians in 1795, he refused to become a Moslem and was murdered in the cathedral. His life, poetry, and music have inspired and continue to inspire many poems, novels, operas, plays, films, and scholarly studies.[26]

Two well-known minstrels from the 14th century are Hovannes Tulkurantsi and Frik. Tulkurantsi authored many love lyrics and a heroic poem on the fall of Sis, capital of Cilicia, in 1369 (see HISTORY), which he probably witnessed.[27]

It is said of Frik that after losing his family and property during the Mongol invasions, he entered a monastery as a lay brother. His lyrics, about 50 in all, are marked by bitterness and irony. "Why, O Lord," he cries out in one of them,

> *Have you no compassion for us?*
> *Are we then made of grass or reeds?*
> *How long, O Lord, must we endure*
> *The torments inflicted upon us?*
> *If we are no longer of any use to you*
> *Then blot us out swiftly*
> *Once and for all!*

The greatest *ashugh* of the 16th century was Nahapet Kouchak, about whom very little is known, except that he wrote so many lyrics that scholars doubt their authenticity and tend to regard them as adaptations of folk songs. In addition to praising the charms of his beloved, Kouchak sang of Christian virtues, extolling humility, resignation, and acceptance of life's injustices. "One must be as humble as the earth underfoot," he says in a song,

*Ignore others' sins
And meditate on one's own;
For life is transient,
Death ever-present
And God our only refuge.*[28]

As conditions in the Caucasus deteriorated however, *ashughs* began to attack these traditional Christian virtues. Djivani (Serop Levonian: 1846-1909) was a singer of social protest. He became very popular in his time and a collection of his songs was published in 1882.

In his lyrics, Djivani—who, like Sayat-Nova, was active mainly in Georgia—sang of the poverty and lack of rights of common people, he condemned assimilation, and went as far as advocating armed revolt against the oppressor. "My father's advice," he says,

*Is much better
Than an odar's philosophy;
I prefer the ruins of Ani
To the splendors of Paris.*

Elsewhere we read:

*Forget the scriptures, my friend;
Read instead books on self defense,
For times are no longer the same.
Let us now arm ourselves
And run to the defense
Of the weak and the needy. . . .*

*The mighty of this world
Crush the humble;
The avaricious
Exploit the poor
And are free to do
What they please.
Be brave, be cunning, be mean!
Don't allow anyone
To ride you like a jackass.
I say, killing is better
Than being killed;
Terrorizing is much better
Than being terrorized.*

Some of the most important authors of travelogues were merchants. Let us cite two representative names from the 17th century: Zakaria Agouletsi and Hovannes Djughayetsi.

In his *Travels of Zakaria Agouletsi in Europe and Asia in the Years 1647-1684,* Agouletsi describes many aspects of life in such countries as Iran, Turkey, Italy, Spain, Germany, and Holland.

Even more interesting is the travel diary of Hovannes Djughayetsi, which came to light and was deciphered only very recently. Djughayetsi was a contemporary of Agouletsi, but unlike Agouletsi, he chose to travel in the opposite direction—to India, Nepal, Tibet. He lived in Lhasa for five years and became fluent in Tibetan. His observations on the life of this remote and mysterious city are of great historical value today.

And here, a word on the important role Armenian merchants played in the economic life of the Middle East, Europe, and Asia. According to Fernand Braudel, their Christianity and in large measure their willingness to take on hard work made them formidable rivals and competitors. Like all mountain people, he writes, ". . . they had great resistance and were very sober. They journeyed to fairs in Germany, to the quaysides of Venice, and to shops of Amsterdam . . . . They dealt with the Indies, Tonkin, Java, the Philippines, and throughout the East except for China and Japan. Some Armenians even owned ships on the Indian Ocean."

Tough and pragmatic, these merchants observed and reported what they had seen without romanticizing. Reading their books, we learn a great deal about the inhabitants of the countries they visited —the way they lived, looked, ate, worked, made love and war, did business.[29]

With minor exceptions, all Armenian writers from the Golden Age to the present day have dedicated an important part of their literary labors to the task of acquainting Armenian readers with works of foreign literatures. There have been a number of writers, however, like the Iranian-Armenian Hovannes Massehian, the Mekhitarist Arsen Ghazikian, and the Soviet-Armenians Khachik Dashtents and Haroutiun Haroutiunian, who are known primarily as translators.

Haroutiun Haroutiunian's (1896-1974) list of translations contains nearly a hundred works, ranging from novels and collections of short stories by Hugo, Defoe, Sholokhov, Saroyan, and Gorky, to Chekhov, Leskov, H.G. Wells, Dreiser, and Turgenev.

In addition to producing a series of original works in verse and prose, Khachik Dashtents (1910-1974) translated over a dozen plays by Shakespeare, along with works by Longfellow, Browning, and Saroyan.

But the translator that is most closely linked with Shakespeare is Iranian-born and Paris-educated career diplomat Hovannes Massehian (1864-1931). Fluent in many languages (in addition to Armenian, English, and French, he knew ancient and modern Persian, Russian, German, Arabic, and Turkish), and a world-traveller (for many years he lived abroad in Berlin, London, Tokyo, Paris), Massehian began to translate early in life. As a close friend of the Shah, he was often asked to translate foreign books on Persia; also French comedies for palace productions. Very probably at this time he also translated some of Shakespeare's plays into Persian. Massehian devoted altogether thirty years of his life to the study of Shakespeare, amassing a valuable library in several languages in the process and eventually translating 14 of Shakespeare's major plays into Armenian—among them *Hamlet, As You Like It, Romeo and Juliet, The Merchant of Venice, King Lear, Othello, Macbeth.* These are translations of such exceptional beauty and power that when, in my twenties, I began to read Shakespeare in the original, I had some trouble dispelling the notion that I was reading a clumsy translation from the Armenian.

In this connection it should be noted that Shakespeare and the Armenians—not just translation, but scholarship and interpretation —is too complex a topic to be summed up in a few paragraphs. To give the reader an idea of this complexity, let me cite some relevant facts. In addition to Massehian and Dashtents, Armenians have had fifty other Shakespeare translators (some of whom, like Vahan Totovents and Vahan Tekeyan, are discussed elsewhere in this chapter); also forty famous Othellos and twenty Hamlets. Some of the better known plays like *Hamlet, King Lear, Othello, Romeo and Juliet,* and *Richard III,* have been translated not just once or twice, but six times—into West-Armenian, East-Armenian, *krapar* (classical Armenian), *ashkharapar* (the spoken idiom), and even a number of dialects. Armenians moreover have translated Shakespeare into several foreign languages. In 1840, a Russian-Armenian scholar by the name of Matvey Ghazamian published a Russian translation of *The Tempest* that was highly praised by Vyssarion Belinsky, among others. Another scholar, Tigran Karapetian, produced a French translation of the *Sonnets* that was of such exceptional brilliance and accuracy that the Oxford University Press issued it in a bilingual edition in order that readers may better appreciate the translator's virtuoso performance. It is to be noted that Karapetian's French was not the modern idiom but the archaic French of Shakespeare's time.

In Shakespeare scholarship, let us mention at least two names: Bedros Adamian (1849-1891), author of an important *Shakespeare's Tragedy Hamlet: Sources and Studies* (Tiflis, 1887), and the Soviet-Armenian Vahram Papazian (1888-1968), author of voluminous essays on *Othello* (Yerevan, 1964; 511 pages), *Hamlet* (Yerevan, 1968; 435 pages), and *King Lear* (Yerevan, 1971; 331 pages). Both Adamian and Papazian were also two of the greatest Shakespearean actors of their time. It is said of Vahram Papazian that he played Othello 3000 times—an unheard of thing in the history of the stage. Everyone who saw him in that role would agree that the part must have been conceived and written especially for him.[30]

The first four decades of the 20th century were a difficult time for Armenian writers. Those who were not persecuted, jailed, and later murdered by the Turks in 1915, eventually perished in the hands of Stalinists during the Great Terror of the 1930s. Of the writers murdered in 1915 by the Turks, let us mention seven representative names: Telgadintsi, Rouben Zartarian, Daniel Varoujan, Siamanto, Rouben Sevag, Krikor Zohrab, and Yeroukhan.

Born in Telgadin in the province of Kharpert, West Armenia, Telgadintsi (Hovannes Haroutiunian: 1860-1915) was a distinguished author and educator. In his novels and plays—*The Capricious Boy* (1904), *Only a Cup* (1907), *The Will* (1911), and many others—he explored marital relations, family life, and provincial mores. His style combines playful charm with acute observation. Telgadintsi also published short stories, travel impressions, popular songs, and lyric poems, all of which are animated by a deep love for the primitive simplicity of Armenian village life—its traditions, proverbs, unique character and patterns of speech. Throughout his life Telgadintsi was also a dedicated teacher. Among his pupils were Vahan Totovents (who was to perish in the Stalinist purges), the Armenian-American short story writer and novelist Hamasdegh, Rouben Zartarian (another victim of the genocide and author of an important monograph on him), and Peniamin Noorigian (under whose editorship his complete works were to appear in Boston in 1927). "I remember him as a man whose eyes reflected a deep sorrow," writes Noorigian. "His integrity and inner strength however would never allow him to give in to defeat and despair...."

Rouben Zartarian may have had his master's sorrowful eyes in mind when he has one of his half-mythical, half-allegorical characters say: "Love may be immortal but the human heart turns into dust. Beauty may be eternal but night places its seal of darkness on the eyes that behold it. Wine cannot dissipate anxiety, and songs of merriment turn invariably into stone...."

Like Telgadintsi, Rouben Zartarian (1874-1915) was born and educated in the West-Armenian province of Kharpert, but was active mainly in Istanbul, whence, following his arrest and imprisonment for political activities (1903-04), he left for Bulgaria. After the revolution of the Young Turks he returned to Istanbul where he published many meticulously crafted prose poems, legends, short stories, and novellas, all of which are allegorical in character and offer a wide range of interpretations. Zartarian also produced a number of literary studies—*Tomorrow's Literature* (1900); *Telgadintsi* (1908); *Avedik Issahakian's Poem, Abou Lala Mahari* (1910); translations (Gorky, Shelley, Victor Hugo, Oscar Wilde, Anatole France, and others); and a large number of political pamphlets. Concerning his work as publicist, Zartarian once said that he had begun his literary career as "an Arabian thoroughbred, but had been coerced into journalism—that is, carrying heavy loads: work fit for a draft horse."

Daniel Varoujan (Cheboukiarian: 1884-1915) was another victim of the Genocide. Born in a small village near Sebastia (Armenia Minor) Varoujan was educated in Istanbul, at the Mekhitarist school of Moorat-Raphael in Venice, and at the University of Ghent (Belgium). "My imagination was shaped by the brilliant colors of Titian and the lusty realism of Van Dyck," he was to write in a letter to a friend. About his childhood, he said: "I spent it daydreaming under willow trees and throwing stones at ducks. During the long winter nights my mother would tell me stories about Janissaries and wolves as the cold wind was howling and wailing outside like the cub of a dragon." He read widely in European literature—Kant, Hugo, the Italians Leopardi and Carducci: "I have read everyone from the Indians to Homer and from Homer to Maeterlinck," he says elsewhere.

Varoujan's contemporaries describe him as a "sweet, modest, candid youth," essentially a dreamer, a man of contemplation who, like so many of his contemporaries, failed to foresee the approaching whirlwind. His love for his country and its traditions was genuine and deep. He loathed the pseudo-cosmopolitan atmosphere of Istanbul (he called it once a sinister caricature of Paris) and preferred to live in the rural hinterland. This contact with village life was to inspire one of his most widely admired works, the posthumously published and unfinished cycle of poems titled *Song of the Bread* (available in French as *Le Chant du pain,* Paris, 1959).[31]

His verse is extraordinary in its complexity and vertiginous energy. It ranges from rousing patriotic poems and the struggle against tyranny *(Heart of the Race)* to elegies on the suffering of his people (*Massacre*) and adult sexual love (*Pagan Songs*). This last cycle of poems led Shirvanzadeh to call him a pornographer.

Varoujan's style is highly idiosyncratic. It contains many striking neologisms, metaphors, and similes. It combines the elegant, classical Armenian he studied under the Mekhitarists, with the spicy vernacular of his province. His authenticity of feeling and daring are spellbinding.

In his reminiscences of Varoujan, Hagop Oshagan writes: "Last time I saw him was in 1915 at Rouben Sevag's home . . . . He read some of his poetry. It was an unforgettable experience . . . . In such moments his body would turn into a musical instrument. And all of us in that room sensed that we were in the presence of one of those truly inspired visionaries from the past. Even Sevag's wife, who being German knew only a handful of Armenian words and expressions which she had learned to please her husband, was so affected by Varoujan's reading that she burst into tears."[32]

Born in Akn (West Armenia) Siamanto (Adom Yarjanian: 1878-1915) was educated in Istanbul and at the Sorbonne in Paris. He travelled widely in France, England, the United States, Austria, Switzerland, Egypt, and Turkey. A consumptive who refused to submit to his fate, according to Rouben Sevag, Siamanto would stubbornly shake the thermometer whenever it reached high levels, shouting: *"I will live! I will live!";* and before facing the weekly ordeal of stepping on a scale to be weighed, he would secrete several books in his pockets.

His verses are pessimistic ("Human Justice—I spit on your face!"), even cataclysmic in tone. Some of his poems—*Flickers of Hope and Agony, Bloody Dispatches from My Friend*—commemorate the Adana massacres of 1909. He also produced many love poems, which (according to Avedik Issahakian) he would invariably destroy after reading them to a close circle of friends, saying he had no business to speak of love in the midst of tragedy. As a result, sorrow, death, and massacre remain the predominant themes of his verse, where he relives the cruel destiny of his people and sings of innocent victims "crazed with suffering," and "cities in flames radiating the heat of a thousand suns." Sometimes realistic, sometimes allegorical, sometimes epic in tone, Siamanto explores new rhythms, tonalities, and modes of expression. He is never melodramatic or monotonous. His cry of anguish never modulates into lamentation, but remains firm, strong, masculine. Though regarded as "the anguished consciousness of his people," he has also been called "a singer of strength, rage, and revenge." In *Heroica* and *Songs of the Knight,* for instance, he chanted the exploits of Armenian guerrilla fighters. Sylva Gaboudikian describes his verse as "a magnificent, polyphonic symphony, a complex, soaring requiem that, even as it speaks of death, promises life, redemption, and ultimate victory."

Known as the founder of the realistic short story in West-Armenian literature, Krikor Zohrab (1861-1915) was also a brilliant orator and lawyer who, in his capacity as member of Parliament for the Young Turk party, became the most eloquent defender of Armenian rights. In his many short stories and novellas—*A Vanished Generation* (1887), *Voices of Conscience* (1909), *Life As It is* (1911), *Silent Griefs* (1911)—Zohrab skillfully analyzed the complexities of urban life. As in Maupassant's work, women play a central role in his fiction. They are as a rule capricious, unfaithful, and irresistibly attractive. Many of his stories are based on real life incidents recounted to him by women friends. "They know that I like to concern myself with their psychological problems," Zohrab once said, speaking of these women; "to be the historian of their inner conflicts. They tend to interpret my tolerant attitude towards their weaknesses as an invitation to confide in me."

Zohrab also published many insightful literary and political essays on a wide range of topics, extending from foreign influences on Armenian intellectual and community life to German Imperialism—both of which he deplored. As a critic he believed that "science and art constantly reorganize and renew our perception of reality."

His commitment to the Armenian cause was firm and uncompromising. He established contact with many foreign embassies and published pamphlets exposing the criminality of the Turkish government. "Had it not been for Zohrab," Yervant Odian said shortly after the Adana massacres of 1909, "the victims would have been declared guilty."

Zohrab foresaw the coming catastrophe ("If, in the next war, Turkey and Germany become Allies," he wrote, "the fate of the Armenians in Turkey will be in mortal peril") but refused to go abroad to save himself, saying that, as a representative of his people, he could not abandon them to the mercy of criminals.

It is said that, after murdering him, the Turks crushed his head between two massive rocks.

Rouben Sevag has already been mentioned in connection with Siamanto and Varoujan. Born in a small village near Istanbul, Sevag

(Chilingirian: 1885-1915) studied medicine at the University of Lausanne where he interned until 1914. Against the better judgment of his friends, he returned to Istanbul on the eve of World War I, was conscripted into the Turkish Army, and shortly thereafter murdered. He was thirty years old. In a collection of short stories titled *From a Doctor's Notebook,* which is based on his experiences with patients, Sevag reveals a remarkable gift for projecting character and outlining a life in a few words. He also authored two collections of verse—*The Red Book* (1910), about the Adana massacres of 1909, and the posthumously published *Book of Love.* His complete works appeared in Yerevan in 1955.

A timid, sickly boy and a slow learner, Yeroukhan (Yervant Sermakeshkhanian: 1870-1915) was able to overcome his own deficiencies and the ridicule of his teachers and classmates by sheer hard work—"to the point," he writes, "that I was reduced to skin and bones"—and eventually become one of the masters of Armenian prose. He began his literary career as a translator of French novels for Armenian periodicals. He himself became an editor and in that capacity, and as a teacher, he was active in Istanbul, Varna (Bulgaria), Cairo, Alexandria, and Kharpert. In addition to a long novel, *Amira's Daughter* (1902), which is his masterpiece, Yeroukhan wrote many short stories and novellas about humble laborers, fishermen, stevedores, washerwomen, street vendors, exiles, and outcasts, whom he observed and described with great compassion and understanding. It has been said of him that "he searches out and exposes diamonds where others see nothing but coal dust."

In April 1915, he was arrested and together with a few other intellectuals paraded through the streets of Kharpert in chains, taken out of town, and murdered in a ditch. He was forty-five years old.[33]

Of the writers who became victims of Stalinist persecution, let us mention seven representative names: Yeghishe Charents, Axel Bakounts, Zabel Yessayan, Vahan Totovents, Drastamat Ter-Simonian, Mkrtitch Armen, and Gourgen Mahari. The first five were either shot or committed suicide; the last two, after spending years in the Gulag and following the thaw of the Khrushchev period in the

1950s, were allowed to return home and resume their literary careers.

Why were these writers persecuted? In his reminiscences, Mahari writes that it didn't even cross his mind to commit the crimes for which he was accused, tried, found guilty, and condemned. He didn't even know, he says, that he was that "terrible monster . . . a member of an underground-nationalist-Trotskyite-terrorist movement! Yes," he goes on. "I was someone important and I didn't even know it. But I know now that I, with a number of other writers, have had secret meetings day and night, and that our sole aim was to sever Armenia from Russia."[34]

Gourgen Mahari (Ajemian: 1903-1969) was born in Van (West Armenia). Orphaned in 1915 as a result of the Turkish massacres, he fled to Yerevan, where he studied literature at the State University. In one of his poems, Mahari describes himself as a proud man whose soul was forged in the dark pits of Tartarus. He may have been helpless as an orphan, he writes, but he was also proud "as only an orphan can be." Unlike some of his contemporaries who sold out, he goes on, he never traded "ink for muck, and pen for intrigue's dagger"; never flattered "the executioners of Bakounts and Charents . . . ." Mahari's veneration for both men knew no bounds. When told by an admirer he could write better than Bakounts, he retorted angrily: "Never say a thing like that again in my presence! Obviously you don't know who Bakounts is." And once, when asked what he considered the happiest event in his life, he replied: "The privilege of having known Charents."

In addition to several collections of verse and short stories, Mahari authored a widely admired autobiographical trilogy and a book of reminiscences of Charents. "The last time I saw Charents," he writes here,

> was in August of 1936 . . . . I was climbing up, past the House of Culture, while he cut across Abovian Street and climbed up Spendiarian. He was walking with his careless gait, one shoulder up, the other down, because his head was leaning on that side. He was going, apparently, home.
> And he's still going, in my brain and soul, across the thorns in my brain and the flowers of my soul, he, elemental, restless, wind-tossed majesty,

luminous child of my people, a pilgrim of the great red pilgrimage, heroic comrade and gentle teacher, Yeghishe Charents . . . .

One of the most dynamic figures of the Soviet-Armenian literary scene, Yeghishe Charents (Soghomonian: 1897-1937) was born in Kars, northeastern Turkey, formerly the seat of an independent Armenian principality. He was active at fifteen publishing poetry and fighting as a volunteer against the Turks in Van. In 1916 he went to Moscow to pursue his literary studies. Following the October Revolution of 1917 he put himself wholeheartedly at the service of the Soviet State. Between 1918 and 1921 he fought with the Red Army in the Russian and Armenian civil wars. To this period belongs *The Frenzied Masses* (1919), which was immediately acclaimed as the greatest poem of the Revolution and prompted the eminent Armenian scholar and critic Nikol Aghbalian to write: "The whole of Russian literature did not produce a poet who could echo in his verse the storm of the Revolution as effectively as Charents."

Between 1924 and 1925, as a Soviet diplomat, Charents travelled widely in Turkey, Italy, France, Germany, and other European countries, in an effort to encourage Armenian writers, musicians, artists, and scholars of the diaspora to come and work in Soviet Armenia.

His satirical novel *Land of Nairi,* where he makes fun of three Armenian prototypes, the shopkeeper, the fighter, and the preacher, appeared in 1926 and enjoyed enormous critical and popular success. He became a director of the State Publishing House and for the next ten years continued to be active editing, translating (Walt Whitman, Pushkin, Mayakovsky, Goethe, Gorky, Erich Maria Remarque, and Verhaeren), and publishing original works, the most important of which are *Rubayat* (1927); *Epic Dawn* (1930); and *Book of the Road* (1933), generally regarded as the masterpiece of his mature years. It contains poetic reflections about Armenia and its past, an adaptation of the Armenian folk epic *David of Sassoun,* verses about love and art, and what at first looked like an eminently mediocre propaganda piece titled "The Message." Apparently a eulogy to the greatness of Stalin, hidden in it was a message in the form of an acrostic constituted by the second letter of each line that read: "Oh! Armenian people, your salvation lies only in your collective powers." Labelled by the Central Committee as a "Trotskyite counter-revolutionary book which slanders the party," *Book of the Road* was banned and Charents himself was savagely attacked in the press. A prominent critic representing the official Soviet position condemned Charents and some of his associates as "saboteurs, counter-revolutionaries, Trotskyites, Dashnaks, agents of international capitalism, whose intention was to deviate the Armenian people from the path of happy life and to lead them back to the miseries of the past." Many Armenian intellectuals protested, including Axel Bakounts, Zabel Yessayan, Alexander Tamanian, and Martiros Sarian. Stalin himself is said to have told an Armenian delegation that had come to see him, that Charents should not be touched; but a few months later Charents was arrested and died on November 29, 1937. Official sources have maintained a deafening silence concerning the circumstances surrounding his death. It is widely rumored, however, that he went on a hunger strike and killed himself by dashing his head against the walls of his cell when he was refused his daily dose of morphine.

After nearly two decades of neglect, Charents was rehabilitated and his complete works in six volumes, and numerous collections of his poems, appeared in large editions and were exhausted in a matter of hours.

Probably no single modern Armenian poet has been written about as much as Charents. Many books and innumerable articles have been devoted to his life and work. In 1977, at the jubilee celebrating the 80th anniversary of his birth, several literary periodicals devoted entire issues to him. Charents has been translated into Russian (by Anna Akhmatova and Boris Pasternak, among others) and into most of the other languages of the Soviet Union. Some poems have also been translated into English but these are too few to give an accurate impression of his range.

Tormented, many sided, complex, and often contradictory, as a man and a poet, Charents is extremely difficult to sum up. It has been said that there are in him five or six different poets each one of whom could have made a name for himself in the literature of any country. He has been described as a generous friend, a loving husband, a tender father, and as a loud-mouth drunkard and obscene junkie leading a rowdy cafe life and, revolver in hand, accusing former colleagues of counter-revolutionary activities. He is also said to have shot at a woman who spurned his attention—an episode that resulted in a short imprisonment in 1926, at the height of his fame. Though in the memoirs of his contemporaries he is often called a man of wide learning and erudition, Charents was not essentially a man of culture and refinement. The primitive element never quite disappeared from his works. His formative experiences were war, famine, epidemic, and revolution. "I sing songs that are made of iron," he said. "Even when my head reaches the stars, my feet remain sunk deep into the earth." What makes his work appealing to both the masses and the intellectual elite is the combination of brutality of expression and hidden emotional sensitivity.

In his revolutionary phase Charents modeled his literary and public *persona* on Mayakovsky, employing direct colloquial means of expression and pouring out topical poems of propaganda—*Lenin* (1924), *Ballad of Vladimir Ilyich, a Peasant, and a Pair of Boots* (1924), *Uncle Lenin* (1924), *Lenin and Ali* (1925), and a few others—which he was later to repudiate. In a poem written in 1930, he said to his muse:

> *You were like a sister to me,*
> *Truthful, pure and bright;*
> *But I spat on your face.*
> *I betrayed you one night*
> *With a cold mistress,*
> *Who sang to me dreams of iron,*
> *And took me into a world without love.*

In his youth, he rejected indiscriminately all the Armenian classics ("My soul was not created to be the slave/ Of gelded words all learned by heart . . ."), but in many poems of his maturity, he paid tribute to an astonishingly large number of them—from Narekatsi and Sayat-Nova to Medzarents, Daniel Varoujan, Hovannes Toumanian, and Avedik Issahakian. In addition to absorbing his native culture in profound and unexpected ways, Charents also learned advanced poetic techniques from the Russian symbolists, imagists, futurists, acmeists, and from poets as varied as Dante, Goethe, Heine, and Whitman.

At first dazzled by the promises of the October Revolution, he pontificated in the self-assertive, dogmatic accents of a universal prophet; but when disillusionment came, he lowered his voice and gradually came nearer earth, man, and truth. His art, though nationalistic in tone, acquired a deep strain of humanitarian philosophy. His works have had a lasting influence not only in Soviet Armenia but on poets writing in the diaspora.

The author of some of the most brilliant short stories in 20th-century Armenian literature, distinguished translator and scholar who brought out of oblivion the works of the 13th-century fabulist Vartan Aykegtsi, Axel Bakounts (Alexander Tevossian: 1899-1937) also played a key role in the struggle against the Communist attempt to make literature an instrument of Party propaganda. "Revolution? . . . Socialism? . . ." one of his characters reflects,

> they are just passing phenomena, a period when history is suffering from a flu, so to speak, a temporary ailment, after which, all the dead cities will come to life again from under the ashes, as long as there are still people in this world like Hovnatan March, who will burst into tears as soon as they hear the word Armenia, and who embrace this ideal as an alcoholic would grab his last bottle of brandy.

Unlike Charents, who at times wavered and adjusted his art to the prevailing winds of the regime, producing a number of politically motivated works that to this day make of him the favorite subject of Party-inspired adulation, Bakounts remained firm in his convictions, dedication, and idealism.

A member of the Armenian Revolutionary Federation (Dashnaktsoutiun) since 1915, Bakounts was willing to cooperate in the "voluntary disbandment" of the party, provided its members were not persecuted. In a speech delivered in 1924 in Yerevan, he declared that it was a mistake to confuse counter-revolutionaries with Dashnaks, who were, in his own words, "politically and socially trained people . . . prepared to take an active part not only in the defense of the political security of the country, but also in our gigantic social struggle and in the reconstruction of the country."

He went on to say: ". . . if any danger threatens our Soviet fatherland, we are ready to defend our new path and, as the Dashnak guerrillas fought with superhuman heroism in the past, we too can prove that we can fight with the same spirit, but this time for the proletariat, for the Revolution."

This oath of loyalty to the New Order postponed but could not prevent his liquidation which occurred when he was not yet forty.

Bakounts's approach to the art of narrative is highly idiosyncratic. He deals with his subject with such warmth and faith that the reader responds with friendship and affection. Writes Levon Mkrtitchian, a contemporary Munich-based scholar and author of a book-length study on Bakounts: "No sign of indifference, boredom or reluctance can be found in any of his writings. His views, for or against all the subjects he deals with, are evident in his writings . . . . Bakounts looks at the world from the vantage ground of a man matured by experience, but still a part of the world and society. It is for that very reason that however full of tragic sorrow they may be, all Bakounts's writings vibrate with lyricism and shine with humor."

The following passage from a story titled "The Rain" illustrates this point. Bakounts is speaking of a newly-built electric generating station in Soviet Armenia. "I look at it," he writes,

> and I remember the ancient history of my country.
>
> The stoves and parchments tell the story of the destruction of its cities, of massacres and of the mass exodus of the people.
>
> Like reeds they bent their heads before the winds and raised them again when peace came. In terror they fled from their villages like herds of cattle from a burning forest, and then built houses on quays, and the rainy wind beat against their mud huts.
>
> Conquerors have boastingly inscribed stories of loot and plunder on the rocks of your country, while in dark cells the chronicler invented equally vain legends about past glories.
>
> The common folk lay silently under the whip of the khan, the beg and the White Czar; sometimes they revolted, but the next day they again relied on their sad songs and continued to bear their burden. They tilled and sweated, and the lion's share went to the village Elder, the monastery, or the moneylender.
>
> The sky poured its rain of sadness on their gray huts.
>
> I look at the eyes of this new man and read a new story. What buildings will yet rise on the slopes of our mountains and in our valleys! Innu-

merable towns will rise again on their ruins to the accompaniment of the merry songs of their builders.
The fecund autumn rain falls on the earth, on men, and on cultivated lands.

In effect Bakounts's message here is very similar to the one embedded in Charents's famous poem "The Message" mentioned above: "Oh! Armenian people, your salvation lies only in your collective powers." In the eyes of Stalinists, this was subversive, counter-revolutionary talk simply because it ascribed progress not to the Kremlin but to the creative genius of the Armenian people.

Before establishing herself permanently in Yerevan in 1933, Istanbul-born and Sorbonne-educated Zabel Yessayan (1878-1943) lived and worked in Iran, Iraq, Egypt, Lebanon, Italy, Switzerland, Russia, and Azerbaijan. An erudite scholar, an influential teacher, and a versatile author, she published works in both French and Armenian. In her autobiographical novels and novellas—*Retreating Forces* (1926), *Shirt of Fire* (1934), *The Gardens of Silihdar* (1935), and others, she draws on her early experiences in Istanbul. Her magnum opus *Barba Khachik* (Yerevan, 1966), a posthumously published unfinished novel of 851 pages, is based on the life of an unconventional uncle, a Zorba-like character whom she adored as a child. Her other works include *Phoney Geniuses* (1909), a satirical novel; *In the Ruins* (1911), eyewitness accounts of the 1909 Cilician massacres; *Contemporary West-Armenian Writers* (1916), literary criticism; and *Prometheus Unchained* (1928), travel impressions of Soviet Armenia. Though dismissed as propaganda, this last book expresses her wholehearted commitment to the new regime. But as a former member of the Armenian Revolutionary Federation and a passionate defender of Charents, Bakounts, Mkrtitch Armen, and others accused of deviationism and anti-Soviet agitation, she too was arrested, exiled, and died under circumstances that have never been disclosed.

A prolific and multi-faceted writer, Vahan Totovents (1893-1938) produced with equal facility poems in prose and verse, short stories, novellas, novels, critical and biographical works, comedies, dramas, translations from Shakespeare, and a widely read and admired autobiographical book titled *Life on the Old Roman Road*. Writes Rouben Zarian in his reminiscences of Totovents: "He wrote fast. He had no trouble finding the right word. His sentences flowed with ease. He didn't try to achieve perfection, only spontaneity. He had something to say and he said it. He was never idle. A born writer and a reporter by training, he never waited for inspiration. And since his urge to write came from deep within and was irresistible, sentences and paragraphs followed one another with phenomenal speed."

Totovents was born in Mezre, a small town on the Euphrates in the province of Kharpert, where he studied under such masters of Armenian prose as Telgadintsi and Rouben Zartarian. In his youth he travelled extensively in the Middle East, Europe, and the United States. After graduating from the University of Wisconsin, he fought as a volunteer in the Caucasus during World War I. "I wanted to see my country liberated," he writes in his autobiographical sketch. "I saw instead its total destruction, and torrents of my countrymen's blood. I saw human suffering of such depth that there can be nothing deeper in this world. I saw nights gorged with blood. I saw men crazed by hunger; I saw bloodthirsty mobs attacking innocent men, women, and children, and I heard the howls of their terrified victims." Another two years (1920-22) of wandering followed—Istanbul, Paris, New York, whence he returned to Yerevan and where, in addition to over a dozen books, he published countless essays and articles in newspapers and periodicals. Criticized for failing to produce works with "proletarian" content, Totovents refused to conform and was eventually arrested and exiled to Siberia. Very little is known about his last year. Sarepig Manoogian, his official biographer, simply informs us that Totovents "died at the height of his creative powers leaving behind many unfinished projects...."[35]

A literary critic of strong Marxist persuasion who published only two short books in his lifetime—a biographical sketch of *Karl Marx* (1933) and a brief outline of *The Literature of Armenia* (1934)—

Drastamat Ter-Simonian (1895-1937) was nevertheless an influential political agitator, commissar, editor, and lecturer active not only in the Caucasus (Yerevan and Tiflis) but also in Paris, Moscow, Kiev, and Kharkov. His most important book, *Essays*, was published posthumously in 1961 and it contains studies of 19th- and 20th-century Armenian revolutionaries, poets, and authors. It is still not clear why he was executed. Probably his close friendship with Charents and Aghassi Khanjian (the leader of the Armenian Communist Party whose "suicide" in the hands of Beria signaled the unleashing of the terror in Armenia) made of him a deviationist by association.

Charents also played a decisive role in the life of Mkrtitch Armen (Haroutiunian: 1906-1972), who was a native of Alexandropol (now Leninakan). In his autobiographical sketch, Armen writes: "In 1925 I left Leninakan and was on my way to Meghri where I had been offered a post as a teacher. I stopped in Yerevan for an hour or two and there I met Charents. He invited me to his place and I have been a Yerevantsi ever since."

A prolific and often brilliant novelist and short story writer, Armen also published collections of verse, children's stories and legends, and some thirty volumes of translations from the Russian. His style is marked by a haunting melancholy and a vagueness that has the undefined quality of a dream. In the preface of one of his most widely acclaimed books *They Asked Me to Deliver This to You* (1964), he writes:

Dear Soviet citizens, countrymen:
Your fathers, brothers and sons, whom I met in 1937 and for eight years thereafter in the camps, when I too was a convict, made me promise on my honor to deliver this to you.

Whereas some convicts passed their entire sentence in one or two camps, chance willed that I should be transferred to sixty different camps in eight years.

And in every camp I went I met inmates who made me promise to write about them; to write the truth and nothing but the truth—write about that which I saw for eight years, continuously, as I wandered like a gypsy through sixty camps, felled trees in sixty forests and rolled logs down sixty rivers. Not for a moment did I let drop the torch held high in my hands, sticky with the resin of pine trees.

And I returned, and wrote this book, which they made me promise on my honor to deliver to you.[36]

Among those who survived the 1915 Genocide and Stalin's purges were the East-Armenians Avedik Issahakian, Derenik Demirjian, Stepan Zorian, and Gostan Zarian, and the West-Armenians Vahan Tekeyan, Levon Shant, and Hagop Oshagan.

Since the publication of his first volume of poems, *Songs and Wounds* (Alexandropol, 1898), Avedik Issahakian (1875-1957) has been one of the most popular poets of Armenia. Though arrested and imprisoned a number of times by the Czarist secret police, he was allowed to write and publish more or less freely even during Stalin's reign. His complete works have had several editions in Soviet Armenia, and collections of his verse have appeared in Boston, Fresno, New York, Paris, Buenos Aires, Cairo, Teheran and a number of other cities with large Armenian communities. Issahakian was popular not only with the masses on both sides of the Iron Curtain and the Soviet establishment but with fellow intellectuals and poets as well. Louis Aragon, Valery Bryusov, Ilya Ehrenburg, and Pablo Neruda, among others, have expressed genuine admiration for his work. "The whole of Europe may not have such a spontaneous talent," Alexander Blok has said of him. And more recently Nikolai Tikhonov, in his introduction to Issahakian's *Selected Works* (Moscow, 1976) writes: "The power of Issahakian's lyrics is that he could turn the most personal into the universal.... His voice travelled far beyond the bounds of Armenia and evoked a very lively response."

In addition to his poems, Issahakian wrote short stories, legends, fables, an unfinished novel titled *Ousda Garo*, reminiscences of his contemporaries, and literary essays. One of his most popular and enduring works, however, is the narrative poem *Abou Lala Mahari* (1909), which has been translated into many languages, including English.[37] Based on the life of the blind Arab poet-philosopher Abou Ala al-Mahari (973-1058), who is said to have distributed his wealth among the poor and retired into the desert, away from the injustice, hypocrisy, and superstition of men, it is an extraordinarily pessimistic and misanthropic work. Here are four random stanzas:

Let me pitch my tent, upon the nests
  of snakes and scorpions let me pitch it:
I am a thousand times safer there
  than among men, deceitful and smiling.

I do not wish to greet people,
  or to break bread at their tables;
I will sit and eat with wild beasts,
  I will receive the greetings of hyenas.

Take me far away from friends
  that like insatiable mosquitoes
Pursue you when you have blood,
  but when you dry up, they forget you.

And what is a woman, but deceitful, cunning
  man-devouring spider, forever vain,
Who likes your bread, lies with her kisses,
  and embraces another while still in your arms?

If Abou Lala Mahari sounds at times like Nietzsche's Zarathustra, it may be because Issahakian was a great admirer of the German philosopher and was deeply influenced by his world-view—though in later life he tended to discount this influence. "When I was young," a biographer quotes him, "I was taken with different philosophical systems: pessimism, anarchism .... I was captivated by Buddha, Schopenhauer, and above all Nietzsche. I was particularly impressed by Nietzsche's laconic, aphoristic style. Later, however, I came to realize that his philosophy was foreign to my temperament. Nietzsche's world favors supermen. I worship heroes myself, but I have no sympathy whatever with Nietzsche's cruel supermen. Nietzsche never thrust deep roots into me. His philosophy is based on cruelty. Our people have been subjected to too much cruelty as it is .... Gogol's *Dead Souls* and Dostoevsky's *Brothers Karamazov*—they are the works that molded me .... And Chekhov—there are some things by Chekhov that I always carry with me wherever I go ...."[38]

Prolific and durable poet, novelist, playwright, and essayist Derenik Demirjian (1877-1956) was born in Akhalkalak and educated at Etchmiadzin, Tiflis, Moscow, and Geneva. He began his literary career as a poet of despair and loneliness and gradually developed into a major playwright and novelist. His most important work is a 2-volume historical novel titled *Vartanank* (1943-1946), based on the life of the 5th century military leader and saint Vartan Mamikonian (see RELIGION), whose heroic struggle against the overwhelming Persian forces has inspired and continues to inspire many poets, playwrights, painters, and composers.

Demirjian's other works include collections of short stories; *Mesrob Mashtots* (1956), an unfinished historical novel; memoirs *(With Toumanian);* plays *(Vassak, National Fiasco, Napoleon Kurtikian,* and the enormously popular *Nazar the Brave,* where he satirizes bourgeois morality and which has been turned into a successful film); essays, whose topics range from literature and linguistics to historiography and art history; and translations of, among others, Gogol's *Dead Souls.*

Demirjian's style is marked by daring similes, unexpected metaphors, and a charm all its own.[39]

Stepan Zorian (Arakelian: 1889-1967) was born in Kirovakan (Armenia) and was mainly self-taught. After working as editor and translator in Tiflis, he moved to Yerevan shortly after the establishment of Soviet rule and lived there until his death.

Though he develops deeply Armenian themes, Zorian's prose bears the influence of Russian and European realistic writers many of whom he translated into Armenian. Some of his best-known works are *Sad People* (1918), a collection of short stories dealing with provincial life; *The Red Stork* (1936), children's stories and fables; *The Girl from the Library* (1925), a novella; and such socialist realist novels as *Chairman of the Revkom* (1923), *The Vartatsor Commune* (1925), *The White City* (1932); also autobiographical novels, *The Story of a Life,* 2 volumes (1935-39); historical novels, *King Pap* (1944), *The Armenian Fortress* (1950), *The Family of Amirians* (1959); and several volumes of memoirs: *A Book of Reminiscences* (1958), *Acquaintances* (1969), and *My Toumanian* (1969). His translations include Harriet Beecher Stowe's *Uncle Tom's Cabin,* Mark Twain's *The Adventures of Tom Sawyer,* Turgenev, Sienkiewicz, Plekhanov, Chekhov, Ostrovsky, Stefan Zweig, and many, many others. Zorian's complete works first appeared in 6 volumes (1940-

1954), and have subsequently been revised and reissued in 10 volumes (1960-64).

Like Shirvanzadeh, whose cousin he was, Gostan Zarian (Yeghiazarian: 1885-1969) was born in Shamakh, Azerbaijan. The son of a prosperous general in the Czar's Army, Zarian was sent to Baku and later to Paris and Brussels for his education. It was only in his twenties that he decided to study Armenian at the Mekhitarist Monastery of San Lazzaro in Venice (1910-1912); after which he dedicated his life to Armenian literature and culture—founding, editing, and co-editing a number of important Armenian-, French-, and English-language periodicals of the diaspora (*Mehian* and *Partsravank* in Istanbul, *La Tour de Babel* in Paris, *The Armenian Quarterly* in New York); teaching Armenian history, culture, and comparative literature in several universities in Yerevan (1922-24), at Columbia University in New York (1944-46), and Beirut (1952-54); and producing works of fiction, nonfiction, and verse. From 1961 until his death he lived in Soviet Armenia. An edited version of his *magnum opus*, *The Ship on the Mountain* (originally published in Boston in 1930) was brought out in Yerevan, and shortly thereafter in a Russian translation in Moscow. Most of his works, such as *The Traveller and his Road* (1927), *Countries and Gods* (1935-38), *The Island and a Man* (1955), are densely-peopled travel impressions which also contain elliptical reflections on the nature of history, philosophy and art. These have not yet been issued in book form and lie buried in the files of the now defunct *Hairenik* Monthly (Boston) where they first appeared.

From the reminiscences of his contemporaries, Zarian emerges as a flamboyant, irrepressible man of infectious enthusiasm and enormous charm who had a phenomenal facility for languages and could speak Russian, French, Spanish, German, English, and Italian.

"There was something of Gargantua in him," writes Rouben Zarian (no kin) in his *Reminiscences*. "Wine was his favorite beverage. But he never got drunk, never lost his self-control. He was gullible and given to easy enthusiasms. And though he loved city life, he always had a deep-seated longing for the earth, stones and greenery of the countryside. He frequently expressed the wish to be taken out of town. And he would stare with wonder at the distant horizon, the mountains, the sky...."

Though intimately acquainted with many foreign literatures and cultures (Zarian counted among his friends Rabintranath Tagore, Verhaeren, Miguel de Unamuno, Celine, Picasso, and Lawrence Durrell), he was more intensely nationalistic than most of his contemporaries. He deplored, for instance, Charents's infatuation with Mayakovsky, saying the Italian futurist Marinetti had gotten rid of his worn-out, threadbare coat and after a detour through Moscow where it had been picked up and used by Mayakovsky, it had reached Yerevan "where it now parades (*man gou ka,* a favorite Zarian expression devilishly difficult to translate) on Abovian Street arguing, threatening, and spitting on Raffi . . . spitting on Aharonian —and that with the consumptive saliva of Muscovite 'masters.' Danger, danger, danger!"

Zarian's style is forceful yet curiously elusive. "It is better not to express an idea fully," he once said, "rather than to repeat it. Repetition wears down the mind. An unfinished thought on the other hand excites the reader's imagination. . . . One should always aim at moving the reader's inner world rather than delivering chewed-up and half-digested ideas for his consumption." Sometimes biased, often emotional, Zarian is never dogmatic, because his extravagances always support an affirmative view of life.[40]

Born, educated, and mainly active in Istanbul, Vahan Tekeyan (1878-1945) survived the Genocide because he happened to be out of the country in 1915. An enormously gifted and many-sided poet, critic, teacher, and community leader, Tekeyan was also a journalist who not only contributed to many of the important Armenian periodicals and newspapers of the diaspora but also edited most of them himself at one time or another. A withdrawn, restless man, and a lifelong bachelor, he spent a good portion of his life in corners of cafes and hotel rooms in Europe and the Middle East. He seems, however, never to have been reconciled with his nomadic, solitary existence. One of his most touching poems, titled "My Child," is an elegy to the child he never had. In another poem he reflects on his "solitary, sad, and unloved" condition and wonders whether his long-departed mother would have abandoned him down below had she known of his fate.

Tekeyan's poetic output is varied, consisting of personal and love lyrics, patriotic verse, where he reflects on the tragic destiny of his people and sings of hope and a utopian world dominated by harmony and love.

> Let us share equally
> The riches of this world;
> Let us open the gates wide
> And let us welcome everyone.
> Let the whole world
> Rush into our garden;
> But let no man
> Harm a single tree
> Or crush a single flower. . . .

Tekeyan's power to manipulate words and the delicate precision of his workmanship are superlative. Because he did not enjoy the early spectacular success of such poets as Bedros Tourian, Medzarents, and Daniel Varoujan, Tekeyan approached his art with a more critical stance. As a result his verse gradually acquired a contemplative calm and detachment denied to most of his contemporaries. It has been said that his style is so dense that it can express a state of mind in a single syllable.

During his lifetime, Tekeyan published no more than six collections of verse and prose—*Anxieties* (1901), *Miraculous Resurrection* (1914), *From Midnight to Dawn* (1919), *Love* (1933), *Armenian Song-book* (1943), and *Hymn-book* (1945). Five years after his death, nine more volumes of prose and verse (of a projected 15 volumes) appeared in Cairo, followed by a 500-page anthology titled *Works* (Yerevan, 1958). Since then several more collections of his verse, prose, and correspondence have appeared in the diaspora and Soviet Armenia.

Tekeyan's work as translator and editor should not be ignored. An accomplished translator, he has left masterful renditions of Shakespeare's *Sonnets* and Baudelaire's *Fleurs du mal*. His selfless dedication and encouragement of contemporaries as well as much younger men could be the topic of an entire volume. His many letters to Daniel Varoujan, Shahan Shahnour, Jacques Hagopian, Vahe-Vahian, Leon Surmelian, and many others, attest to this aspect of his wonderful personality. Of these writers, the last three are still active in the diaspora, and one of them (Surmelian) has chosen English as his medium (see below).[41]

Poet, novelist, playwright, essayist, diplomat, and educator Levon Shant (Seghbossian: 1869-1951) was born in Istanbul and educated at Etchmiadzin and at universities in Jena, Leipzig, and Munich. After the establishment of Soviet rule in Armenia he lived in exile in France, Iran, Egypt, and Lebanon. He died in Beirut at the age of 82. His creative life spanned half a century and during that time he produced works of an astonishing variety and versatility. He is best known, however, for his dramas which were staged frequently and enjoyed great popularity. Five of his most admired plays are *Ancient Gods* (1909), *The Emperor* (1914), based on the life of the Byzantine emperor Nicephorus Phocas (see HISTORY), *In Chains* (1918), *The Princess of the Fallen Castle* (1921), and *Oshin Bail* (1929). His other works include *Our Independence* (Boston, 1925), a political essay; many novels, short stories, poems, and such scholarly studies as *Psychological Development of Man* (Beirut, 1948), *Formation of Words in Armenian and the Emotive Connotations of the Language* (Beirut, 1950), and *A Grammar of Western Armenian*, 4 volumes (Beirut, 1950). "Without struggle and hard work," Shant has said, "without a single-minded dedication to a goal, death would be preferable to life." This may also be said to be the central theme of his oeuvre.[42]

A figure of comparable eminence and versatility was Hagop Oshagan (Kufedjian: 1883-1948), an often brilliant, sometimes controversial man of letters who produced with equal ease novels, short stories, essays, plays, critical studies and reminiscences of his contemporaries. His works have been divided into three more or less equal parts: those that appeared in book form (enough to fill a small library), those that were lost, and those that lie buried in defunct periodicals. His 5-volume *Panorama of Western Armenian Literature* (Jerusalem, 1945-56), is a seminal work and essential reading on the subject. Though highly respected as a critic, Oshagan, unlike most critics, approached his task with a sense of detached irony. "A hundred critics of genius," he once said, "aren't worth a single poet."

Born in Brussa (Turkey), Oshagan was active mainly in Istanbul, Cyprus, Jerusalem, and Aleppo, where he died.

One of the most highly regarded teachers of his time—it has been said that single-handed he has produced more writers than all the other teachers put together—Oshagan seems to have had a Nabokovian intolerance for general ideas and abstractions and constantly urged his students to develop a taste for the specific detail and the unique image. "You are lucky enough to have come from villages with their own colorful assortment of rogues, eccentrics, and idiots," he is quoted by one of his students. "Some of you may even have overheard family quarrels between irritable in-laws. Concentrate on these and similar events. . . . Never describe something you haven't seen with your own eyes!"[43]

Other influential names in the field of modern scholarship are philologists and linguists Hrachya Ajarian and Nikol Aghbalian, historiographer Nicholas Adonts, and literary historian and folklorist Manoog Abeghian.

Famous polyglot, eminent authority on the Armenian language, literary historian, and educator, Hrachya Ajarian (1876-1953) was born to a humble family (his father was a shoemaker) in Istanbul, and educated in French and German universities. Two of his teachers were H. Huebschmann and Antoine Meillet (author of an *Esquisse d'une grammaire comparee de l'armenien classique,* and several other works). Ajarian authored close to 200 monographs: critical works on the history of Armenian literature, the definitive classification of Armenian dialects, a 2-volume *Complete Grammar of the Armenian Language* (Yerevan, 1955), which contains references to 562 languages, and a 7-volume *Etymological Dictionary of the Armenian Language* (1926-1935), about which Meillet has said: "In the entire history of the human race, no man, not even a nation, has ever produced such a masterpiece."[44]

The dean of modern Armenian historiography, Nicholas Adonts (Nikoghayos Ter-Avedikian: 1871-1942) was born in Zankezur (Armenia) and studied at universities in St. Petersburg, Munich,

Paris, and London. His often daring and sometimes controversial works, written in Russian, French, and Armenian, include the magisterial study *Armenia in the Period of Justinian* (1908), originally written in Russian; *Histoire de l'Armenie* (Paris, 1946), which covers the periods from the 10th century B.C. to the 6th century A.D.; *Origins of the Armenian Feudal Nobility* (Beirut, 1949); and about eighty other important essays dealing with medieval Armenian history, literature, linguistics, folklore, and related topics. Of particular interest are his pioneering studies devoted to Armenian contributions to and relations with the Byzantine Empire.[45]

One of the most important and prolific figures in Soviet-Armenian scholarship, Manoog Abeghian (1865-1944), produced definitive works on Armenian grammar and medieval literature, dictionaries, studies on German, French, and English literatures, reminiscences of contemporaries, and a monumental collection of variants of the epic poem *David of Sassoun* in two volumes (Yerevan, 1936-1951). His complete works in eight thick volumes have been published by the Manoog Abeghian Literary Institute of the Armenian SSR Academy of Sciences in Yerevan. He also saved from oblivion priceless treasures of Armenian folk poetry.

Philologist, literary critic, educator, Minister of Culture in the short-lived Republic of Armenia, and later a community leader active mainly in the Middle East, Nikol Aghbalian (1873-1947) was born in Tiflis and studied linguistics in St. Petersburg under the celebrated Nikolai Marr, also philosophy under Bergson at the Sorbonne in Paris. His works include *The Diary of a Philologist* (Beirut, 1942), *An Introduction to the History of Armenian Literature,* monographs on the 5th-century historian Movses Khorenatsi and the 19th-century *ashugh* Sayat-Nova; and many essays and reviews on contemporary Armenian literature and linguistics.[46]

In the immediate post-Genocide years, Istanbul continued to be the most important center of Armenian culture in the diaspora. But gradually this center shifted to Paris, and then to Beirut.

Among writers active in Paris, there were such poets, essayists, critics, and novelists as Shahan Shahnour, Shavarsh Nartuni, Arshak Chobanian, Zareh Vorpuni, Vazken Shoushanian, Neshan Beshigtashlian, Puzant Topalian, and Nigoghos Sarafian.

Shahan Shahnour (Kerestedjian: 1904-1974), also known in French literary circles as Armen Lubin, is regarded by many as the most original and powerful novelist of the French diaspora. Born and educated in Istanbul, he spent most of his life in Paris where he made a living as a photographer and occasional contributor to French literary journals.

Retreat Without Song (1929), one of Shahnour's best-known novels, which bears the ironic subtitle *An Illustrated History of the Armenians,* is a brief and painful, even cruel account of half-a-dozen Armenian boys in Paris grappling with the complexities of adjusting to their new environment. Most of them eventually sink into an alienated mode of existence and become assimilated.

Like Raffi, Shahnour blamed the Church for the state of Armenian decline. At one point, one of his characters calls Narekatsi's *Book of Lamentations* an "unhealthy" and an "immoral" book. It was Christianity that made Armenians "passive, resigned, and submissive," he adds. Another Shahnour character describes his compatriots as "peddlers instead of fighters—a decrepit, doddering breed. There's no gun-powder in their blood—no guts, no desire to beat and bite those who hurt and humiliate them. They have never conquered. They have never knocked down anyone. They are weaklings no one can respect. O Lord, if you have a particle of strength left in you, sweep away this ugly, disgusting pile of old women, these refugees, these exiles and orphans—cleanse the world by getting rid of us; or else give us strength and courage!"

Shahnour's work may be regarded as an indictment and a warning to those dedicated yet misguided political activists who cannot read the writing on the wall and in their obsessive efforts to settle old, intramural scores, ignore the fact that their nation is gradually sinking into anonymity. Needless to add, critics and party functionaries (two roles that are frequently assigned to the same individual not only in Soviet Armenia but in the diaspora as well) were nearly unanimous in condemning Shahnour's novel, which, to make matters worse, contained daring and sometimes sordid scenes. Echoing the words of the 19th-century revolutionary thinker Mikael Nalbandian—who had urged writers "to show the greatness of virtue, the baseness of vice, to encourage the former and warn against the latter," and who had further warned against "inculcating into the Armenian family the vice and dissolution of family morals which the European home received from Civilization"—one critic (H. Aghbashian) wrote: "Shahnour's description of 'life as it is' is devoid of moral value. A writer should not simply record that which he observes. He should instead kill that which is condemned to die, and give life to that which is destined to live."

Edward Topchian, a Soviet-Armenian critic, said: "Shahnour's fictional characters are men without vision, men who lost all feeling of national pride and are gradually sinking in the quagmire of an alienated existence." Topchian went on to point out that Shahnour could very easily have saved his characters by letting them join the French proletarian movement of the 1920s.

These attacks may have had something to do with Shahnour's decision to adopt French as his medium—though he continued to write in Armenian, and after a lapse of nearly two decades, several more volumes of his fiction and nonfiction appeared in Beirut and Paris.

Shahnour is now considered one of the masters of 20th-century fiction and one of those rare social observers who gave expression to a problem that still haunts the Armenian diaspora.[47]

Shavarsh Nartuni (Aivazian: 1898-1968) was born in a small village near Istanbul but spent most of his life in Paris. "I came to France at the age of 25," he writes in an autobiographical essay. "I came with an insatiable thirst for knowledge. Dissatisfied with my medical studies at the university, I would spend my free daytime hours at the Sorbonne, and my evening hours in libraries. There was fire in my blood—an all-consuming, devouring green flame which made me find time even for the *Opera*, the *Comedie Francaise*, and the *Opera Comique*. . . . " After receiving his medical degree, Nartuni became involved in community affairs, edited several publications, the most important of which was *Haipouj* (The Armenian Cure), the only Armenian-language health magazine of the diaspora, and contributed to the press a ceaseless flow of literary essays, short stories, prose poems, fables, and articles on linguistics, history, and different aspects of Armenian culture, some of which were later collected and published in some 20 volumes.

Throughout his life Nartuni was tempted and often urged by friends to isolate himself and live "in solitary confinement with his inspiration," but his many obligations as physician, editor, and activist prevented him from doing so. Late in his life however, he travelled as far as Iran to the East and the Americas to the West. He died shortly after his return in 1968, as he was about to write of his many experiences and impressions.

Nartuni's style has been described as a bitter-sweet yet irresistible mixture of intense passion and detached irony (see *LANGUAGE*).

Arshak Chobanian (also Archag Tchobanian: 1872-1954) is highly regarded as a critic who produced penetrating studies of the 16th-century *ashugh, Nahapet Kouchak* (1902), the 18th-century poet and painter *Naghash Hovnatan* (1912), and the 19th-century lyric poets *Bedrous Tourian* (1894), and *Mkrtitch Beshigtashlian* (1907). He devoted a large portion of his life to the task of acquainting the French with Armenian culture. His French translations of Armenian literary works, of which he compiled several volumes, are unexcelled and were greatly admired by Anatole France, Valery Bryusov, and Emile Verhaeren. "Through your voice," said Verhaeren, "we heard an entire nation—its speech, its passion and suffering." For nearly three decades, Chobanian edited *Anahid*, one of the most influential literary periodicals of the diaspora, which he founded and published himself from 1898 to 1949 (with two wartime interruptions). Among contributors to *Anahid* were Issahakian, Varoujan, Zohrab, Shirvanzadeh, Toumanian, Zartarian and Gostan Zarian.

Chobanian's other works include a large quantity of original verse and prose; *Profiles*, 2 volumes (Paris, 1924-29); and an essay in French, *Victor Hugo, Chateaubriand et Lamartine dans la litterature armenienne* (Paris, 1935).

As a critic, Chobanian was by no means doctrinaire in his tastes. "It is the work of art," he said, "that makes the rules and not the rules which make the work of art."

When, following his death in a traffic accident in Paris, his manuscripts and papers were collected and shipped to Soviet Armenia, they filled 35 cases.[48]

After Stalin's death in 1953, and following a speech by Anastas Mikoyan (on March 11, 1954) which criticized those who regarded writers like Raffi and Charents as bourgeois nationalists, literary life in Armenia revived rapidly. Exiled authors were allowed to return home and resume their literary activities. Banned books and many translations from foreign literatures were published. Political control of the arts was openly discussed in literary periodicals and newspapers, some of which, like *Kragan Tert* and *Karoun*, were widely read by the general public. "I no longer live in terror of you," Kevork Emin declared in a poem titled "Conversation with a Pharisee"; and speaking in the name of an entire generation that suffered at the hands of ruthless men in the service of an unscrupulous regime, he took to task those writers who had cautiously kept quiet during the Great Terror. Elsewhere he also attacked "demagogic and nihilistic critics" for failing to understand nationalistic literature, and for removing "from our ranks some of our finest writers by denouncing their work."

A prolific poet and critic, Kevork Emin (Karlen Muradian: b. 1919) studied engineering in Yerevan and literature in Moscow. The author of some thirty volumes of verse and translations from the Russian, he has himself been translated into Russian by Boris Pasternak and Yevtushenko. One of his recent cycle of poems, *Time-Earth-Love* (1976), described by a Russian critic as "a monologue of filial devotion to one's native land," received the prestigious USSR State Prize.

Sylva Gaboudikian (also Kaputikian: b. 1919) is another prolific and influential poet whose patriotic verse and love lyrics have been collected in some twenty volumes and enjoy wide popularity in Soviet Armenia and the diaspora. Though on certain occasions she has criticized the Kremlin for failing to take a firmer anti-Turkish stand, she reveals an authoritarian temperament in complete harmony with the *status quo* in other areas, especially in her rambling travelogues, *Caravans Are Still on the Way* (1964), and *Mosaic of My Soul with the Colors of the Map* (1976) (the first dealing with her impressions of the Middle East, the second with Canada and the United States), which contain frequent political and autobiographical divagations.⁴⁹

The poet who represents the peak of post-war Soviet-Armenian poetry however is Baruir Sevag (also Paruir Sevak: Ghazarian: 1924-1971). Born in a small village in the district of Ararat, Sevag studied literature at the State University of Yerevan and at the Literary Institute of Gorky in Moscow. A member of the executive of the Union of Soviet-Armenian Writers for many years, and on the editorial board of several literary journals, he was an erudite critic as well as a brilliant poet. Perhaps his greatest achievement is the creation of an idiom at once traditional, modern, and personal—indebted to the folk poetry of the bards (Sayat-Nova), to the medieval mystic Narekatsi, and to such modern poets as Charents, and yet unmistakably his own. Some of his best-known cycles of poems are *The Immortals Command* (1948), *Irreconcilable Proximity* (1953), *Love's Road* (1954), *With You Once More* (1957), *The Man in the Palm of the Hand* (1963), *The Never Silent Bells* (1966), which is based on the life of composer Komitas (*see* MUSIC), and *Let There Be Light* (1971). In these works Sevag achieves a rare lyrical intensity, evoking the history, traditions, nature, and life of Armenia, and searching for ultimate values. Sevag also collaborated in the revised translation of the Bible for the 1970 edition; produced two important film scripts on historical themes, *Mesrob Mashtots* (1962), and *Sayat-Nova* (1965), about whom he also wrote a 500-page monograph; and translated from the Russian Pushkin, Bryusov, Yessenin, Lermontov, and many others.

Sevag's work aroused a profound and widespread mood of soul-searching throughout the nation. Publicly criticized for his nationalist and modernist inclinations, he died tragically in a car accident at the age of 47 at the height of his powers, full of new projects and never more conscious of his own capacity for development. His collected works in six volumes were issued in 1972-74 in Yerevan.⁵⁰

Other well-established poets whose collections of verse appear more or less regularly are Hamo Sahian (b. 1914), Maro Markarian

(b. 1915), Hovannes Shiraz (b. 1915), Vahagn Davtian (b. 1922), and Razmik Davoyan (b. 1940).

In his last collection of verse, *Hot Anvils* (Yerevan, 1978), Davoyan writes:

Like the echo of a whisper
I search
for a little silence
in the midst of confused
uncertain noises.

I search for a little silence
in order that I may listen
to myself
feel myself
in its fullness.

I search for a little silence
when I shall smile
a silent smile
like the smiling stars above
when I shall believe
without shouting
and afterward
I shall disappear
in complete silence
like mist in the valley ....

As these lines suggest, there is no discernible "ideological content" in Davoyan's verse. This is also true of the prose of such contemporary short story writers and novelists as Vakhtang Ananian, Sero Khanzadian, Shahen Tatikian, and Grant Matevossian.

Sometimes referred to as "Armenia's oldest writer," Vakhtang Ananian (1905-1980) was born to a peasant family and began his literary career as a journalist. He has published several volumes of war sketches (*In the Circle of Fire, On the Battlefield*), also short stories, novels, and pamphlets, but is best known for his 4-volume *Animal World of Armenia* (Yerevan, 1961-67), and 7-volume *Stories of a Hunter* (1947-1977), which, in addition to encounters with bears, wolves, and a wide assortment of other wild beasts, contains autobiographical fragments, anecdotes, sketches, and reminiscences of such contemporaries as Avedik Issahakian,

Charents, and Bakounts. In one of these fragments, recalling the circumstances surrounding his decision to become an author, Ananian writes that one day, when he was young, an editor overheard him tell a hunting story to a friend and asked him to write it down for his magazine. Ananian refused saying he had never written anything in his life. He was urged to write it exactly as he had recounted it. "Writers do not fall from heaven," he was told. Throughout his prolific career, Ananian seems to have kept that advice constantly in mind. Accessible, unaffected, conversational in tone, at his best Ananian is an irresistible combination of local color, charm and down-to-earth wisdom. He has been translated into as many as 25 languages, including English.[51]

Even more successful is novelist Sero Khanzadian (b. 1915). Though occasionally criticized for "distortions of Soviet reality," Khanzadian's novels on historical and contemporary themes—*The Land* (1954), *General Mekhitar* (1962), and others—are probably the most widely read and admired.

Notwithstanding official criticism for "a tendency for psychological quests not connected with social relationships and a disposition to interpret reality through old romanticism," Shahen Tatikian (b. 1924), in addition to being active in journalism, radio, and television, has produced a steady stream of books—averaging one a year—some of which come near being fully satisfying. The recurring motif in his fiction is urban man in crisis—often precipitated by a terminal disease, an accident, or obsessive love. His style, though far from flawless, has a curiously artless charm of its own. At critical points, Tatikian has a way of allowing the reader's imagination to fill in the details by saying very little or nothing. When one of his fictional characters, an articulate young doctor, for instance, finally has a chance to speak on the telephone with a girl whose image has haunted him ever since he saw her in the street, all he can say is: "I would like to see you." "I know," she replies. "Would you like to see me too?" "Of course." Next we watch them together at a party, and out-Chekhoving Chekhov, the narrator/protagonist informs us: "We kept looking at each other. We drank. We looked at each other and we drank."

One of the most promising Soviet-Armenian writers, Grant (or

Hrant) Matevossian (b. 1935) was born in a small village called Akhnitsor, not far from Yerevan. In 1961 he published a sketch of village life entitled "Akhnitsor," which became the center of considerable controversy. Satirical and comic in tone, this short piece depicted village life with unprecedented and, by Soviet standards, unusual honesty. Eventually the editors of *Sovetakan Grakanoutiun* (Soviet Literature), the literary journal where the story appeared, were removed, and Matevossian himself was severely reprimanded by the Party leadership. In his collection of short stories and novellas titled *August* (Yerevan, 1967), available in English as *The Orange Herd* (Moscow, 1976), where Akhnitsor has become Tsmakut, Matevossian reveals a fondness for describing a series of people, events and conversations that are exaggerated and at times bizarre. His prose teems with details and seems to be riding madly off in all directions in a whirlwind of dust. And in the eye of this whirlwind stands the narrator: sensitive, vulnerable, often confused and exasperated by the obtuse villagers, but above all ambitious and drunk with the wine of future glory.

> *Alexandre Dumas wallowed in fame and was surrounded by adoring women, and that was me; Fieldmarshal Kutuzov slept through a decisive battle, and that was me; our king Artavast walked proudly to the executioner's block, past that slut Cleopatra, and that was me too. There was my Nobel Prize, a cozy supper in the Latin Quarter . . . and that kitten Brigitte Bardot. And various snatches of conversation: "I despise you," "The Emperor has asked you to come," "Tell his majesty that I shall be detained for an hour."*[52]

Other novelists that merit mention: Zorair Khalapian (b. 1931), author of many novels, novellas, and plays where he probes the mysterious interconnections between reality and human desires; Zarzant Darian (b. 1912), a prolific author of a two-volume historical novel based on the life of *Sayat-Nova* (Yerevan, 1961-63), also plays and several collections of short stories; Angela Stepanian (b. 1917), author of *Sisters* (1947), *On the Threshold of Summer* (1959), and many other novels.

A poet and essayist whose work has shown a steady advance towards maturity and complexity, Vartkes Bedrossian (also Petrossian: b. 1932) was born in Ashtarak, near Yerevan, and began to publish in 1947. His first book, a cycle of poems titled *Ballad About Man*, came out in 1958. Other books, seven in all, followed—essays, fiction, verse, autobiographical writings. Bedrossian's most important work to date is *Equations with Many Unknowns* (Yerevan, 1977), which contains reminiscences of contemporaries, literary studies, polemics, and travel impressions of Canada, Italy, Turkey, Syria, and many other places. From these pieces, Bedrossian emerges as the type of writer, or rather conversationalist—since his prose has the informality of a friendly chat—who has been everywhere, read everything, met everyone worth meeting, and as a result, has acquired a limitless store of anecdotes and stories with which to illustrate a point. He is literate but never erudite or academic. As he himself observes at one point, one of the unique features of 20th-century Armenian literature is that the overwhelming majority of Armenian writers entered the literary field not from universities but orphanages. Consequently the stress has been on accessibility and individuality rather than the cultivation of a colorless academic jargon that may tend to disguise instead of revealing a writer's emotional make-up and bias.

Bedrossian reveals himself in every line he writes—an intelligent, energetic, sensitive man who loves books and learning but not necessarily libraries and schools. Like Thoreau, he believes before one sits down to write one must stand up and live; and it is no use trying to change the world if you are not willing to begin with yourself. Bedrossian can be as tough as Solzhenitsyn on the degeneracy of the West, but has no sympathy and tolerance either for certain facets of Soviet life—things like pollution, decline of academic standards, indifference towards cultural values, materialism. . . "These," he writes, "are red-hot issues, but one must not be afraid to burn one's hands. . . . "

In the field of literary criticism and scholarship, Sooren Aghababian (b. 1922) occupies a place of undisputed eminence. A leading figure in the numerous discussions that have occurred in the past three decades, Aghababian has authored several school texts, edited works on the history of Soviet-Armenian literature, and contributed numerous articles to both Russian- and Armenian-language encyclopedias. He has also published important monographs on

Stepan Zorian, (1955), *Axel Bakounts* (1959), *Gourgen Mahari* (1959), and *Yeghishe Charents* (1973), among others. His approach is analytical in character with a marked predilection for broad generalization.

Other contemporary Soviet-Armenian critics and scholars that deserve mention: Aram Injikian (1910-1975), a specialist on Avedik Issahakian and author of three books about him; Almast Zakarian (b. 1924), editor of Charents's *Complete Works* (1962-68), and author of the magisterial 2-volume *Armenian Poetry at the Beginning of the 20th Century* (1973-77); Levon Hakhverdian (b. 1924), author of voluminous studies on contemporary Armenian drama and biographies of Hovannes Toumanian and Avedik Issahakian; Hrant Tamrazian (b. 1926), whose works include meticulously researched studies on Shirvanzadeh, Siamanto, Derenik Demirjian, and Charents; Sevak Arzoomanian (b. 1929), author of a 582-page essay on *The Soviet-Armenian Novel* (1967), and biographies of *Vahan Totovents* (1961) and *Zabel Yessayan* (1965).[53]

The situation in the diaspora is difficult to assess because of the absence of up-to-date reference works, and the increasing fragmentation of themes, styles, and preoccupations.[54]

One important factor that hampers the development of contemporary Armenian literature in the diaspora is the lack of commercial or trade publishers. As a result writers act as their own publishers and distributors. Few books sell well enough to assure their authors an adequate income. As elsewhere, Armenian writers get along by taking jobs in cultural and educational institutions. Some, like poets Haroutiun Berberian of Detroit, and Garo Armenian of London, are successful businessmen or executives. Critic and short story writer Hampar Kelikian is a renowned bone surgeon. Novelist and short story writer Hagop Garabents was, until very recently, a broadcaster in the Armenian Department of Voice of America, Washington, D.C. Others are active in political parties or edit newspapers, of which there are over twenty in the United States alone, or teach at universities.[55]

On rare occasions, writers neutral or sympathetic to the regime, are published in Soviet Armenia. A writer who has been accorded this honor is the Armenian-American Peniamin Noorigian (b. 1894). Born in Husenig (West Armenia), Noorigian was educated in Kharpert, under Telgadintsi, whose works he edited (see above), and at the Columbia University in New York. For sixteen years (1939-54) he was editor of *Nor Kir* (New Letters), a literary quarterly published in New York. He is best known for his short stories, a volume of which, titled *Fatherland Longing,* was issued in Yerevan in 1978. In a diary entry dated April 29, 1969, Noorigian writes: "I have lived in the United States for 55 years now, yet I still feel like a stranger in a strange land—a lost traveller who, like Homer's Ulysses, has not yet given up searching for his home." [56]

This refusal to accept the American ethos is shared even by the fictional characters of writers, like the above-mentioned Garabents, who have successfully adjusted to the demands of the New World.

Born in Iran, Hagop Garabents (Jack Karapetian) was educated in American universities. Though fluent in English, he prefers to write in Armenian. He has published several meticulously crafted collections of short stories and a novel titled *Daughter of Carthage* (1972). One of the most perceptive observers of the Armenian-American scene of the 1960s and '70s, in his last collection of interrelated stories, *Old Sowers of the New World* (Washington, 1975), Garabents attempts, in his own words, "to capture a moment in the history of the Armenian diaspora." After giving us a panoramic view of a typical American city and its inevitable Armenian community, Garabents proceeds to speak of its composition and character. "There are Armenians," he writes,

> from Western Armenia, from the Middle East, and from Europe. There are Armenians even from India and Java. A veritable festival of dialects and traditions. Some of them can't even understand one another. But they are Armenians. That is enough. They smell each other out. They communicate with their eyes and eyebrows. What is even more incomprehensible is that they are all Americans now, as American as any Joe Smith or Jim Brown. Our Minas from Bitlis for example is an astrophysicist. Mrs. Parantsem, an opera singer. As for Manoog from Van, he is an executive at Chase Manhattan. The Armenians from our town are important fellows now. They speak with big, confident movements. But scratch their skin and you will come face to face with the enterprising

Kharpertsi, the daring Sassountsi, the polished Bolsetsi, and Marash, Moush, Erzerum, and Trabizond, and places so obscure and remote that their origins must be known only to Xenophon.

Garabents goes on to speak of other Armenians,

> who have not yet come to terms with the world, or with themselves for that matter. They are fatalists who view the world with mistrust. Their souls have been shattered, and like men possessed they relive the experiences of the martyrs and die a thousand deaths every day. They are in America but not of America. Let Americans go to the moon. What of it? They don't care. It is of no use to them. They read Armenian papers from one end to the other, not out of curiosity or to satisfy an inner need, but to fulfill a national duty. In order that Armenian literature and culture may continue to live in their lives and in the lives of their offspring . . . .

Their offspring however do not share their fears and obsessions.

> They are proud of their origin without being chauvinistic about it. They neither hate nor envy the foreigner. They regard themselves as human beings first, as Armenians or Americans second. They feel no need to prove constantly that they belong to a great nation. As a result they are more tolerant and self assured. They are what they are—neither more nor less. . . .

The parents cannot understand their children, whom they regard as radicals, even anarchists. They nevertheless continue to "sow seeds and transform deserts into orchards; they hew stones in quarries, melt down iron in foundries, erect sky-scrapers in cities. They fill the academies of science and the temples of art with their children. And they do these things in order that Armenia may be eternal. In order that our faith in Armenia and Armenianism may remain indestructible."

Armenia and Armenianism is one of the central themes of another leading Armenian-American novelist, poet, critic, and educator, who has been active for three decades now and on as many continents. Born in Aintab (Cilicia) shortly before World War I, Puzant Granian (Chekidjian) was educated in Alexandria (Egypt) and New York. He now lives in Los Angeles. Two of his most important works are the long, autobiographical novel, *The Armenian Comedy* (Beirut, 1965) and *Armenia and the Armenian* (Los Angeles, 1977), which he wrote after visiting Soviet Armenia for the first time in 1974 and which may be described as either a book of travel impressions with autobiographical divagations or a long poem in prose, a wild declaration of love to Armenia—its people, monuments, mountains, valleys, poets and martyrs. "Exile is a mode of existence that is filled with uncertainty, bitterness, confusion, and pain," Granian has said. "To return to Armenia was like regaining a lost paradise...."[57]

This malaise of confusion, pain, and bitterness is a *leitmotiv* that surfaces again and again in the fiction of Noubar Aghishian of California, author of two highly regarded collections of short stories, *Down the Current* (1976) and *Insulted Men* (1978). Aghishian's twice-deracinated Armenian-Americans—first time from their ancestral lands, second time from the Middle East—seem to be unanimous in their rejection of the American way of life. "People here have hearts of concrete, just like their surroundings," remarks a typical Aghishian character. "Aleppo may not be heaven on earth but at least we had friends and neighbors there, we concerned ourselves with each other's problems." Another character delivers the following diatribe: "No one cares about literature and writers here; people are judged by their financial income rather than moral worth. Understanding, enjoyment, appreciation—these things don't exist here. You all live in an abysmal void, a void that cannot be filled with dollars. I feel sorry for you. You are pitiful, and the tragedy of it is that you are not even aware of your own degradation."

A twice-deracinated Armenian-American writer who seems not to have allowed the American ethos to drive him to such harsh conclusions and who continues to produce a steady stream of poems, textbooks, plays, and essays, is Zareh Melkonian of Detroit. "I can write about anything," asserts Melkonian in his last collection of verse, *Mountains in Abysses* (Los Angeles, 1978); "I can even write about not being able to write." His range is nothing short of Balzacian—from atomic and subatomic motions of the human psyche to stars and galaxies, from intimate lyrics to long poems of an epic cast. His explorations of love in its many guises are handled with the type of confidence and penetration that come only through intensely lived experiences. He is an unashamedly autobiographical writer unafraid to deal with the raw data of life—anxiety, fear, passion, man's inhumanity to man.

Other Armenian-American writers briefly noted: poet, short story writer, and novelist Hamasdegh (Hampartsoum Kelenian: 1895-1966), who was born and educated in Kharpert. A resident of the United States since 1913, he never fully adapted to the New World, and following a meeting with Shirvanzadeh in New York, during which Shirvanzadeh advised him to write about his native village, Hamasdegh began to publish a series of sketches and anecdotes providing a carefully detailed account of country life at the turn of the century. His published books include three collections of short stories and verse *(The Village, The Rain, My Prayer)*, and a two-volume novel, *The White Horseman* (1953), which is based on the life of a fedayee or freedom fighter and is generally regarded as his masterpiece;[58] Aram Haigaz (Chekemian: b. 1900), author of about a dozen volumes of fiction and reminiscences;[59] prolific author and editor of several newspapers and periodicals of the diaspora, Antranig Antreassian (b. 1909) whose fiction, reminiscences, and literary criticism have appeared in the United States, Armenia and the Middle East. His most recent novel, *Through the Long Night,* deals with the McCarthy era. He is currently working on a long novel, planned as a trilogy, tracing Armenian life and events from 1895 to the present;[60] Vahe Haig (Tinchian: b. 1896), whose work includes a novel, ethnographical and literary essays, translations, and five volumes of short stories published under the general title of *Ancestral Hearth*; literary historian Minas Tololian, novelist Arpine (Aprahamian), short story writer Sooren Manuelian, poets Shahan Natalie and Jacques Hagopian; and Hagop Asadourian, Lutfi Minas, Garabed Sidal, among many others.

Other writers of the diaspora briefly noted:

The Munich-based broadcaster, journalist, and essayist Levon Mkrtitchian, author of *The Concept of Sovereignty Thoughout the Centuries* (Beirut, 1977), a philosophical study; *Voices from the Fatherland* (Munich, 1978), an anthology of Soviet-Armenian dissenters; also of book-length studies on Axel Bakounts and Solzhenitsyn.[61]

Antranik Zaroukian (b. 1913) of Lebanon, whose works include poems (*Letter to Yerevan*), satirical and autobiographical novels (*The Ashtray; Men Without Childhood*), travel impressions of Armenia (*Old Dreams, New Roads*), and a large quantity of essays and criticism published in *Nairi*, a monthly periodical which he began to edit in 1941. [62]

Others in Lebanon: playwright, poet, literary scholar, novelist, and educator Moushegh Ishkhan (Djenderedjian: b. 1913); poets and critics Vahe-Vahian (Sarkis Abdalian: b. 1907), and Karnig Attarian (b. 1925); also Boghos Snabian, Levon Vartan, K. Ajemian, Keghart, A. Tarian, N. Charkhoudian, and Vehanoush Tekian. [63]

In Istanbul: poets Zahrad (Zareh Yaldesjian: b. 1924), [64] and Zareh Khrakhouni (Arto Jumbashian: b. 1926).

In Iran: Zorair Mirzayan (1918-1946); in Portugal: Vahram Mavian (b. 1926); in France: Krikor Beledian (b. 1945); in England: Garo Armenian, and many others in Egypt, Syria, Austria, Italy, Argentina, and Greece. [65]

In the following few pages, let us consider a handful of writers whose medium of expression is other than Armenian.

In English, one of the first to achieve both fame and fortune was Michael Arlen (Dikran Kouyoumdjian: 1895-1956). Born in Bulgaria, Arlen spent most of his life in England and the United States. His many stories, plays, and novels are now neglected, but enjoyed wide popularity in the 1920s, influencing such writers as Hemingway (especially his *Sun Also Rises*) and F. Scott Fitzgerald (*The Great Gatsby*). It is said that after reading *The Green Hat,* one of his most spectacularly successful novels, Stalin's wife committed suicide. Rebecca West called Arlen "every other inch a gentleman." Irwin Cobb professed to admire him for being "the only Armenian I have met who has not tried to sell me a rug." Someone else suggested he was really Turkish propaganda sent to the United States to justify the Armenian massacres. Everyone—his teachers, his friends, and later his readers—had trouble pronouncing his real name, so he changed it to Michael Arlen. Arlen's attitude towards his "background" was a contradictory tangle of pride and self-contempt. As a young man in London he published articles that were aggressively nationalistic in tone. At a critical moment in his life, however, one of his fictional narrators delivers the following diatribe: "Son of an incapable race, born in the musty twilight of an outcast people, inheritor of centuries of ignoble martyrdoms and mean escapes, what did I deserve but the anxious and helpless solitude of an unwanted servant? What art could come from an Armenian? What greatness?—what, even, of worth?"

The flaw in Arlen's character was a consuming ambition to join the English aristocracy. Being Armenian eventually became a dark secret to be hidden and forgotten. "He pined to be where he didn't belong," D. H. Lawrence said of him, ". . . among the English upper classes. And how they enjoyed the various kicks they got at him! And how he hated them." "You are a foreigner," Churchill once told Arlen in the presence of others, "an intruder, an Armenian who dares to come to this country and write books purporting to be about the manners and behavior of its aristocracy. You do not belong and never will belong to the classes in this country which you are so profitably describing. You have, in point of fact, no right to be sitting at this table."

Arlen is the subject of an excellent biography by an Armenian-American professor of English at Fairleigh Dickinson University, Harry Keyishian, and two memoirs by his own son Michael J. Arlen, *Exiles* (1970), and *Passage to Ararat* (1975).

Though he became a household name to most Armenians here and abroad only after the publication of *Passage,* Michael J. Arlen was already well known to Americans as the television critic for *The New Yorker* magazine and the author of *The Living-Room War* (1969), a collection of *New Yorker* pieces, and *An American Verdict* (1973), an account of the Black Panther shooting in Chicago and its aftermath. He has since published another volume of television criticism, *The View from Highway 1* (1976). His prose has been called "deft, graceful, entirely under control, and satisfyingly intimate." John Updike has called Arlen's television pieces ". . . among the best prose poems being written on life, love, war, and the state of the nation."

William Saroyan (b. 1908) is without any doubt the most widely recognized figure among American-born Armenian writers. Mainly self-taught, Saroyan began to write early and has written steadily since—short stories (*My Name is Aram*), novels (*The Human Comedy, Papa You're Crazy, Mama I Love You*), plays (*The Time of Your Life*, for which he was awarded the Pulitzer Prize), autobiographies *(Here Comes/There Goes/You Know Who)*, most of which have been translated into all the major languages of the world. An American critic has called Saroyan "a conscious spokesman for a people who survived a genocidal holocaust—but throughout his life he has chosen to write not of despair and dadaism and devastation, but joy." [66]

Though he understands and speaks Armenian well, Saroyan writes exclusively in English. Before adopting English as his medium, however, Levon Zaven Surmelian (b. 1907) was an accomplished Armenian lyric poet and author of a highly regarded volume of verse titled *Joyful Light* (1924). Uprooted from his native Trabizond during the Turkish massacres, Surmelian wandered through Russia and Armenia (where, at the age of sixteen, he became an assistant secretary in the Commissariat of the Interior) before making his way to the United States. After writing his best-selling autobiography *I Ask You Ladies and Gentlemen* (New York, 1945), Surmelian went on to produce a novel titled *98.6* (New York, 1950), many short stories, an adaptation of the Armenian national epic *Daredevils of Sassoun* (1964), a collection of Armenian folktales, *Apples of Immortality* (1968), and the highly popular *Technique of Fiction Writing: Measure and Madness* (1968).

Another Armenian-American writer who has produced works of fiction as well as nonfiction is Marjorie Housepian. The author of a Saroyanesque novel, *A Houseful of Love* (New York, 1957), Housepian has also published a widely-read and much quoted essay, "The Unremembered Genocide," which first appeared in *Commentary* (XLII, September 1966), and *The Smyrna Affair* (1971), an account of the burning of Smyrna in 1922 and the expulsion of the Christian minorities from Asia Minor. [67]

According to a survey published in 1974 by the Armenian Assembly in Washington there are over a thousand Armenian-

American scholars actively engaged in education and research. Among these let us note a few eminent names in economics, theology, literary scholarship, sociology, and the sciences.

One of the nation's most distinguished economists, Armen Alchian (b. 1914) has been a professor of economics at the University of California since 1946. He is the co-author of the famed text *University Economics: Elements of Inquiry* (1964), which has been called one of "the best introductory textbook(s) on the subject" (*Encyclopaedia Britannica*). Other works include *Costs and Output* (1958), *Pricing and Society* (1967), *Exchange and Production* (1969), and *Economics of Charity* (1974).

Gabriel Vahanian (b. 1927) is a renowned theologian whose books—*The Death of God* (New York, 1961), *Wait Without Idols* (1964), *No Other God* (1966), and others—have been highly praised by such authorities as Reinhold Niebuhr and Rudolf Bultmann.

Anna Balakian (b. 1916) is a widely respected authority on French symbolist and surrealist literature and the author of a definitive study on *Andre Breton* (New York, 1971). Her works have been translated into many languages, including Japanese. Her sister, Nona Balakian (b. 1919), has been called "perhaps the best-informed person in the United States about the changing fortunes of newspaper and magazine book reviewing, both as an art and as a profession." Since the 1940s, Nona Balakian has held a post on the staff of the *New York Times Book Review,* and authored and edited several collections of essays on contemporary American, English, and French fiction.

Sociologist Edward Tiryakian (b. 1929) is well known for his extensive researches and writings on the social consequences of modernization and industrialization in underdeveloped areas, especially sub-Sahara Africa, and on the development of systematic sociological theory: studies in which an effort is made to relate sociology to neighboring disciplines like history, social psychology, anthropology, economics, and the occult sciences. His *Theoretical Sociology: Perspectives and Developments* (New Jersey, 1970), has been called "easily the most authoritative reference volume on the present state of sociological theory in anglophone North America" (*Choice*).

Born in Hadjen (Armenia Minor) and educated in the United States, Dr. Hampar Kelikian is a noted orthopedic surgeon and literary scholar. He has published stories, poems, and essays in *Ararat* (New York), *Nairi* (Beirut) and many other periodicals; two monumental works of medical scholarship, *Hallus Valgus: Allied Deformities of the Forefoot* (Philadelphia, 1965), and *Congenital Deformities of the Hand and Forearm* (1974); and a collection of literary essays titled *A Doctor and Modern Literature* (Jerusalem, 1964).

One of the leading media critics in the United States, Ben Bagdikian (b. 1920), was born in Marash (Western Armenia), came to the United States when he was less than a year old, and now lives in California. The recipient of numerous prizes, including the Pulitzer Prize (for articles on race relations, American news commentators, the internal security system, and other topics), Bagdikian is the author of *The Information Machine: Their Impact on Men and the Media* (New York, 1971), which, in the words of John Chancellor, "is one of the very best books ever produced about the past, present and the future of American journalism"; *The Effete Conspiracy and Other Crimes of the Press* (1972); *In the Midst of Plenty* (1964), where he exposed the plight of 36,000,000 Americans who live in poverty in the slums of Chicago, on the reservations, in Appalachia, and in migrant workers camps; *The Shame of Our Prisons* (1972, with L. Dash), and *Caged: Eight Prisoners and Their Keepers* (1976), about the uselessness of the American prison system and the criminality of the respectable, law-and-order prison authorities. As part of the research done for his prison books, Bagdikian allowed himself to be committed to one of the state prisons and lived for some months as an inmate. "Compelling," "a journalistic gem," "a must," are some of the words used by critics in connection with his works.[68] "The most compelling principles in my life have been, in private life the pervasive need of love and trust in human relations," Bagdikian has said, "in public life the dignity and freedom of the individual, in intellectual life a distrust of the arcane and detachment from the human condition, and in journalism honesty and clarity."

Two French-Armenian university teachers who have produced works in both French and English are Byzantinist Sirarpie Der Nersessian and Maupassant specialist Artin Artinian.

A resident of the United State since 1951, Artinian (b. 1907), was born in Bulgaria and educated in Paris. His field is modern French literature with particular emphasis on Guy de Maupassant, about whom he has published several important works in both French and English—*La Correspondence inedite de Guy de Maupassant* (1951), *Pour et contre Maupassant* (1955), *From Victor Hugo to Jean Cocteau* (1965), and others.

A recipient of France's highest scholastic degree from the Sorbonne, Istanbul-born Sirarpie Der Nersessian (b. 1896) is an internationally recognized Byzantinist and expert in Armenian and Greek manuscript painting. It is extremely difficult to find a work on Armenian and Byzantine art and civilization that does not include in its bibliography one or more of her works—most of which have already been mentioned in the notes of the present work (*see* HISTORY, LITERATURE, ART & ARCHITECTURE).

Other distinguished names in 20th-century French literature: playwrights Arthur Adamov and Gabriel Arout, novelists Vahe Katcha and Jean-Marie Carzou, and literary scholar Charles Dedeyan.

The son of a wealthy Armenian businessman, Arthur Adamov (1908-1970) was born in Kislovodsk (Caucasus) and educated in Switzerland, Germany, and France. The Russian Revolution and the subsequent nationalization of oil fields in Baku (which plunged the Adamovs into abject poverty), his father's gambling and suicide, and his own arrest by the Vichy government and internment in a French prison camp as a dangerous alien during World War II, were some of the formative events of his life. Except for short trips abroad, Paris remained the center of his activities.

A tormented, Dostoevskian character, Adamov experienced a long series of spiritual, psychological, and ultimately physical crises, which he was to describe in great detail in his three autobiographical books:*L'Aveu* (1946), *L'Homme et l'enfant* (1968), and *Je... ils...* (1969). Long before R. D. Laing, Adamov defended the idea of neurosis, stressing its ability to provide a sharp lucidity inaccessible to the ordinary man; ". . . the neurosis which exaggerates man's particular vision," he said, "defines more clearly his universal significance."

Adamov began to write at an early age (mostly surrealist poetry and autobiographical and critical prose) but became known as a playwright only in the late 1950s. Three of his best-known plays are: *Le Professeur Taranne* (1953), *Le Ping pong* (1955), and *Paolo Paoli* (1957).

In the 1960s, critics and literary historians often joined his name with those of Samuel Beckett (who won the Nobel Prize), Eugene Ionesco (who became a member of the French Academy), Jean Genet (who was canonized by Sartre), and a number of other lesser known absurdist or avant-garde or anti-theater playwrights whose works were a response to a post-Dachau and post-Hiroshima world from which traditional moral values had disappeared.

Though his plays often end in insanity, murder, and suicide, Adamov did not regard human life and the world as an absurdity. Shortly before he committed suicide, he was willing to admit: "Life is not absurd. It is difficult, just very difficult." Life seemed to him, he said elsewhere, like a "monstrous beast which penetrates and surpasses me, and which is everywhere, within and outside." He did have one way, however, to rid himself of the terror which gripped and enveloped him: "My only recourse is to write, to make others aware of it, so as not to have to bear all of it alone, to get rid of a part of it, however small it may be."

Competent in several languages, Adamov also translated into French C. G. Jung, Rilke, Buechner, Kleist, Dostoevsky, Gogol, Gorky, Chekhov, Strindberg, Goncharov, and others.

Adamov was not as successful as Beckett, Ionesco, and Genet in capturing the imagination of the public, though he was admired by fellow playwrights and critics as dissimilar in temperament as Gide, Camus, and Sartre. In his recently published interviews and lectures on the theater—*Sartre on Theater,* edited by Michel Contat and Michel Rybalka (New York, 1976)—Sartre makes numerous references to Adamov's contributions to the contemporary French theater.[69]

Born in Nakhichevan, French playwright and director Gabriel Arout (Arouchian: b. 1909), emigrated to France from Yerevan in 1921. He has scripted many films, dramatized short stories by Chekhov, novels by Dostoevsky, authored original plays, and translated and adapted plays by English, American, and Russian authors.[70]

Vahe Katcha (Katchadourian: b. 1928) was born in Damascus and educated in Paris. He has published about twenty novels, some of which (*The Hook, Fatal Journey, An Eye for an Eye, Don't Look Down*) have been translated into English or made into successful films. The *Larousse Dictionary of Contemporary French Literature* (Paris, 1966), describes him as "a powerful novelist of classic restraint with a remarkable ability to analyze the cultural and psychological evolution of the new generations of the Middle East." One of his novels was recently issued in an Armenian translation in Yerevan. He has also been translated into Russian, Dutch, Portuguese, Swedish, Italian, German, and several other languages.

Son of the well-known painter Jean Carzou (see ART), Jean-Marie Carzou (b. 1938) was born and educated in Paris. He began his literary career as a journalist contributing to such prestigious Parisian dailies as *Le Monde*, *Combat*, and *Quotidien de Paris*. He went on to publish works of nonfiction and fiction—*Cinquante Vietnam* (Paris, 1969), *Armenie 1915: un genocide exemplaire* (1975), *Caida* (1977). He has also written, directed, and produced many television documentaries on subjects that range from Nietzsche, Vermeer, and Malraux to composers Olivier Messiaen, Boulez, and to such classics of French literature as Madame de Sevigne and George Sand.

Charles Dedeyan (b. 1910) was born in Smyrna and educated at the Sorbonne in Paris where he is now a professor of comparative literature. He is the author of *Le Theme de Faust dans la litterature europeenne* (1954), *Dante en Angleterre* (1958), *Chateaubriand et Rousseau* (1972), and dozens of other works on French, English, Italian, and German literature of the Classic, Romantic, and Modern periods.[71]

Two Armenian writers whose medium is Russian are Marietta Shaginian (or Shahinian) and Nina Berberova—the first resides in the Soviet Union, the second in the United States.

Extremely prolific and many-sided, Marietta Shaginian (b. 1888) has authored works in many genres—plays, collections of verse (before the Revolution she was a poet on the fringes of the Symbolist movement), travelogues (*A Trip to Weimar*), critical works (*On Art and Literature*), biographies and reminiscences of contemporaries (*Goethe, Recollections of Rachmaninov*), psychological novels (*One's Own Fate*), traditional novels (*Adventures of a Lady in Society*), experimental novels (*K. and K.*), American style thrillers (she is regarded as one of the founders of the detective novel in the USSR), and Soviet-style socialist-realist novels (*The Hydroelectric Plant*), which is based on the building of an electric power station on the River Mizinko in Armenia. Though she has been accused of opportunism for her extreme pro-Soviet stance during and after the Great Terror, Shaginian has written some penetrating and eloquent pages on Armenia (see my *Armenia Observed*) and on such Armenian cultural heroes as Khachatur Abovian (in her *Journey Through Soviet Armenia*, which is available in English) and Yeghishe Charents (in her introduction to the Russian translation of Charents's novel *Land of Nairi*). According to Konstantine Serebryakov, the author of several essays on Shaginian (one of which was published in *Ararat*, Summer 1973), in her nineties, she is as restless and active as ever.

The author of a remarkable autobiography titled *The Italics Are Mine* (New York, 1969), and a resident of the United States since 1951, Nina Berberova (b. 1901) was born and educated in Russia (Goncharov is said to have modeled Oblomov on her Armenian great-grandfather). Most of her Russian works, which include short stories, novels, essays, memoirs, biographies (of among others Tchaikovsky, Borodin, and Blok), have not yet been translated into English.

Vittoria Aganoor's (Aghanoorian: 1855-1910) collections of verse—*The Eternal Story* (1905), *New Lyrics* (1908), *New Songs* (1910)—were highly considered in their time in Italy. She was born in Padua but spent most of her life in Venice. Some of her poems have been translated into Armenian by the prolific Mekhitarist scholar Arsen Ghazikian. [72]

In the field of Italian scholarship, there is Edoardo Arslan (1899-1968), educator, museum curator, and author of numerous studies on Italian and Byzantine art and architecture. His father, Yervant Arslan (1865-1948), was a renowned otorhinolaryngologist and author of 74 monographs.

Two pioneers of the Arabic literary revival are Rizqallah Hassun (1825-1880), poet, translator of Biblical books, and author of a short life of Christ, [73] and Adib Ishak (1856-1885), poet, novelist, playwright, and critic. Others include historian Iskandar Abicarius, his brother John Abicarius, compiler of the first English-Arabic dictionary, and John Wortabet, author of *Syria and the Syrians*, 2 volumes (London, 1855), and other works.

Armenian contributions to the literatures as well as the arts, economy, and governance of such countries as Rumania, Poland, Hungary, and the Ukraine, have a long history because the Armenian diasporas here date as far back as the 11th century—that is, following the Seljuk invasions and the destruction of Ani in 1045 (see HISTORY). At first farmers, artisans, and merchants, Armenians gradually became the main intermediaries in trade between East and West. In the 16th century nearly all trade in these countries was in the hands of the Armenians, who, after acquiring some degree of prosperity, intermarried with the local gentry and assumed a more active role in the cultural and political life of their country of adoption. [74]

The history of the Lukacz family (Ghougassian) in Hungary is a typical case in point. Originally from Ani, the Ghougassians emigrated to Hungary and played such a prominent role in the enonomic life of the country that Empress Maria Theresa raised them to the aristocracy, which in turn allowed them to be active in politics and the arts. One of the first to achieve eminence was Mauritz Lukacz (1812-1881), who became a noted philologist, historian, author of an important study on Roman history, and translator of Lord Byron and Cervantes. Another was Denesh Lukacz (1816-1868), an important educator who counted among his students the future Emperor Franz-Josef. Bela Lukacz (1847-1901) was a historian, economist, publisher of an influential daily, and author of many works of fiction and non-fiction. University teacher and statesman Laszlo Lukacz (1850-1932) was Prime Minister of Hungary from 1912-13. Georg Lukacz (1865-1950) was Minister of Culture from 1905-06. Miklosz Lukacz (b. 1905) is now a professor of music and director of the Budapest State Opera. His interpretations of Wagner have been highly praised throughout Europe.

Two eminent names in Rumanian literature are Mihai Eminescu and Garabed Ibraileanu.

Known as "Rumania's Hoelderlin," Eminescu (1850-1889) is generally regarded as the founder of modern Rumanian literature. Writes Martin Seymour-Smith: "Mihai Eminescu constructed a body of Rumanian poetry that has never been equalled. The enchanted quality that his marvellous and original handling of the language produces is inevitably lost in translation. Eminescu established Rumanian as a literary language." Elsewhere we read: "Eminescu concentrated in his work the entire evolution of Rumanian national poetry" (Z. D. Busulenga). Struck by insanity in 1883, Eminescu lived until 1889 in a dramatic alternation between lucidity and madness. In addition to verse, his work includes a large quantity of prose (short stories, novels, plays, articles, letters).

Ibraileanu (1871-1936) was a critic, editor, novelist, and educator whose collections of essays, of which he published several, and his autobiographical novel *Adela* (1933), which was awarded the most prestigious literary award of the country, had a decisive influence on the development of 20th-century Rumanian literature. Like Eminescu, Ibraileanu maintained strong ties with the Armenian communities of Rumania, publishing many articles and essays on Armenian history and culture. [75]

---

[1]Until now I have referred to Istanbul as Constantinople. It is interesting to note however that Greeks themselves called Constantinople New Rome, and the origin of the name Istanbul is neither recent nor Turkish. Istanbul stands for the Greek words "Is tin poli," meaning "To the city." Writing in 1403, the Spanish traveller Gonzalez de

Clavijo says: "The Greeks do not know the city by the name of Constantinople, but Estombol."

²*Sassna Dzerer* has inspired several English-language adaptations or retellings, the best of which are: Leon Surmelian, *The Daredevils of Sassoun* (Denver, 1964); Mischa Kudian, *The Saga of Sassoun* (London, 1970); Aram Tolegian, *David of Sassoun* (New York, 1961); A. K. Shalian, *David of Sassoun* (Ohio, 1964). See also *David de Sassoun*, French translation by Frederic Feydit (Paris, 1964). For an excellent critical study, see Chake Der Melkonian-Minassian, *David de Sassoun: L'Epopee populaire armenienne* (Montreal, 1972).

³Some of these manuscripts have been listed, annotated, and described by Sirarpie Der Nersessian (b. 1896), an internationally recognized expert in the field: See *Manuscrits armeniens illustres de XII, XIII, et XIV siecles de la Bibliotheque des peres Mekhitaristes de Venise,* 2 volumes (Paris, 1936-1937); *Armenian Manuscripts in the Freer Gallery of Art* (Washington, 1965); *Armenian Manuscripts in the Walters Gallery* (Baltimore, 1974); *The Chester Beatty Library: Catalogue of the Armenian Manuscripts,* 2 volumes (Dublin, 1958). See also, M. Brosset, *Catalogue de la Bibliotheque d'Etchmiadzin* (St. Petersburg, 1840); F. C. Conybeare and J. O. Wardrop, *A Catalogue of the Armenian Manuscripts in the British Museum* (London, 1913); S. Baronian and F. M. Conybeare, *Catalogue of the Armenian Manuscripts in the Bodleian Library* (Oxford, 1918); F. Macler, *Catalogue des manuscrits armeniens et georgiens de la Bibliotheque Nationale* (Paris, 1908); A. Surmeyan, *Grand catalogue des manuscrits armeniens des collections particulieres d'Europe* (Paris, 1950); Avedis K. Sanjian, *A Catalogue of Medieval Armenian Manuscripts in the United States* (Los Angeles, 1976).

⁴Goghpatsi's *Refutation of the Sects* is discussed by Zaven Arzoomanian, *Studies in Armenian Historiography* (New York, 1974). See also L. Maries, *Le De Deo d'Eznik de Kolb connu sous le nom de Contre les sectes* (Paris, 1924).

⁵These and a number of other historians have been translated into French by Victor Langlois, *Collections des historiens anciens et modernes de l'Armenie,* 2 volumes (Paris, 1867-1869). *History of Armenia* by Faustus of Byzantium has been translated into French by the eminent 19th-century historian, educator, philologist and translator Mkrtitch Hovsep Emin (Karapetian: 1815-1890).

⁶See M. Khorenatsi, *History of the Armenians,* English translation by R. W. Thomson (New York, 1978). In his commentary, Thomson dismisses the autobiographical details of Khorenatsi's account of his travels and studies as a "patchwork of quotations" from the *Autobiography* of Anania Shirakatsi (*see* SCIENCE*)*, the Armenian version of the Alexander Romance, and the various homilies of St. Gregory Nazianzus. Another American scholar finds Thomson's conclusions irrefutable and comments: "To refer to Khorenatsi as the Armenian Herodotus is to do a distinct injustice to the true Father of History." This scholar seems to be unaware of the fact that Herodotus himself is often referred to as "the Father of Lies."

⁷See Aram Raffi, "Armenia: Its Epics, Folk-Songs, and Medieval Poetry," in Zabelle Boyadjian's *Armenian Legends and Poems* (New York, 1916).

⁸Nikol Aghbalian, *Movses Khorenatsi,* English translation by Armine Manoukian Sarian, in *The Armenian Review* (July 1979).

⁹Agathangelos, *History of the Armenians,* Armenian text with English translation *en face,* edited and translated by Robert W. Thomson (New York, 1977). See also A. A. Bedikian, *The Golden Age in the 5th Century: An Introduction to Armenian Literature in Perspective* (New York, 1963); G. Garitte, *Documents pour l'etude du livre d'Agathange* (Vatican City, 1946).

¹⁰Sebeos, *Histoire d'Heraclius,* French translation by F. Macler (Paris, 1904). Fragments from Sebeos are translated and paraphrased by Enno Franzius, *A Short History of the Byzantine Empire* (New York, 1967).

¹¹Several Armenian historians of this and following centuries (Asoghik, Samuel of Ani, Nerses Shnorhali, Nerses Lambronatsi, Sempat Sparabed, Matthew of Edessa, and others) have been translated into French by the eminent 19th-century Armenologist Jean-Paul E. Dulaurier (1807-1881). See his *Recherches sur la chronologie armenienne technique et historique* (Paris, 1859); *Recueil des historiens des Croisades: Documents armeniens* (Paris, 1869). Dulaurier travelled widely in the Middle East and Russia, also Vienna and Venice, researching and writing many studies on Armenian history and culture. See also, M. F. Brosset, *Collection d'historiens armeniens,* 2 volumes (St. Petersburg, 1847-46); V. Langlois, *Collection des historiens anciens et modernes de l'Armenie,* 2 volumes (Paris, 1868-69).

¹²The first 25 prayers of *Narek* are available in English. See *Lamentations of Narek: Mystic Soliloquies with God,* translated by Mischa Kudian (London, 1977). For general background, see Karekin Sarkissian, *A Brief Introduction to Armenian Christian Literature* (New Jersey, 1974).

¹³See Arshak Sahakian, *St. Nerses, the Gracious* (New York, 1973). For English translations, see *Anthology of Armenian Poetry,* translated and edited by Diana Der Hovanessian and Marzbed Margossian (New York, 1978).

¹⁴See *Ararat* (Fall 1980) for English translations of several fables by Gosh.

¹⁵Several collections of Armenian folktales are now available in English: Mischa Kudian, *Three Apples Fell From Heaven* (London, 1969); Leon Surmelian, *Apples of Immortality* (Berkeley, 1968); Virginia Tashjian, *Once There Was and Was Not* (New York, 1966); Susie Hoogasian-Villa, *100 Armenian Tales* (Detroit, 1966).

¹⁶See *Seven Bites from a Raisin: Proverbs from the Armenian,* translated by P. M. Manuelian (New York, 1980).

¹⁷For more on the Mekhitarists, see A. Goode, *A Brief Account of the Mekhitarist Society* (Venice, 1835), and Kevork Bardakdjian, *The Mekhitarist Contributions to Armenian Culture and Scholarship* (Cambridge, 1976); also *Ararat* (Spring 1977).

¹⁸Abovian is discussed by Baron August von Haxthausen, *Transcaucasia* (Leipzig, 1856), Friedrich Parrot, *Journey to Ararat* (New York, 1970, originally published in 1846), and Marietta Shaginian, *Journey Through Soviet Armenia;* see also my *Armenia Observed* (New York, 1979).

¹⁹It is to be noted that "the only place on earth where Kurds are now recognized as an ethnic group, and where they are allowed to know themselves and study their cultural heritage is Soviet Armenia"—this according to a contemporary Kurdish spokesman. There are today over 40,000 Kurds in Soviet Armenia, where they

have their own schools, theaters, newspapers, and publishing houses. The establishment of these institutions was made possible only after Armenian scholars had devised a new alphabet for them. Though most Kurdish authors now write in their own language, some have also produced significant works in Armenian.

[20] As if to conform with Vartan's dreams, these dusty roads are now tree-lined avenues, one of which leads to a highway that reaches the border of Turkey. The Turkish government, however, for reasons that have not yet been made public, has consistently refused to open its frontier.

[21] See Mikael Nalbandian, *Agriculture as the True Way*, English translation by Leon Megrian, in *The Armenian Review* (issues 106-109).

[22] Hagop Baronian, *Honourable Beggars*, edited and translated by Mischa Kudian (London, 1978). Also, *The Honorable Beggars*, translated and adapted into a play by Jack Antreassian, with an introduction by Bedros Norehad, illustrations by Alexander Saroukhan (New York, 1980).

[23] Yervant Odian, *Comrade Panchoonie*, translated by Jack Antreassian, with an Introduction by Michael Kermian, illustrated by Alexander Saroukhan (New York, 1977).

[24] *For the Sake of Honor*, translated into English by Nishan Parlakian (New York, 1975). One of his novels is available in French—*L'Artiste* (Paris, 1909).

[25] See Mischa Kudian, *The Bard of Loree: Selected Works of Hovannes Toumanian* (London, 1971); Virginia Tashjian, *Once There Was and Was Not* (Based on stories by Toumanian) (Boston, 1966); Hovannes Toumanian, *David of Sassoun*, bilingual edition, English translation by H. S. Varvarian (New York, no date).

[26] See *Sayat-Nova: His Life and Some Poems* (Yerevan, 1963).

[27] See James Russell, "Hovannes Tulkurantsi: Master Minstrel," *Ararat* (Summer, 1979).

[28] For translations of Kouchak's lyrics, see Desmond O'Grady, *Off License* (Dublin, 1968). *Anthology of Armenian Poetry*, edited and translated by Diana Der Hovanessian and Marzbed Margossian (New York, 1978). See also *Les Trouveres armeniens*, traduction francaise avec une introduction par Archag Tchobanian (Paris, 1906).

[29] For a short and informative monograph on this topic, see K. S. Papazian, *Merchants from Ararat: A Brief Survey of Armenian Trade Through the Ages*, edited and revised by P. M. Manuelian (New York, 1979). For general background see Fernand Braudel, *The Mediterranean and the Mediterranean World in the Age of Philip II*, 2 volumes (New York, 1972-73). See also H. A. Manandian, *The Trade and Cities of Armenia in Relation to Ancient World Trade*, translated by Nina G. Garsoian (Lisbon, 1965), and Jean-Baptist Tavernier, *The Six Voyages of Jean-Baptiste Tavernier*, translated by John Phillips (London, 1677).

[30] For more on this fascinating topic, see Rouben Zarian, *Shakespeare et les armeniens*, translated by N. Haroutiunian, with an introduction by Vahe Godel (Geneva, 1973).

[31] Vahe Godel (b. 1931), the French translator of Varoujan's *Song of the Bread*, is also the author of a number of studies on Armenian literature and a poem titled *Armenie* (Paris, 1967), commemorating the 50th anniversary of the Genocide. He is the son of Robert Godel, a distinguished Swiss linguist and Armenologist. Born in Geneva and educated in Istanbul, where he studied Armenian, Robert Godel (b. 1902) has taught Classical Armenian *(Krapar)* at Harvard (1964) and at universities in Geneva (1951-68) and Los Angeles (1968). He is the author of among others, *An Introduction to the Study of Classical Armenian* (Wiesbaden, 1975), the seminal *Les Sources manuscrites du cours de linguistique general de F. de Saussure* (Paris, 1957), and editor of *Cahiers Ferdinand de Saussure*.

[32] For more on Varoujan, see Shoghere Markarian, "Veronica Varoujan Remembers." *Ararat* (Winter 1978).

[33] Daniel Varoujan, Siamanto, Rouben Zartarian, and Krikor Zohrab are discussed in *Ararat* (Autumn 1976), a special issue devoted exclusively to the writers murdered by the Turks in 1915. The issue also contains translations from the works of these four writers. Short stories by Zartarian, Yeroukhan, Zohrab, and Sevag are also included in *Classical Armenian Short Stories*, translated by Sarkis Ashjian (Beirut, 1959).

[34] It is to be noted that in 1936 Armenia became a "sovereign" Soviet Republic, "voluntarily" united with—and constitutionally guaranteed the right to secede from—the Soviet Union. And yet, an entire generation of Armenian political leaders and intellectuals was purged for *allegedly* desiring to secede from Russia. This period of Armenian history is competently discussed by Manuel Sarkisyanz, *A Modern History of Transcaucasian Armenia* (Leiden, 1975). See also Roy Medvedev, *Let History Judge: The Origins and Consequences of Stalinism* (New York, 1971).

[35] In addition to *Scenes from an Armenian Childhood* (London, 1962), English title for *Life on the Old Roman Road*, Mischa Kudian has translated a collection of short stories by Totovents, titled *Tell Me, Bella* (London, 1980, originally issued in 1972).

[36] *Ararat* (Winter 1979) is our main English-language source for the seven writers discussed in this chapter. In addition to biographical and autobiographical sketches, critical evaluations, reminiscences by contemporaries, and translations, this special issue of 120 pages contains a brief bibliography, some background material, and many illustrations.

[37] An English translation of *Abou Lala Mahari* is included in *Avedik Issahakian, Selected Works: Poetry and Prose*, translated by Mischa Kudian (Moscow, 1976) which also contains a lengthy introduction by the Russian poet and critic Nikolai Tikhonov. See also *Avedik Issahakian: Scent, Smile and Sorrow—Selected Verse (1891-1957) and Jottings from Notebooks*, translated with an introduction by E. B. Chrakian (Watertown, 1975).

[38] As quoted by Aram Injikian, *Avedik Issahakian* (Yerevan, 1977), English translation *Ararat* (Spring 1978). Issahakian is also discussed in Ilya Ehrenburg's *Memoirs* (see my *Armenia Observed*).

[39] For more on Demirjian, see Leo Hamalian, "Spokesmen of the Spirit," in *Burn Af-*

ter Reading (New York, 1978). See also Derenig (or Terenig) Demirjian, *Vartananc*, French translation by Dikran Kirazian (Paris, 1964).

⁴⁰Gostan Zarian is one of the major characters in Lawrence Durrell's *Prospero's Cell* (London, 1945), and to a lesser extent in *Spirit of Place; Letters and Essays on Travel* (London, 1969). See also *Ararat* (Autumn 1973 and Summer 1974) for two excellent essays on Zarian by Dr. Hampar Kelikian and Lemyel Amirian.

⁴¹See Kohar Tololyan, "Vahan Tekeyan: The Poet and the Poetry" in *Ararat* (Autumn 1977). See also Vahan Tekeyan, "Two Letters to Daniel Varoujan," in *Ararat* (Winter 1978).

⁴²See Levon Shant, *The Princess of the Fallen Castle*, English translation by Hagop Baytarian (Boston, 1929).

⁴³*Ararat* is preparing a supplement devoted to Oshagan's life and work, edited by his son Vahe Oshagan, himself a noted poet, critic, and teacher of Armenology at the University of Pennsylvania.

⁴⁴See John A. C. Greppin, "Armenia's Greatest Linguist," *Ararat* (Spring 1979).

⁴⁵See Nicholas Adonts, *Armenia in the Period of Justinian*, English translation by Nina G. Garsoian (Lisbon, 1970); also Moushegh Ishkhan, *Professor Nicholas Adonts: Remembrances and Impressions*, translated by Rouben Adalian, serialized in *The Armenian Observer* (Los Angeles, January/February, 1977).

⁴⁶See Nikol Aghbalian, *Movses Khorenatsi*, English translation by Armine M. Sarian, in *The Armenian Review* (June 1979). Aghbalian is discussed by Puzant Granian, *My Land, My People* (Los Angeles, 1978).

⁴⁷Shahnour is further discussed by Hampar Kelikian, "Shahnour: Novelist of Exile," *Ararat* (Summer 1977); Arthur Adamov, "L'Oeuvre d'Armen Lubin," *Andastan: Arts et Lettres* (Paris, No. 18). See also *French Poetry Today: A Bilingual Anthology*, edited by Simon W. Taylor and Edward Luci-Smith (New York, 1972), which contains a number of Shahnour-Lubin's poems in French.

⁴⁸These and other writers of the French diaspora are discussed by H. Kurkjian, *Essai sur l'exil* (Paris, 1978).

⁴⁹For a review of and translations from *Mosaic of My Soul with the Colors of the Map*, see *Ararat* (Winter 1978).

⁵⁰For more on Baruir Sevag, see *Fifty Soviet Poets*, compiled by Vladimir Ognev and Dorian Rottenberg (Moscow, 1969), which also contains translations from Sylva Gaboudikian.

⁵¹See Vakhtang Ananian, *Steep Paths: Hunting Stories* (Moscow: Progress Publishers).

⁵²Grant Matevossian, *The Orange Herd*, English translation by Fainna Glagoleva and Igor Kravtsov (Moscow, 1976).

⁵³Recent trends in Soviet-Armenian literature are examined in *Discordant Voices: The Non-Russian Literatures, 1953-1973*, edited by George S. N. Luckyj (Toronto, 1975). For translations, see *New Writing from the Middle East*, edited with an In-

troduction and Commentary by Leo Hamalian and John D. Yohannan (New York, 1978); *Anthology of Armenian Poetry*, translated and edited by Diana Der Hovanessian and Marzbed Margossian (New York, 1978); *Soviet Armenian Poetry*, translated and edited by Mischa Kudian (London, 1973); *Soviet Literature Monthly* (Moscow, March 1966).

[54] For short sketches of recent trends in the United States, Lebanon, and Iran, see Sooren Manuelian, "There May Yet Be Hope," in *Ararat* (Winter 1977); Vahe Oshagan, "Armenian Literature in Lebanon," in *Ararat* (Summer 1978), and "The Literature of the Persian Armenians," *Ararat* (Summer 1979).

[55] See Bedros Norehad, "The Armenian-American Press," in *Ararat* (Winter 1977).

[56] English translations of Peniamin Noorigian's stories are included in *Tales from the Armenian*, translated by Jack Antreassian (New York, 1955), which also contains translations of stories by Antranig Antreassian, Vahe Haig, and Sooren Manuelian.

[57] Puzant Granian's *Armenia and the Armenian* is available in English as *My Land, My People* (Los Angeles, 1978), translated by Ara Baliozian in collaboration with the author.

[58] For a better understanding of the role of Armenian fedayees or freedom fighters in the struggle against the Ottoman Turks ranging from the first major uprising in 1862 to the massacres of 1896, see Louise Nalbandian, *The Armenian Revolutionary Movement: The Development of Armenian Political Parties Through the 19th Century* (Los Angeles, 1963). Gabriel Bagradian, the protagonist of Franz Werfel's *Forty Days of Musa Dagh*, is based on a real life fedayee. So is Saroyan's short story "Antranik of Armenia," in *Inhale and Exhale* (1936). Rouben Der-Minassian, another fedayee, became an eminent man of letters producing several scholarly works and a monumental 7-volume memoir titled *Reminiscences of an Armenian Revolutionary* (Los Angeles, 1962), which has been abridged and translated into English by James Mandalian as *Armenian Freedom Fighters* (Boston, 1963).

[59] Aram Haigaz, *The Fall of the Aerie*, translated into English by H. Baghdoian (Boston, 1936).

[60] A volume of Antranig Antreassian's fiction is available in English. *The Cup of Bitterness and Other Stories*, translated by Jack Antreassian (New York, 1980).

[61] For English translations, see *Discordant Voices: The Non-Russian Soviet Literatures, 1953-1973*, edited by George S. N. Luckyj (Toronto, 1975), which contains a contribution on Soviet-Armenian literature by Mkrtitchian; and "Axel Bakounts As Champion of the True Concept of the Popular Basis of Literature in Soviet Armenia," in *The Caucasian Review* (Munich, VII, 1958, 66-91). Both translations are anonymous.

[62] For English translations of Zaroukian's verse, see *New Writing from the Middle East*, edited by Leo Hamalian and John D. Yohannan. See also *Ararat* (Spring 1979).

[63] Some of these writers are now residents of the United States.

[64] See *Zahrad: Selected Poems*, English translation by Ralph Setian (Ottawa, 1974).

[65]Translations of some of these writers are included in *Anthology of Armenian Poetry*, translated and edited by Diana Der Hovanessian and Marzbed Margossian (New York, 1978). *Further Reading:* Most of the writers mentioned in this chapter are discussed by H. Thorossian, *Histoire de la litterature armenienne* (Paris, 1951); K. A. Sarafian, *History of Education in Armenia* (La Verne, 1930); James Etmekjian, *French Influence on the Western Armenian Renaissance* (New York, 1964); *Dictionary of Oriental Literatures, volume 2: West Asia and North Africa*, edited by Jaroslav Prusek and Jiri Becka (New York, 1974); *Great Soviet Encyclopedia*, editor in chief A. M. Prokhorov (New York, 1973).

[66]The standard work on Saroyan is Howard Floan, *William Saroyan* (New York, 1966); see also David Kherdian, *A Bibliography of William Saroyan* (1965), and *An Evening with Saroyan* (1970). Saroyan is also discussed in some detail by Nona Balakian, *Critical Encounters* (New York, 1978); *The Armenian-American Writer* (New York, 1958); and "Writers on the American Scene," *Ararat* (Winter 1977); and by Alfred Kazin in *Starting out in the Thirties* (New York, 1965).

[67]Marjorie Housepian, Leon Surmelian, and a number of other Armenian-American novelists—among them, Richard Hagopian, Peter Sourian, Peter Najarian, Emanuel Varandyan, the half-Greek A. E. Bezzerides, Harry Barba, Fred Ayvazian (also known as Fred Levon and Kenneth Flagg), Vartanig Vartan, and Charles Tekeyan; also playwrights Ralph Arzoomanian, Nishan Parlakian, and Charles Gregory—are discussed by Nona Balakian, "Writers on the American Scene," *Ararat* (Winter 1977). The list of Armenian-American novelists has now been augmented by Aram Saroyan (son of William), Laura (*Beggars and Choosers*) Kalpakian, Lucik (*Forbidden Days of Ramazan*) Melikian, John (*Extreme Remedies*) Hejinian, and a number of others.

[68]These and many other Armenian-American scholars are discussed in *Ararat* (Winter 1977). See also *Armenian-North American Poets*, edited by Lorne Shirinian (Quebec, 1976); *Armenian-American Poets: A Bilingual Anthology*, edited, and translated by Garig Basmadjian (Detroit, 1976).

[69]For more on Adamov, see John H. Reilly, *Arthur Adamov* (New York, 1974); John J. McCann, *The Theater of Arthur Adamov* (North Carolina, 1975); Rene Gaudy, *Arthur Adamov: Essais et documents* (Paris, 1971); Martin Esslin, *The Theater of the Absurd* (New York, 1961); G. E. Wellwarth, *The Theater of Protest and Paradox* (New York, 1967); Pierre Melese, *Arthur Adamov* (Paris, 1973).

[70]For a complete list of Gabriel Arout's works, see *Who's Who in France, 1977-1978* (Paris, 1977).

[71]For a complete list of Dedeyan's books see *The International Who's Who 1978-79* (London, 1978).

[72]See *Enciclopedia Italiana* (Milan, 1929).

[73]See John A. Haywood, "Rizqallah Hassun: A Pioneer of the Arabic Literary Revival," in *Ararat* (Autumn 1979).

[74]See W. E. D. Allen, *The Ukraine: A History* (London, 1940); Francis Dvornik *The Slavs in European History and Civilization* (New Jersey, 1962); *The Cambridge His-*

tory of Poland: From the Origins to Sobieski, edited by W. F. Reddaway, et alii (London, 1950). There are many books documenting Armenian presence in these countries, most of which however have not yet been translated into English. In this connection, see Gromniki, *The Armenians in Poland: Their History, Rights and Privileges* (in Polish: Warsaw, 1889); Cz. Lechicki, *The Armenian Church in Poland: Its Historical Survey* (also in Polish: Lvov, 1928). See also Dr. E. Sluzkiewics's epilogue to the Polish-language edition of David M. Lang's *Armenia: Cradle of Civilization* (Warsaw, 1976). A distinguished orientalist, Sluzkiewics asserts here that the great 19th-century poet and playwright Juliusz Slowacki (1809-1849), one of the dominant figures in the Romantic movement of Polish literature, whose plays are still staged frequently in Poland, was of wholly or partly Armenian descent. It is to be noted that Armenians and the Middle East play a central role in Slowacki's works, many of which are available in English: See *Anhelli*, translated by Dorothea Radin (Westport, 1979); *Mary Stuart: A Romantic Drama*, translated by Arthur and Marion Coleman (Westport, 1978); see also *Five Centuries of Polish Poetry*, translated by Jerzy Peterkiewics and Burns Singer (Philadelphia, 1962).

[76] See *Poems of Mihai Eminescu*, translated by Sylvia Pankhurst and I. O. Stefanovici (New York, 1930); E. D. Tappe, *Rumanian Prose and Verse* (New Jersey, 1956). For an excellent biographical sketch of Eminescu, see *The McGraw-Hill Encyclopedia of World Biography*, edited by David I. Eggenberger (New York, 1973). Both Eminescu and Ibraileanu are cited in "Rumanian Literature," *Encyclopedia Americana*, vol. 23 (New York, 1976); see also Martin Seymour-Smith, *Guide to Modern World Literature* (London, 1975).

Music

Armenia is a country whose inhabitants are musically gifted to an unusual degree. Music thus holds an important place both in the past and present history of the nation. Her folksongs, words and music alike, are of such power and beauty that they enthral even the European listener.

Grove's Dictionary of Music and Musicians

We shall never be able to understand fully the development of Eastern church music until we know more about Armenian music and its role in the development of Eastern chant.

Egon Wellesz

It is often forgotten that Western liturgical music—the Ambrosian, Mozarabic, Gallican, and Gregorian chants (to which musicians from Frescobaldi to J. S. Bach and Berlioz returned time and time again for refreshment and inspiration)—has melodic formulas and cadences that show a distinct kinship with Byzantine melody; and that the source of both Byzantine and Western music is generally considered to be in the Near and Middle East.

The Armenian hymnary contains 1,200 songs. "In the setting of these hymns," says *Grove's Dictionary*, "Armenia possesses a school of church music which ranks among the most beautiful of all the known oriental styles: the music of the utmost expressiveness, and in wealth of invention the only school which can compare with it is the Byzantine, which in many ways it excels."

Not bound by barlines and the rules governing polyphonic music, Armenian melodies move with unlimited freedom. Their intervals and ornamentations are far more complex and varied than those of Gregorian chant, with which however, they share a moving spontaneity and authenticity of feeling.[1]

Like medieval Armenian art and architecture, these melodies were completely ignored by scholars for a long time. It was musicologist (also singer, conductor, and composer) Komitas Kevorkian (Gomidas Vartabed: 1869-1935), who through his lecture tours in Europe created a widespread interest and thus gave a new impulse to research work on Armenian liturgical music and folksongs—some of which, it is to be noted, had already been transcribed by, among others, Mussorgsky, Balakirev, and Ippolitov-Ivanov. Komitas' pioneer work can be compared to that of Bartok and Kodaly in Hungary. He collected, wrote down, harmonized, and interpreted many folksongs. Claude Debussy and Romain Rolland were two of his most devoted admirers.

Komitas' efforts however were tragically interrupted in 1919, when as a result of the Turkish atrocities (he was himself arrested, interrogated, tortured, and deported) he became mentally afflicted and died a few years later.[2]

The task of making Armenian modes and folk melodies known throughout the world fell to other composers, two of whom—Aram Khachaturian in Russia, and Alan Hovhaness (Haroutiun Chakmakjian) in the United States—are generally regarded as 20th-century musical giants.

The son of a bookbinder who showed no musical ambition or talent until he was nineteen, Khachaturian (1903-1978) was born in Tiflis and educated in Moscow, where he also lived and worked as teacher and conductor until his death. His frequently performed *Piano Concerto* (1936), *Violin Concerto* (1940), and *Cello Concerto* (1950); also ballet suites *Masquerade* (1939), *Gayane* (1942), and *Spartacus* (1956), are gems of craftsmanship and melodic exuberance. Connoisseurs can appreciate some of their intricate rhythms and harmonies, but the less knowledgable are pleased too without needing to know why. In his music we hear once again the brilliant improvisations of the *ashughs* (see LITERATURE), and the piercing beauty of Armenian folk melodies. Khachaturian's music is cheerful and sensuous. It speaks of the joy and happiness of life. Its optimistic, holiday spirit is only occasionally interrupted by melancholy interludes lacerating in their tender simplicity. Writes James Bakst: ". . . the folk character of his music often leaves a listener feeling the universality, rather than the specific national aspect of his art."[3]

This observation could apply to another Soviet-Armenian composer whose works are still widely performed today in the Soviet Union and occasionally in the West—Alexander Spendiarian (1871-1928). Born in the Crimea, Spendiarian (also Spendiarov) studied with Rimsky-Korsakov in St. Petersburg. Some of his better-known orchestral compositions are: *Concert Overture* (1901), *Three Palm Trees* (1905), *Crimean Sketches* (revised a number of times), *Yerevan Sketches* (1925), *Garib Bulbul* (1925, and the posthumously produced and enormously popular opera *Almast* (1930), based on a narrative poem by Hovannes Toumanian. He also revised and elaborated the songs of Sayat-Nova.

Like Khachaturian, Spendiarian made use of both Crimean Tartar and Armenian folk melodies.

Alan Hovhaness (b. 1911) has made use of Oriental melodies with particular emphasis on Armenian liturgical music. Hovhaness's temperament and use of these ancient melodies, however, are totally different from Khachaturian's. Khachaturian is an extrovert, Hovhaness an introvert, a mystic, but no less universal. "His is a tranquil, contemplative music that often takes on the character of mystic incantation," writes Joseph Machlis. And Virgil Thompson:

He writes in the early Christian, the medieval, and the modern Armenian technique, possibly even a little in the pre-Christian manner of that ancient and cultivated people. . . . The expressive function of his music is predominantly religious, ceremonial, incantatory. . . . The high quality of this music, the purity of its inspiration, is evidenced in the extreme beauty of the melodic material. . . . It brings delight to the ear, and pleasure to the thought. Among all our American contributions to musical art, it is one of the most curious and original.

Hovhaness shares with Khachaturian another important quality: accessibility. Speaking of "The Mysterious Mountain," Hovhaness's best-known tone poem, whose source of inspiration is Mt. Ararat, and which was first performed by Leopold Stokowski in 1955, Miles Kastendrick writes:

Its beauty, its serenity of spirit, its "sweet consonance" brought accolades of praise as further performances took place. The superb double fugue of the second movement evoked the greatest admiration for contrapuntal craftsmanship. Enjoyment of the work as a whole even inspired an editorial in the Cleveland News, which said in part: "Surprise, surprise. Here was a modern piece full of melody and pleasant to the ear. No dissonance, no noise, no discord—just beautiful, sweeping harmony."

Born in Somerville, Massachusetts, Hovhaness taught himself to improvise at the piano before he ever had any lessons on the instrument. By the age of thirteen, he had composed two operas as well as many shorter pieces. Mozart, Handel, Bartok, and Sibelius were his principal early influences. In 1940, shortly after he became organist of the Armenian Church of St. James in Watertown, Hovhaness destroyed almost all the Western-type music he had until then composed—symphonies, operas, quartets, piano works. . . more than a thousand pieces—and devoted himself to the study of Armenian liturgical music and the works of Komitas. The titles of many of his works reveal their Armenian sources of inspiration—the "Saint Vartan," "Etchmiadzin," and "Ani" Symphonies, "Lousadzak" Piano Concerto, "Arevakal" Suite for orchestra, "Nerses Shnorhali" Fugue for strings, for example.

An extremely prolific composer, Hovhaness completed work on four symphonies, toward the end of 1976 alone. His total catalogue exceeds 300 opus numbers, which doesn't include the works destroyed in 1940. "I write every day," Hovhaness has said: "I have more ideas than I can use." Writes Oliver Daniel: "When he does not have a blank music notebook with him, a menu, the reverse side of a bill, or any piece of paper with adequate white space becomes something on which to write his music." Daniel goes on to describe Hovhaness as "a blend of saintly El Greco mysticism, Oriental resignation and Western dynamics."[4]

Other important musicians who played a prominent role in the development of Armenian music:

Hampartsoum Limondjian (1768-1839), a composer of church music, educator, and musicologist who developed a new system for transcribing orally transmitted traditional melodies;

Tigran Chukadjian (1836-1898), composer of the first Armenian opera *Arshak II* written in the 1860s in Istanbul:

Christopher Kara-Murza of the Crimea (1854-1902), transcriber and popularizer of many folk songs;

Organist, conductor, educator, and composer Nathan Amirkhanian (1872-1949) who was active in Turkey, Iran, Georgia, Finland, Germany, Bulgaria, Russia, and the United States and whose works include operas (*Ivanko, Ralitsa*), 200 songs, the oratorio *Christos* (1936) and the operetta *Bouff* (1940);

Armen Tigranian (1879-1950), whose lyrical folk-opera *Anoush*, based on a narrative poem by Hovhannes Toumanian (*see* LITERATURE) and first performed in 1912, is one of the most popular and frequently staged works in the Armenian musical repertoire;

Makar Ekmalian (also Yegmalian: 1856-1905), whose works include in addition to many arrangements of Armenian folk songs and liturgical melodies, cantatas, symphonic overtures, choruses, songs, and piano pieces.

Sarkis Barkhudarian (b. 1887), influential teacher at the conservatories of Tiflis and Yerevan, and composer of ballets, symphonic works, romances, piano pieces, incidental music for plays and films, and many arrangements of folk songs. One of his students, the Armeno-Georgian Vano Muradeli (1908-1970) acquired international reputation shortly after the premiere of his opera *The Great Friendship* (1947), which initiated the crackdown by Soviet officials on liberal trends in the arts. Muradeli, together with Khachaturian, Shostakovich, Prokofiev, and a number of others, were attacked for their "formalism" and unmelodic music. After Stalin's death however, Muradeli was rehabilitated and served as head of the Moscow Composers' Union. His other works comprise three symphonies, cantatas, songs, film and theater music, symphonic dances, and the chamber opera *October* (1964).

Among composers active in Soviet Armenia today, let us mention Alexander Haroutiunian (also Aroutiunian: b. 1920). In the 1940s, Haroutiunian became acquainted with Kabalevsky, Shostakovich, and Khachaturian, all of whom had a decisive influence on his future development. He has composed piano and trumpet concertos, orchestral overtures, symphonies, symphonic poems, cantatas *(About the Motherland)*, operas *(Sayat-Nova)*, and piano pieces, all of which are marked by melodic richness and the creative use of folk intonational material.

Composer-pianist Arno Babajanian (b. 1921) whose romantic *Heroic Ballad* for Piano and Orchestra (1950) earned him the prestigious State Prize of the USSR in 1951, has also composed a *Sonata* for Violin and Piano (1959), a *Cello Concerto* (1962), *Six Pictures* for Piano (1965), and many film scores and popular songs. [5]

Unlike their Soviet counterparts, Armenian composers of the diaspora have been free to experiment with atonal or avant-garde music, though most of them have preferred the tonal mode. Richard Yardumian, Rouben Gregorian, Grant Beglarian, Avedis Nazarian, Vazken Muradian, Hampartzoum Berberian, Loris Tjeknavorian, Sahan Arzruni, to mention only a handful that come readily to mind, are predominantly tonal composers.

"I think of myself as one of many baroque style composers," Yardumian (b. 1917) has said, "who worked anonymously to enrich a field of common practice by slight degrees. Their practice was based on what the public liked and understood."

Often based on old traditional church melodies, Yardumian's accessible and tuneful compostions (orchestral suites, choral preludes, symphonies, concertos, and oratorios) enjoy steady performances on the international scene. As an organist and choirmaster (he is the son of a Protestant minister), Yardumian has also harmonized some fifty hymns.

A resident of the United States since 1950, Vazken Muradian (b. 1921) was born in Ashtarak (Armenia) and educated in Yerevan and Venice (Italy). His many compositions include sonatas, songs, symphonies, piano pieces, and concertos for such exotic instruments as the *oud* (an Arabic variant of the lute) and the viola d'amore.

Grant Beglarian (b. 1927) is a noted Armenian-American educator, conductor, and composer who in addition to a large quantity of orchestral, chamber, and band music, has authored many important essays on musical education. [6]

Requiem for the Massacred (1974) is one of Loris Tjeknavorian's (b. 1937) better-known compositions. A strikingly original piece scored for trumpet and 27 percussion instruments such as bells, cymbals, and drums, it utilizes several chants and hymns from the Armenian liturgy and it has been described as "a work of great emotional impact. . . . that attempts to depict the chaotic feeling and horror of the massacre in all its inhuman stages, including fear, tortures, humiliations, degradations, deprivations, and the tribulations of the survivors." [7]

Among composers of avant-garde and experimental music, mention should be made of Cathy Berberian and Alicia Terzian.

Originally from the United States and now living in Milan, Cathy Berberian is an internationally respected singer and composer whose works include recordings of songs by Stravinsky, Monteverdi, and Luciano Berio (with whom she was married for a time), and such curiously titled original compositions as *Stripsody* (1966), *Magnificathy* (1971), and *Readjoice* (1971). She has appeared on all the major stages of Europe and the United States including La Scala (Milan) and Covent Garden (London).[8]

Alicia Terzian (b. 1936) of Argentina has produced works for orchestra, chorus, ballet, brass band, piano, chamber music, songs, and electroacustic music often accompanied by visual effects.

In the related fields of musical education and criticism there are a number of internationally respected names. Among these let us mention cellist Diran Alexanian, violinist Ivan Galamian, and critic Felix Aprahamian.

Born in Istanbul, Diran Alexanian (1881-1954) was educated in Germany. He taught the cello in Paris and New York; conducted orchestras; composed (songs, *Armenian Suite* for cello, and others); transcribed melodies by Komitas; edited J. S. Bach's *Suites* for cello; and authored two important texts, *L'Enseignement du violoncelle* (Paris, 1914), and *Traite theoretique et pratique du violoncelle* (Paris, 1922). [9]

Ivan Galamian (b. 1903), was born in Tabriz (Iran), and graduated from the Philharmonic School in Moscow. He began to teach the violin when he was fourteen and he has taught in some of the most prestigious conservatories in Moscow, Paris, New York, and Philadelphia. The author of the widely used text *Principles of Violin Playing and Teaching* (New York, 1962), Galamian has been called "the most effective violin teacher in the country" (Isaac Stern); "at quick consensus the world's greatest violin teacher" (Faubion Bowers); and "one of the great teachers of our time" (Joseph Wechsberg). According to *Time* Magazine, "most of the brightest young soloists in the United States are Galamian products." Efrem Zimbalist, himself one of the greatest violinists of recent times, has said of Galamian: "He can make a violinist out of a table."[10]

Music critic for the London *Times*, Felix Aprahamian has also published childhood reminiscences (*When I Was Young: Memories of London Childhood*, edited by Valerie Jenkins), translations from the French (*Conversations with Olivier Messiaen* by Claude Samuel), and memoirs of contemporaries (*Beecham Remembered*, edited by H. P. Gregg).

In the field of popular music, Cher (Sarkissian) and Ross Bagdassarian have achieved prominence in the United States; and Georges Garvarents, Charles Aznavour, and the half-Armenian Michel Legrand in France.

Garvarents (b. 1932) began his musical career as a composer of songs for Aznavour and Sylvie Vartan (another enormously popular singer and entertainer of Armenian origin), and went on to become a prolific composer of film music with over 60 scores to his credit.

In addition to being a very popular crooner and actor (*see* CINEMA) Charles Aznavour (b. 1924) is a versatile and prolific composer of songs, musical comedies, and film scores. [11]

[1] See Egon Wellesz, "Music of the Eastern Churches," in *Early Medieval Music up to 1300*, edited by Dom Anselm Hughes (London, 1954); *Essays on Armenian Music*, edited by Vrej Nersessian (London, 1978); Amy Abgar, *Melodies of the Holy Apostolic Church of Armenia* (Calcutta, 1897); Pierre Aubry, *Le Systeme musical de l'Eglise armenienne* (Paris, 1903); Pietro Bianchini, *Les Chants liturgiques de l'Eglise armenienne traduits en note musicale europeenne* (Venice, 1977); Makar Ekmalian, *Chants of the Divine Liturgy of the Armenian Church* (Detroit, no date); Nerses Ter-Mikaelian, *Das Armenische Hymnarium* (Leipzig, 1905); Egon Wellesz, *Die Armenische Messe und ihre Musik* (1920).

[2] See Komitas, *Musique populaire armenienne* (Paris, 1925); *Gomidas Vartabed* (New York, 1969), issued on the 100th anniversary of the birth of the musicologist, this volume contains biographical and incidental pieces by various hands.

[3] See Ivan Martinov, *Aram Khachaturian* (Moscow, 1947); Gustav Schneerson, *Aram Khachaturian* (Moscow, 1958); Stanley Dale Krebs, *Soviet Composers and the Development of Soviet Music* (New York, 1970); James Bakst, *A History of Russian-Soviet Music* (New York, 1962); Boris Schwarz, *Music and Musical Life in Soviet Russia: 1917-1970* (New York, 1972). Other Soviet-Armenian composers discussed in this last work: Arno Babajanian, Alexander Haroutiunian (also Aroutiunian), Karen Khachaturian, Edward Mirzoyan, Sergei Balasanian, and Edgar Hovanesian (also Oganessian). See also *Testimony: The Memoirs of Dmitri Shostakovich*, as related and edited by Solomon Volkov, translated from the Russian by Antonina W. Bouis (New York, 1979).

[4] For more on Hovhaness, see Joseph Machlis, *Introduction to Contemporary Music* (New York, 1961); David Ewen, *Composers Since 1900* (New York, 1969); Nicolas Slonimsky, *Music Since 1900* (New York, 1971); *Ararat* (Autumn 1960, Winter 1971, Autumn 1977); *Saturday Review* (Feb. 22, 1959); *Time* (March 29, 1958).

[5] These and many other Soviet-Armenian composers are discussed in *Who's Who in the Socialist Countries*, edited by Borys Lewytzkyj and Juliusz Stroynowski (Munich, 1978); and *Great Soviet Encyclopedia*, editor in chief, A. M. Prokhorov (New York, 1973).

[6] These and other Armenian-American composers and interpreters (Maro and Anahid Ajemian, Ani and Ida Kavafian, Lili Chookasian, Sahan Arzruni, Berj Zamkochian, Varoujan Kodjian, and many others) are discussed by Armine Dikijian, "The Music and the Musicians," in *Ararat* (Winter 1977).

[7] For more on Tjeknavorian, see John Sarian, "Master Musician," in *Ararat* (Summer 1978).

[8] There are a number of other Berberians active on the American and international

musical scene: composers Onnig and Shahan Berberian, cellist Vahe Berberian, and operatic basso Ara Berberian.

[9]Diran Alexanian is discussed and quoted at some length in J. M. Corredor, *Conversations with Casals*, translated by Andre Mangeot (London, 1956). See also Elizabeth Cowling, *The Cello* (London, 1975); H. L. Kirk, *Pablo Casals* (New York, 1974).

[10]See Joseph Wechsberg, *The Glory of the Violin* (New York, 1972); Samuel and Sada Applebaum, *The Way They Play it, Book 1* (New Jersey, 1972); *The Atlantic Monthly* (Feb., 1972); *Time* (Dec. 6, 1968).

[11]Garvarents, Aznavour, Sylvie Vartan, and Michel Legrand are discussed in the *Larousse dictionnaire de la chanson francaise* (Paris, 1968). The recordings of these and many other contemporary Armenian musicians are listed and discussed by John M. Sarian, *Record Guide* (New York, 1979). Most of the composers, interpreters, and educators mentioned in this chapter are discussed in *Grove's Dictionary of Music and Musicians*, edited by Eric Blom (London, 1954); *The International Cyclopedia of Music and Musicians*, edited by Oscar Thompson and Bruce Bohle (New York, 1975); *International Who's Who in Music*, edited by Ernest Kay (Cambridge, 1975); *Dictionary of Contemporary Music,* edited by John Vinton (New York, 1974).

Art & Architecture

Mother's Armenian eyes they call Picasso's, Armenian melancholy they term Byzantine and Russian. . . . We are a people who have never understood commercial publicity. The great art of our people lies hidden in ruins and amid the daily life of remote villages.

Arshile Gorky Adoian

Greek genius at Haghia Sophia and Italian genius at St. Peter's only realized more fully what the Armenians had originated.

Josef Strzygowski

The history of fine arts in Armenia (metal, wood and stone carving, ceramics, painting, sculpture), have a millenial tradition that antedates the history of Urartu. Scholars now agree that Urartian architecture itself owes little or nothing to outside influences and it very probably influenced the architecture of neighboring kingdoms including that of the earliest Achaemenid kings. "In the craft of building in stone," writes Toynbee, "the Urartian masons surpassed their Assyrian masters and attained almost an Egyptian standard—not in massiveness, but in precision." The Urartian fort of Teishebaini (Fortress of the god of war Teishebas), on the hill of Garmir Plur (Red Hill) near Yerevan, is an outstanding example of Urartian architecture. Founded in the 7th century B.C., this fortress and government center, with towers and buttressed perimeter wall, massive gateway, parade ground within the wall and ground floor entirely occupied by storerooms, was destroyed by Scythian hordes in the 6th century B.C. Recent excavations have brought to light the citadel with a two-storied building consisting of about 150 rooms (some with wall paintings), and a town with a very regular layout.

Urartian cups, engraved bronze shields, cauldrons decorated with heads of griffins, sirens, and bulls, and supported on tripods, and numerous other artifacts, were widely exported and imitated as far away as Greece.[1]

Of Armenian art from the 5th century B.C. to the introduction of Christianity in the 3rd century A.D., very little remains. Tigranocerta (Dikranagerd), the celebrated capital of Tigran II the Great, with its magnificent palaces, temples, and fortified wall, has been destroyed so thoroughly that archaeologists cannot even agree on its site.

After a period of decline, Armenian architecture reached its Golden Age in the Middle Ages, more precisely from the 6th to the 13th century.

The design and construction technique of Armenian fortifications of this period have excited the interest of many architectural historians, and Armenian influences have been traced as far as the British Isles. Many developments in Western systems of fortification resulted from experience gained on the Crusades and especially through the opportunities for examining Armenian defenses and interrogating local craftsmen.[2]

Khachkars, often erroneously referred to as "grave-stones" or "tombstones," represent a uniquely Armenian medieval art form.

Some *Khachkars* (Literally "cross-stones") were in fact used as grave-stones, but many others were built to commemorate important historical dates in the life of the nation (a military victory for example), or the community (the completion of a church, a fountain, a bridge). They are thus of artistic as well as historical interest.

Constructed on regular flagstones or carved on rocks, inside churches, or on their walls, near entrances, in cemeteries, or plinths on the ground, or directly on rocks, *khachkars* come in many sizes, shapes, and styles. In their final form they are stone slabs sometimes reaching large dimensions, having twice their width in height or more. One facade is completely covered with delicate networks of botanical or geometrical patterns with a cross in the center, the other may be either smooth or covered with inscriptions bearing the name of the commissioner, the stonemason, and sometimes the occasion for which they were erected. [3]

In Armenia and the neighboring republic of Azerbaijan, *khachkars* are a common sight. *Khachkars* may also be seen in Ireland, where they are called "high crosses." In their efforts to explain the origins and development of high crosses and the stylistic affinities of certain Irish churches and abbeys with those of Armenia, archaeologists and architectural historians have advanced different theories. The French archaeologist Francois Choisy believes that Armenian architectural techniques travelled along the Dniester (Russia) and the Vistula (Poland) to Scandinavia and from there to Scotland and Ireland. Others have divided the exportation of architectural and artistic forms from Armenia to western Europe and Ireland into two phases: the first at the end of the 8th century when Charlemagne attracted to Aix, clerics, artists, scholars, and artisans from many countries including those of Asia Minor; the second in the 11th century when, following the Muslim conquest of Ani in 1064, refugee monks with their own masons fled to the West reaching Ireland, where they built on models of their homeland. [4]

As we have seen, it was under the Armenians that Byzantium reached its summit of political power and artistic splendor (*see* HISTORY). Practically nothing survives of the countless churches and palaces which were the ornament of Constantinople in this era.

A ray of that splendor, however, can still be seen today in Venice. The 11th-century basilica of Saint Mark with its five domes, the polychromatic marbles inside and outside, the finely carved screens and tall nave-pillars, reredos of enamel and rich mosaics, the gold and purple, is Byzantine in conception and execution; and a visible reminder of the fact that Venice was subject to Byzantium before she became independent.

But the subject of Byzantine influence on Europe—its art and architecture, as well as law, literature, drama, and music—is too complex and vast to be compressed into a few paragraphs. The view expressed in 1923 by the eminent Byzantinist J. B. Bury (1861-1927) that Constantinople "was no more than a dream-name of wealth and splendor to Englishmen, except to the few adventurers who travelled thither to make their fortune..." has begun to crumble away. It is now generally admitted that Byzantium played a highly important role not only in Russia and the Balkans, but also in England, which was then the remotest state of the West. For more than a thousand years Byzantium not only defended Christianity and Western Civilization against attacks of innumerable barbarians, but it also preserved and enriched the heritage of the ancient world. Writes Paul Lemerle:

> From a pagan civilization in the grip of decadence and incapable of self-renewal, Byzantium created a Christian one, more humane and responsive to the dictates of a critical conscience.... The Slavs owe the whole of their religion and institutions to it. Western countries, through merchants, monks, pilgrims and Crusaders, never ceased to be under the magic of far-off and beguiling Constantinople....

According to Strzygowski, Romanesque builders received from Armenia the stone technique and the articulation of the wall by blind arcades resting on colonnettes. Gothic builders acquired the rib-vault by way of Armenia; Byzantine architects, the dome placed on squinches to cover an octagon; and Leonardo and Bramante, the central plans of their churches, including St. Peter's in Rome. Even those who have questioned Strzygowski's sweeping claims are willing to concede "... it would be foolish to deny that Armenian architecture could occasionally have exerted its impact on Western, and, above all, on Byzantine building"; and, "Of all the border countries of the Empire, Armenia is the only one to deal with Byzantine architecture on an equal footing" (Krautheimer).[5]

Jacques Benoist-Mechin believes that the Armenian basilica of Aghtamar, which was built between 914 and 921, is almost certainly the origin of Romanesque art. Recently it has been discovered that certain French churches were built on the same plan.

Many other churches and cathedrals in France, Italy, and the Balkans not only bear witness to the popularity of the Armenian style, but were actually built by Armenian masons. In particular one may mention St. Chapelle in Paris, where in three medallions illustrating the story of Noah's ark appears the silhouette of the famous 7th-century Zvartnots cathedral (the largest round church in the world), complete in every detail; St. Germain-des-Pres and the belfry of Charlemagne's palace in Aachen—both built by the 9th century Armenian architect Oton Matsaetsi. We also know that it was Trdat, the builder of the great cathedral of Ani (completed in 1001), who was invited to Constantinople to repair the dome of Haghia Sophia. Manuel was another great architect of the 10th century. He is the builder of the basilica of Aghtamar on Lake Van, mentioned above.[6]

It was also in a village not far from Lake Van that Sinan (1489-1588), the greatest "Ottoman" architect, was born. The son of Christian parents (Sinanian is a common Armenian name), he is called the "Great" Sinan to avoid confusion with two other architects who bore the same name. It is to him that Istanbul owes its reputation as the most brilliant shrine of Islamic architecture.

Drafted into the Janissaries at the age of twenty-four, Sinan first revealed his extraordinary engineering talents in 1534, in the course of a campaign against Persia, by building a bridge of boats across Lake Van so cleverly that the leaders of the expedition were amazed. Shortly thereafter he became the chief architect of Suleiman the Magnificent and for the next fifty years served three sultans. He was nearly a hundred years old when he died in 1588. His biographers attribute 360 buildings to him—mosques, schools, palaces, mausoleums, hospitals, bridges, granaries, aqueducts, and fountains—some of which still adorn places as remote from Istanbul as Bosnia (Yugoslavia) and Mecca.[7]

In addition to architecture, Armenians excelled in fresco painting, ceramics, metal and repousse work, and above all manuscript illumination (miniature painting).

At first eclectic, the art of manuscript illumination developed a richly imaginative and unique style, especially in Armenia Minor, where contacts with the Crusaders and the Mongols resulted in works that surpass in beauty anything the Latin West and the Far East have produced.

Toros Roslin (13th century), who has been hailed as a true precursor of the Italian Renaissance, and Sarkis Pidzak (14th century), deserve particular mention. Write Burney and Lang: "Though of miniature proportions, Roslin's work is comparable to that of Cimabue or Giotto, and merits a prominent place in the history of world art." T. S. R. Boase: "Toros Roslin is by any standards one of the great figures of 13th-century art. His range of expressions and poses has a new humanity far removed from Byzantine formulas, and his colors are vividly contrasted." Arshile Gorky: "Toros Roslin is the Renaissance. What electricity the man contains! For me, he is the greatest artist the world produced before the modern age." [8]

An Armenian painter whose very name became a synonym for art and beauty in 19th-century Russia was Ivan Aivazovsky (1817-1900). As official painter to the Navy, Aivazovsky was commissioned by Czar Nicholas I to paint a series of views of the Russian ports of the Baltic and the Black Sea. He was admired by Turner (who dedicated a poem to him), and Chekhov. His house in Feodosia, in the Crimea, where he was born, is now a museum. [9]

Less well known today but highly regarded in his time, Istanbul-born Zakar Zakarian (1849-1923) was active mainly in Paris, where he had his first exhibition in 1879, after which he decided to interrupt his medical studies and devote his full time to art. He was on friendly terms with some of the most illustrious names in French art, including Edgar Degas who painted his portrait. Zakarian's favorite painter, however, was Jean-Baptiste Chardin, and his works, mainly still lifes and musical instruments, have the refinement, deceptive simplicity and charm of this 18th-century French master. "They are haunted by the spirit of distant songs and forgotten melodies," a contemporary French critic wrote; "and they continue to vibrate with an inner harmony." [10]

Among French painters and engravers of the early 20th century, Edgar Chahine (1873-1947) became well known for his masterful studies of the Paris masses. The winner of numerous prizes, he illustrated such classics of French literature as Verlaine and Anatole France (whose portrait he also painted) [11]

Other Armenian artists who lived and worked in Paris at one time or another: Hovsep Pushman, Sarkis Khachadourian, and Haroutiun Ajemian. Both Pushman (also Puchmann: 1877-1966) and Khachadourian (1886-1947), in addition to producing a large number of original works, recreated many works of Iranian and Indian art and were thus instrumental in introducing new motifs in the world of design and fashion. [12]

Born in Brusa and educated in Venice, Haroutiun (Ariel) Ajemian (1904-1965) was active in Paris (1931-38) as well as New York, where he died. Many of his paintings develop Armenian themes ("Sharakan," "The Massacre," "Armenian Pantheon"). Ajemian was also an influential teacher, one of whose students, Jansem, still lives and works in Paris today.

The paintings of Jansem's (Jean Semerjian: b. 1920) initial phase ("The Armenian Girl" of 1946, for instance, and "Armenian Wedding" and "Funeral" of 1948) likewise celebrate Armenian life and traditions. The winner of numerous prizes, Jansem has had more than 50 personal exhibitions in Moscow, New York, London, Tokyo, and other major cities throughout the world. Jansem has also been active in such fields as fashion and furniture design, cartoons, and illustrating books. Like Carzou, another well-known contemporary of his, Jansem has so far shunned avant-garde tendencies and seems more interested in conveying emotional qualities rather than in experimentation. His favorite subjects are women from all walks of life who look from his canvasses as if begging for sympathy. [13]

Jean Carzou (Carnig Zouloumian: b. 1907) was born in Aleppo and educated in Cairo, and later in Paris, where he had his first exhibition in 1939. His style has changed very little since then. A Carzou painting—with its brilliant reds, greens, and blues, closely woven lines, mysterious shadows and perspectives, which create a strangely poetic atmosphere closer to romantic nostalgia than metaphysical anguish—can be as easily recognized as a Van Gogh or a Renoir. In the 1950s, Carzou became famous as a stage designer for the Paris Opera and the Comedie Francaise. In addition he has illustrated books by, among others, Maurois, Camus, and Hemingway. His wife, Nane Carzou, is the author of a fascinating diary titled *Voyage en Armenie* (Paris, 1974), and his son, Jean-Marie Carzou, is the author of several works of fiction and nonfiction (*see LITERATURE*).[14]

Three modern sculptors who have achieved international standing are the Armenian-American Reuben Nakian, and the Soviet-Armenians Hagop Gurdjian and Yervant Kochar, whose splendid equestrian statue of David of Sassoun in Yerevan has acquired archetypal dimension.

Hagop Gurdjian (1881-1948) was born in Shoushi (Armenia) and lived and worked in Yerevan, Tiflis, Moscow, and Paris where he studied under Rodin and was overwhelmed by his spiritual intensity. Thereafter his work developed an intense emotional expressiveness and his powerful busts of Tolstoy, Rachmaninov, Chaliapin, Shirvanzadeh, and General Antranik, and many other Russian and Armenian contemporaries illustrate his identification of composition with psychological content. In addition to portraits, Gurdjian's works, which number over 300, include animal subjects, and mythological, historical and allegorical figures. Versatile, prolific, enormously gifted, he was highly regarded by his contemporaries and his works were exhibited in nearly all the major cultural centers of the world from Tokyo to New York.[15]

Born in Long Island, New York, Nakian was encouraged in his artistic interests by his parents. At the age of ten he was studying drawing as other children study the piano. In the mid-1930s he met Arshile Gorky, who had a profound influence on him. Thenceforward Nakian's works became more improvisatory and his full, rounded forms and highly finished surfaces, which had been widely accepted, became less smooth. His style came to be known as a sculptural equivalent of action painting, in which roughly textured abstract forms achieve a spontaneous monumentality. A meticulous craftsman who has destroyed a staggering number of works because they didn't "work out," Nakian is a colorful, flamboyant character, whose personality is as intriguing as his art. Writes Frank O'Hara: "Nakian is unrepressed, un-neurotic, unabashed in his approach to sensuality. One finds no guilt or masochism in a Nakian. This remarkable artist. . . has the energy of a young man and a confidence more sure for having included defeat, rejection, and triumph. . . . Nakian has achieved a relationship with physical truth that is both stoic and sybaritic, wherein the dead live and the living wait in a kind of despairing sensual delight." [16]

Three outstanding architects of the modern era are Toros Toromanian, Alexander Tamanian, and Raphael Israelian.

Known as the father of modern Armenian architecture, Toros Toromanian (1864-1934) was also a noted art historian and archaeologist. He spent nearly thirty years travelling throughout Armenia, studying, photographing, and describing churches and monuments. It was mainly as a result of these labors that architectural historians like Strzygowski recognized the unique style and contribution of Armenian architecture. Toromanian's role in this field is similar to that of Komitas in music.

In addition to being a brilliant architect, Alexander Tamanian (1878-1936) was a competent administrator who undertook such large schemes of work as the reconstruction of Yerevan and a number of other Soviet-Armenian towns. He also designed hospitals, city halls, libraries, hydroelectric plants, theaters, schools and many other buildings in both Russia and Armenia. Tamanian borrowed freely from Armenian sources, skillfully adapting them to modern requirements. When Pablo Neruda said: "I think Yerevan is one of the most beautiful cities I have seen; built of volcanic tuff, it has the harmony of a pink rose," he was paying tribute to Tamanian's genius. [17]

The extremely many-sided and prolific Raphael Israelian (1908-1973) is the designer of the Arch of Charents, facing Mount Ararat on the road leading to the pagan temple of Garni, the five-spanned bridge over the River Hrazdan, the famed bell-tower of

Sardarabad, many museums, warehouses, apartment buildings, and memorial fountains.

There are several dozen Soviet-Armenian painters who have achieved some status in the Soviet Union. Among these, however, only one (Martiros Sarian) is widely recognized in the West, and another (Minas Avetissian) deserves to be better known.

The works of Martiros Sarian (1880-1972), which depict the typical features of his native Caucasian mountains, are distinguished by the bold use of strong, fresh, freely applied and contrasting colors. Writes S. V. Utechin: "His style is unique among Soviet landscapists, who since the triumph of Socialist Realism have, as a rule, worked in a vein of timid monotonous illusionism." Sarian himself has said: "Land is like a living being: it has a soul of its own. And without a native land, with no close bond with his country, no man can know himself and his soul." All of Sarian's works celebrate his passionate love for the land of his ancestors, the land where, in his own words: "I saw the sun for the first time and felt its warmth intensely. Camel caravans and tinkling bells coming down the slopes of the hills; shepherds with sun-browned features leading their flocks of sheep, cows, horses, donkeys and goats; street life; Turkish women gliding away in their black and pink veils and violet pantallettes and wooden sandals; Armenian women with large black almond-shaped eyes; these and many more things were the realities I had dreamed of since my early childhood." Like all highly gifted individuals, Sarian, though he lived to be 92, never grew old, never lost his productivity. He seemed to undergo a temporary rejuvenation over and over again. This may explain the astonishing variety of styles that is apparent even in a limited collection of his reproductions. Some of his landscapes have the playful, elusive charm of Paul Klee; others the monumental permanence of Cezanne. In his fondness of raw colors, Sarian at times reminds one of German expressionists. He was as fascinated with masks as James Ensor. He could capture a bull's dark strength and menacing silhouette against a moonlit white wall with the daring of a Picasso. Sarian is a perfect illustration of Bergson's philosophy of "perpetual becoming." He absorbed many influences but always preserved his identity and uniqueness. [18]

A painter, muralist, and stage designer who inherited from Sarian his versatility and bold use of pure colors was Minas Avetissian (1925-1975). Like Sarian, Avetissian delighted in glorifying the Armenian landscape, and more particularly the small village, near Leninakan, where he was born. Writes Puzant Granian, himself an accomplished painter, "Avetissian is the sun-god of contemporary Armenian painting. A modern, versatile, exuberant brush. . . using different styles and techniques, projecting visual and emotional climates of astonishing variety. The sun, the magic of light, mountains, villages, people, animals, seasons, and interior scenes where he turns into an introvert, a mystic." Avetissian died in a car crash. [19]

The Armenian landscape haunted the works of another painter who spent most of his life in the United States. "In my art there will always be the soul of Armenia," wrote Arshile Gorky (Vosdanig Adoian: 1904-1948) in a letter. "I shall resurrect Armenia with my brush for all the world to see and when we return to clay as well we must, then perchance they might say, 'as a son of the Armenian mountains he offered his modest share to the accumulation of our world's great culture.'"

To the question: "What has the Armenian experience to add to modern life?" Gorky once replied:

> *Sensitivity. That is the main, the unforgettable word that has been engraved in my memory of it. Sensitivity to beauty, sensitivity to sadness and melancholy, sensitivity to the frailty as well as the nobility of life. Sensitivity to intellectual progress. It is such an important contribution. Sensitivity in the day of de-humanization. Therein lies our contribution to all art. Our Armenia should not belong to Armenians alone. Our Armenia, the sensitivity of Armenia, its understanding and immense experience of bad and good, of the beautiful and ugly, the dead and living is needed by all the world. The humanity of Armenia is our homeland's book. It is an art that should be offered so others may share it and learn from it.*

It is now generally agreed that Arshile Gorky Adoian played an important historical role in the birth of the New York School of Abstract Expressionism and was instrumental in introducing European influences (Cezanne, Picasso, Miro, Kandinsky) to the United States.

He was born near Lake Van. His childhood left a permanent nostalgic mark on his paintings. Though he was sixteen when he arrived in the United States, he never adjusted to the demands of the New World and was in constant conflict with his surroundings. "One must recognize," he writes in another letter to his family, "that an Armenian in America is indeed a strange creature." Money was a lifelong problem. For a while he earned his meals washing dishes. His last years—"when his art blazed out in passionate fulfillment of his great promise"—were filled with tragedy. It was discovered that he had cancer; his neck was broken in a car accident; a fire destroyed 27 of his sketches and drawings; his wife left him; and at the age of 43, Gorky took his own life by hanging himself in his studio. Writes Julien Levy: "Arshile Gorky achieved a critical mixture of form and abandon, tragedy and humor, ferocity and tenderness, organization and dream, abstraction and Surrealism, resulting in a series of drawings and paintings that announce greatness for the art of his century." [20]

Photography is another field in which Armenians have excelled. Some of the most familiar names here are Yousuf Karsh of Ottawa, Cavouk of Toronto, Garo of Boston, Arto DeMirjian, Arthur Tcholakian, and Armen Kachaturian of New York.

A superb technician whose careful use of light to create atmosphere and reveal character is without rival, Yousuf Karsh (b. 1908) is undoubtedly one of the greatest portraitists of our time. His classic portraits of Churchill, Sibelius, Shaw, Einstein, and Hemingway are as penetrating studies as, say, Picasso's portrait of Gertrude Stein, Renoir's of Wagner, and Graham Sutherland's of Churchill—to mention only three modern masterpieces. (It is interesting to compare Sutherland's Churchill with Karsh's. In Sutherland's famous portrait, Churchill is made to look, in the words of an English critic, "like an evil, bilious toad"; in Karsh's even more famous photograph, on the other hand, he is the quintessential statesman-hero.)

"All I know," Karsh has said, "is that within every man and woman a secret is hidden, and as a photographer it is my task to reveal it if I can." In addition to writing the captions in his many photographic albums—the best known of which are: *Faces of Destiny* (Toronto, 1947), *Portraits of Greatness* (1959), *Faces of Our Time* (1971), *Karsh Portraits* (1976)—Karsh has published a poignant autobiography titled *In Search of Greatness* (Toronto, 1962). [21]

Though John H. Garo (Garoian) is remembered today mainly as Yousuf Karsh's teacher, he was in his time a highly respected portraitist who photographed many nationally and internationally known personages. "He did not travel to find them either; they sought him out in Boston," writes Karsh, who devotes many pages of his autobiography to his reminiscences of Garo. [22]

In addition to portraits (*The Majesty of the Black Woman*), Jerusalem-born Arthur Tcholakian excels in photographing landscapes, panoramas, and daily activities (*Israel: Land of Promise; Armenia: State/People/Life*). His work has achieved national repute. [23]

A resident of Canada since 1958, Cavouk (Artin Cavoukian: b. 1915) has photographed many internationally recognized celebrities and his works have been exhibited in galleries throughout the world. In 1974, his photograph of Elizabeth II of England was adopted as the official portrait of the Queen by the Canadian Government.

[1]For more on the art and architecture of this period, see G. Asratian, *Yerevan and its Environs* (Leningrad, 1973); Charles Burney and D. M. Lang, *The Peoples of the Hills: Ancient Ararat and Caucasus* (London, 1971); Sir Banister Fletcher, *A History of Architecture* (New York, 1975). The best work on Urartian art and architecture, however, is by B. B. Piotrovskii, *Urartu: The Kingdom of Van and Its Art* (New York, 1967).

[2]John Harvey, *The Master Builders: Architecture in the Middle Ages* (New York, 1971).

[3]For a magnificently illustrated text on *khachkars*, see Levon Azarian and Manoug Alemian, *Armenian Khachkars* (Yerevan, 1976).

[4]Armenian influence on Irish as well as European art and architecture is discussed by Francoise Henry, *La Sculpture irlandaise pendant les douze premiers siecles de l'ere chretienne* (Paris, 1932); *Irish Art*, 3 volumes (Cornell University Press, Ithaca, New York, 1967); H. G. Leask, *Irish Churches and Monastic Buildings Prior to 1530*, 3 volumes (Dundalk, 1955-1960); Brian De Breffny and George Mott, *The Churches and Abbeys of Ireland* (London, 1976).

[5]See Richard Krautheimer, *Early Christian and Byzantine Architecture* (London, 1965); J. Strzygowski, *Origin of Christian Church Art* (Oxford, 1923); S. Der Ner-

sessian, *Armenia and the Byzantine Empire* (Cambridge, Mass., 1945); *Great Architecture of the World*, edited by John Julius Norwich (London, 1975); Edouard Utudjian, *Les Monuments armeniens du IVe siecle au XVIIe siecle* (Paris, 1967); Giovanni T. Rivoira, *Moslem Architecture: Its Origins and Development*, English translation by G. McN. Rushforth (New York, 1975) with an excellent section on Armenian churches; Lawrence K. Cone, *Armenian Church Architecture* (New York, 1974); Karoly Gombos, *Armenia: Landscape and Architecture* (New York, 1975).

[6]See Sirarpie Der Nersessian, *Aghtamar: Church of the Holy Cross* (Harvard, 1965); *Documents of Armenian Architecture:* volume 1, *Haghbat;* volume 2, *Khachkars;* volume 3, *Sanahin;* volume 4, *St. Tadei of Van;* volume 5, *Amberd;* volume 6, *Geghart;* volume 7, *Goshavank;* volume 8, *Aghtamar;* volume 9, *Ererouk;* issued by the Faculty of Architecture of the Polytechnical School and the Armenian Academy of Science of Milan, under the direction of the distinguished Italian architect and art historian Adriano Alpago Novello (Ares, 1970-77).

[7]See Arthur Stratton, *Sinan* (New York, 1972); B. Unsal, *Turkish Islamic Architecture in Seljuk and Ottoman Times, 1071-1923* (London, 1959); S. K. Yetkin, *L'Architecture turque en Turquie* (Paris, 1962).

[8]For a lengthy discussion of Toros Roslin's life and work, see Sirarpie Der Nersessian, *Armenian Manuscripts in the Walters Art Gallery* (Baltimore, 1974); also by the same author, *Armenian Manuscripts in the Freer Gallery of Art* (Washington, 1965); and *Armenian Art* (London, 1979). See also, Lydia Dournovo, *Armenian Miniatures* (New York, 1961); *Armenian Art Treasures of Jerusalem*, edited by Bezalel Narkiss and Michael E. Stone (New York, 1979).

[9]For more on Aivazovsky, see Rosa Newmarch, *The Russian Arts* (New York, 1916); Helen Rubissow, *The Art of Russia* (New York, 1946); S. N. Barsamov, *Ivan Konstantinovich Aivazovsky* (Moscow, 1965). For a penetrating sketch of Aivazovsky, see *Letters of Anton Chekhov*, English translation by M. H. Heim and Simon Karlinsky (New York, 1973).

[10]See F. Macler, *La France et l'Armenie a travers l'art et l'histoire* (Paris, 1917), and *Dictionnaire biographique des artistes contemporains, 1910-1934*, 3 volumes (Paris, 1930-34).

[11]Chahine and many other Armenian painters, sculptors, designers, and engravers are discussed by E. Benezit, *Dictionnaire des peintres, sculpteurs, dessinateurs et graveurs* (Paris, 1949). See also Onnig Avedissian, *Peintres et sculpteurs armeniens du 19eme siecle a nos jours, precede d'un apercu sur l'art ancien* (Cairo, 1959)—not to be confused with the Soviet-Armenian painter Minas Avetissian, Onnig Avedissian was himself a distinguished painter active mainly in Egypt; Garig Basmadjian, *A Century of French Armenian Painting* (New York, 1979).

[12]For more on Sarkis Khatchadourian and Pushman, see M. Fielding, *Dictionary of American Painters, Sculptors, and Engravers* (Philadelphia, 1926), and *Ararat* (Spring 1973).

[13]Jansem is further discussed by M. Zahar, *Jansem* (Geneva, 1964), P. Mazars, *Jansem* (Monte Carlo, 1974). See also *Ararat* (Winter 1978).

[14]There are several works in French on Carzou's life and work but none so far in English. See F. Fels, *Carzou* (Geneva, 1959); R. Rey, *Carzou* (Monaco, 1959); P. Lambertin, *Carzou* (1962). See also my *Armenia Observed* (New York, 1979).

[15]See M. Gautier, *H. Gurdjian* (Paris, 1954).

[16]See Frank O'Hara, *Art Chronicles 1954-1966* (New York, 1975). Nakian and many other Armenian-American artists (among them Khoren Der Harootian, Siroon Mangurian, Edmund Yaghjian, Kero Antoyan, Manuel Tolegian, Anahid Janjigian, Simon Samsonian, Martin Barooshian, Mary Melikian, Vava Sarkis Khatchadourian, Salpi Mavian, Mariam Attarian-Bryer, Puzant Godjamanian, Richard Kevorkian, Adrina Zanazanian) are also discussed in *Ararat* (Winter 1977), and *Who's Who in American Art*, edited by the Jacques Cattell Press (New York, 1978). See also *Simon Samsonian: His World Through Paintings*, edited by M. Haigentz (New York, 1978).

[17]See Pablo Neruda, *Memoirs*, English translation by Hardie St. Martin (New York, 1977). Though Armenia and Armenians are not mentioned in the index, Neruda devotes a whole section of his memoirs exclusively to his impressions of Armenia.

[18]Martiros Sarian, *Fragments de ma vie* (Moscow, 1976); Shahen Khachatrian, *Martiros Sarian: Masters of World Painting* (Leningrad, 1975); S. V. Utechin, *Concise Encyclopedia of Russia* (London, 1961).

[19]See G. Igitian, *Minas Avetissian* (Leningrad, 1976).

[20]See Julien Levy, *Gorky* (New York, 1968); Karlen Mooradian, *Arshile Gorky Adoian* (Chicago, 1978); Harold Rosenberg, *Arshile Gorky: The Man, the Time, the Idea* (New York, 1962); Ethel K. Schwabacher, *Arshile Gorky*, (New York, 1957); William Seitz, *Arshile Gorky: Paintings, Drawings, Studies* (New York, 1962); *Ararat* (Fall 1971).

[21]See Aylesa Forsee, *Famous Photographers* (Philadelphia, 1968), and *Current Biography*, Charles Moritz editor (Feb. 1980, volume 41, No. 2).

[22]See Yousuf Karsh, *In Search of Greatness* (Toronto, 1962).

[23]These and other Armenian-American photographers are discussed by Arto De-Mirjian Jr., "Artists of the Camera," in *Ararat* (Winter 1977).

Cinema

Like all Soviet republics, Armenia has a prolific film industry about which the West knows very little. Even such renowned film-makers as Hamo Bek-Nazarov, a leading pioneer of Soviet cinema, and the critically acclaimed Sergei Paradjanov, are known only to the happy few.

Before he became a pioneer of Georgian, Azerbaijani, and Armenian cinemas, Yerevan-born and Moscow-trained Hamo Bek-Nazarov (Hampartsoum Beknazarian: 1892-1965) was a highly respected actor in the Russian film industry with nearly a hundred roles to his credit. Some of his better-known films are *Namous* (1925), after Shirvanzadeh's play, *David Beg* (1944), *Land of Nairi* (1930), and *Pepo*, which was originally filmed in 1934 and later refurbished and reissued in 1964. Based on Sundukian's famous play, and with a moving musical score by Aram Khachaturian, *Pepo*, like his other films, is marked by authentic settings, dynamic montage, and a well-crafted script. In his *Soviet Cinema*, Alexander Birkos writes: "Hamo Bek-Nazarov was one of the few pre-revolutionary artists that succeeded in breaking out of the confines of melodramatic romanticism." [1]

Born in Tiflis, Sergei Paradjanov (Sarkis Paradjanian: b. 1924) studied music in Kiev and cinematography in Moscow. His *Shadows of Our Forgotten Ancestors* (1964) won 16 prizes at international festivals and, according to a number of Western critics, is one of the best Soviet films of the 1960s. His other films include: *Golden Arms* (1957), *The First Boy* (1959), *Ukrainian Rhapsody* (1961), *Street Flower* (1962), and *Sayat-Nova* (1969). Arrested as a dissident and sent to a labor camp in 1974 for breaking the Soviet moral code, Paradjanov was freed in January 1978, no doubt as a result of world-wide publicity and a petition for his release signed by, among others, Fellini, Jean-Luc Godard, Luis Bunuel, Rossellini, Joseph Losey, Noam Chomsky, and Michelangelo Antonioni. [2]

Moscow-born and educated Lev Atamanov (Atamian: b. 1905), is one of the pioneers of the Soviet cartoon film. His creations, some of which are occasionally televised in the United States and Canada with English soundtracks, include *A Dog and a Cat* (1938), based on a story by Hovannes Toumanian (see LITERATURE), *The Magic Carpet* (1948), *The Yellow Stork* (1950), *The Golden Deer* (1954), and *The Snow Queen* (1957). Atamanov has been awarded many prizes at international film festivals in Venice, Cannes, Rome, London, Moscow, Belgrade, Delhi, and other places. [3]

Another well-known figure in Soviet cinema is Nina Aghadjanova-Shutko (Aghadjanian: b. 1889) who has scripted many classics of the Russian cinema, including Eisenstein's celebrated *Battleship Potemkin* (1925). [4]

Among film-makers of Armenian origin, active outside the Soviet Union, the two best known are Rouben Mamoulian and Henri Verneuil.

Born in 1899 in Tiflis (Georgia), Rouben Mamoulian studied under Stanislavsky in Moscow and later in Paris. After directing his first play in London in 1922, he emigrated to New York and from there to Hollywood where he soon became one of the great names in the industry. Less meretricious than Cecil B. DeMille, as meticulous a craftsman as Hitchcock, Mamoulian's films are marked by technical ingenuity and skillful direction of actors and more particularly actresses. He broke the sound barrier to liberate both camera and soundtrack by putting wheels on the camera (which until then had to be enclosed in a booth to block out noise); he experimented with subjective sounds, subjective camera, nonrealistic sounds, dramatic use of color—it was Mamoulian who directed the first picture in the new Technicolor process. In addition to many operas, operettas, plays, and musicals, he directed five spectacularly successful films: *Golden Boy* with William Holden (in his first starring role); *Dr. Jekyll and Mr. Hyde* with Fredric March (the best adaptation so far of Stevenson's masterpiece); *The Mark of Zorro* and *Blood and Sand* with Tyrone Power, and *Queen Christina* with Greta Garbo at her most radiant. This last film also contains the most famous of all Garbo images—the final close-up as she stands at the ship's prow, her face, according to Mamoulian's instructions a perfect blank into which the audience might read what it would. [5]

"It was after I had seen *Queen Christina* that I decided to become a film director," Henri Verneuil has said in an interview. "I was fourteen when I went to see that film and when I read 'Directed by Rouben Mamoulian' on the screen, I had this feeling I too would become a director someday. Was I serious? Of course! I remember to have said to myself: 'Mamoulian is an Armenian, so am I.' This may not seem like a good enough reason, but there it is. What counts is that I did become a director. . . ." One of the most successful and prolific film directors of our time Henri Verneuil (Ashod Malakian) was born in Rodosto (Turkey) in 1920 and educated in France. He began his career as a journalist in Marseilles. An accomplished craftsman, he has produced, scripted, and directed many elegant comedies, thrillers, adventure stories and dramas starring such internationally recognized performers as Anthony Quinn, Fernandel, Trevor Howard, Jean Gabin, Jean-Paul Belmondo, Charles Boyer, and Daniel Gelin.

In a recently published article Verneuil has described the circumstances surrounding his adoption of a pseudonym. As a journalist in Marseilles, he writes, when he submitted a series of articles on the Turkish massacres, his editor suggested he publish them under an assumed name in order to forestall any charges of pro-Armenian bias. Malakian agreed provided the articles were printed without cuts. The temporary pseudonym that his editor chose for him was Henri Verneuil. [6]

Among actors, the most widely recognized are Gregoire Aslan, Charles Aznavour, and Alice Sapritch in France; and in the United States: Akim Tamiroff, Arlene Francis, and Mike Connors.

Like Alice Sapritch (b. 1919), Gregoire Aslan (b. 1908) is not as well known in the United States as Charles Aznavour—though he has appeared in over forty plays and seventy films, some of which, like Claude Autant-Lara's *Oh Amelia* (1949), and *The Red Inn* (1951), were widely viewed here.

Singer, composer, and now author (*Aznavour by Aznavour: An Autobiography*) Charles Aznavour's (b. 1924) film credits include such classics of the French cinema as Franju's *La tete contre les murs* (*The Keepers* in English: 1958), Jean Cocteau's *The Testament of Orpheus* (1960), and Francois Truffaut's *Shoot the Piano Player* (1960). He has also appeared in several international films like *The Games* (1969), *The Adventurers* (1970), and others. [7]

Throughout his life Akim Tamiroff (Tamiriants: 1898-1973) was in great demand as a character actor and appeared in films by Preston Sturges, Jules Dassin, Vittorio de Sica, Orson Welles, and Jean-Luc Godard, among others.

Author of *That Certain Something: The Magic of Charm* (New York, 1960), and an autobiography titled *Arlene Francis: A Memoir* (New York, 1978), Arlene Francis (Kazanjian: b. 1908) has appeared in many Broadway plays and Hollywood films including one opposite Jimmy Cagney in Billy Wilder's hilarious farce *One, Two, Three* (1961).

Mike Connors (Krikor Ohanian: b. 1925) is of course the very popular star of *Mannix*.

In the related field of film education and criticism, let us mention two Armenian-Americans: Haig Manoogian, producer, educator, and author of the widely used text *The Film-Maker's Art* (1966), and Jack Shadoian, author of a fascinating study titled *Dreams and Dead Ends: The American Gangster/Crime Film* (Cambridge, 1977).

[1] Bek-Nazarov's contributions to the Soviet cinema are cited in Jay Leyda, *Kino: A History of the Russian and Soviet Film* (London, 1960); Thorald Dickinson and Catherine De la Roche, *Soviet Cinema* (New York, 1972).

[2] See *S. Paradjanov*, edited by A. J. Liehm (Venice, 1977); Jeanne Vronskaya, *Young Soviet Film Makers* (London, 1972); Marco Carynnyk, "S. Paradjanov in Prison," *Journal of Ukrainian Graduate Studies* (Spring 1978); Paradjanov's case as a dissident is further discussed by Leonid Plyushch, *History's Carnival: A Dissident's Autobiography*, edited and translated by Marco Carynnyk (New York, 1979). See also *Ararat* (Spring 1971), and my *Armenia Observed* (New York, 1979).

[3] Atamanov and a number of other Soviet-Armenian directors (among them, Y. Erzinkian, G. Balasamian, L. Issahakian, P. Barkhudarian, A. Martirossian, G. Oganissian, S. Kevorkov, M. Darbinian, Funze Dovlatian, Bek-Nazarov, and Paradjanov) are discussed by Alexander S. Birkos, *Soviet Cinema: Directors and Films* (Connecticut, 1976).

[4] See *The Battleship Potemkin*, edited by Herbert Marshall (New York, 1978).

[5] The standard and most readable and complete work on Mamoulian is Tom Milne, *Mamoulian* (Indiana, 1970); another useful work is Richard J. Anobile, *Rouben Mamoulian's Dr. Jekyll and Mr. Hyde* (New York, 1975). For a lengthy interview with Mamoulian, see Andrew Sarris, *Hollywood Voices: Interviews with Film Directors* (New York, 1971). As the author of two books—*Shakespeare's Hamlet: A New Version* (New York, 1966), and *Abigail: Story of a Cat at the Manger* (New York, 1964)—Mamoulian is one of the few film directors listed in *Contemporary Authors*, vols. 25/28 (Detroit, 1971). Mamoulian, together with some other Armenian-American film-directors (Aram Boyajian, Richard Sarafian, Aram Avakian) are discussed by Peter Manuelian, "In the Spotlight," in *Ararat* (Winter 1977).

[6] This story however has a typical sequel that is worth recounting. "A couple of days after these articles appeared," writes Malakian,

> an official from the Turkish embassy knocked at my door. "Monsieur Verneuil," he said speaking with a soft, kindly voice, "recently you published a series of pro-Armenian articles which may tend to mislead public opinion. As a Frenchman you were very probably taken in by Armenian lies. I am here to expose these lies in order to prevent any future misunderstanding between our two friendly governments."
>
> "Listen, my friend," I said when the Turk was through delivering his prepared speech, "you have come all this way to expose lies and correct errors without realizing that I happen to be the son of Hagop Effendi Malakian from Rodosto. What the Turks have done to Armenians is neither massal [Oriental tale] nor fic-

tion. We, West-Armenians, have felt the Turks' deeds on our skins and we still bear deep scars in our souls. I shall therefore ask you to be kind enough to spare your time as well as mine, because whatever you have to say won't change the tragic reality that exists between our people. Unless the Turks admit their responsibility and make reparations by returning our lands, the gap that exists between us will not only remain wide open but it will grow wider and deeper with time."

Without saying a word, the Turkish official simply turned on his heels and left never to appear again.

After the publication of these articles I became known as Henri Verneuil. Shortly thereafter I was called to Paris under that name and that's how I have been called ever since.

[7] For more on Aznavour and Tamiroff, see *The Oxford Companion to Film,* edited by Liz-Anne Bawden (New York, 1976). See also Philippe Bouvard, "Alice Sapritch," in *Paris-Match* (Novermber 20, 1979).

Science & Technology

New techniques of agriculture, animal husbandry, metallurgy, and engineering began to emerge in Armenia in the 4th millenium B.C. Not far from Yerevan, close to the village of Metsamor, there stands to this day a massive rocky hill, half a mile in circumference. The hill is riddled with caves, underground storage vaults, and prehistoric dwellings. It is now believed to have been an important pre-Urartian scientific, astronomical, and metallurgical center (probably 4th millenium B.C.).

Shengavit, another ancient settlement on the outskirts of Yerevan, has been assigned by archaeologists to the 4th/3rd millenium B.C. Excavations have brought to light many houses and temples built of large stone slabs, and a secret underground passage leading to the Hrazdan River.

Urartians themselves were great masters in the construction of artificial lakes, roads, fortified citadels, and vast irrigation canals. Their settlements are distinguished from Assyrian settlements by vast irrigation systems. In the words of Arshile Gorky, "Armenia has not only been at the crossroads of the world, but has built them with its own sinews. Our forebears hung irrigation canals like necklaces around mountain throats."

Built in the 9th century B.C., the Canal of Meinua, also called Shamiram Su (because, according to an Armenian legend, Queen Semiramis spent much time here in building, landscape gardening, and debauchery, to console herself after the death of King Ara) still bears fresh water over a distance of about 46 miles from a spring to the southern edge of Van. The artificial Lake of Rusas and the Canal of Rusas were both built by King Rusas II in the 7th century B.C.

The royal citadel in the hills above Lake Van is an impressive example of Urartian military engineering. The fortifications consist of massive blocks of basalt laid without mortar in courses from half to one meter deep to a thickness of three or four meters, surmounted by courses of brick to a total height of some twelve meters.

In the Van region alone, more than forty such sites have been discovered. A great many other sites remain unexplored because they lie on the frontiers of Turkey, Iran, and Russia, and tend to fall in areas of military security.

Armenia's first great scientist is Anania Shiragatsi (also Ananias of Shirak: 600-670 A.D.). Shiragatsi was a prolific encyclopedic writer who has left works on astronomy, metaphysics, geography, mathematics, music, chronology, and a great variety of other subjects. His textbook on arithmetic, *Questions and Answers*, which contains materials on the art of computation in tabular form, is one of the most ancient works on arithmetic to be handed down to us. Shiragatsi's sources include Ptolemy, Thales, Hippocrates, Democritus, Plato, Aristotle, Zeno the Stoic, and Epicurus.

In an autobiographical essay, Shiragatsi tells us he was dissatisfied with the schools in his province and determined to become a true scholar, he decided to study in the "land of Greeks." After travelling for three years in search of a good teacher, he finally found one in Trebizond, Tychicus by name, a brilliant man not only "renowned among kings," but also possessing a knowledge of both the Armenian language and literature. Shiragatsi studied with Tychicus for eight years, after which he returned to Armenia and devoted the rest of his life to writing and teaching. His school gained an excellent reputation and attracted many students. His works had widespread use as basic textbooks.

Some of Shiragatsi's theories are worth mentioning. He believed, for example, that the Milky Way was a mass of dense but faintly luminous stars; that the moon was a dark body by nature whose only light was that which it reflected from the sun; that the sun was bigger than the moon—their different distances from the earth making them appear the same size; that the earth was held up by the atmosphere and the winds: "The earth is the center," he writes. "All round the earth is the air, and the heavens surround the earth on every side." And: "Birth is the beginning of annihilation, and annihilation in its turn is the beginning of birth. From this immortal paradox, the earth derives its eternal existence." [1]

Surgical tools made of obsidian (a black stone that can be honed to great sharpness) and dating back to the second millenium B.C. have been found on the shores of Lake Sevan. Also skulls that bear evidence of delicate surgery "equal to anything doctors can do today," according to a Soviet surgeon and anthropologist. In the Matenadaran Library of Yerevan, there are manuscript texts on applied medicine, anatomy, physiology, and diagnosis dating back to the 10th century A.D. The dissection of bodies for educational and research purposes was in wide use in Armenia by the 13th century—about three centuries earlier than in Europe.

Mekhitar Heratsi (12th century) and Amirtovlat Amassiatsi (15th century) wrote encyclopedic works on many aspects of medicine, including psychotherapy. Speaking of Heratsi's *Relief Against Fevers* (Chermants Mekhitaroutiun), Burney and Lang write:

> For the first time in the history of medicine Mekhitar Heratsi introduced the notion that typhoid, malaria, and septic fevers were infectious 'mouldy fevers,' as he aptly termed them.... Heratsi mastered the technique of surgical operations, and used silk thread for sewing up wounds. He employed mandragora for an anaesthetic. He carried out experiments on animals, and was aware of the value of special diets in treating dis-

orders, and of music and psychotherapy for the relief of nervous complaints. ²

As Mehmed II's court physician, Amirtovlat Amassiatsi (ca. 1422-1496) had access to the sultan's vast library and seems to have read all the Greek, Latin, and Arabic works on medicine. His elegantly illustrated works cover an astonishing range of topics: anatomy, physiology, obstetrics and gynecology, venereal diseases, hygiene, therapy, toxicology, infantile diseases, otolaryngology, neurology, and mental illnesses. In one of these encyclopedic works, Amassiatsi lists no less than 3700 prescriptions prepared with herbs and medicinal plants.

Amassiatsi's work was continued and edited by Buniat Sebastatsi, a distinguished 17th-century physician and scholar, himself the author of a famous medical text containing 50 sections, each devoted to diseases of specific organs of the human body. ³

Armenian contributions to modern science are too many to enumerate here. Again let us mention a few representative names. In the Soviet countries, four widely recognized names are Leon Orbeli, Artem Mikoyan, Victor Ambartsumian, and Ana Aslan.

One of the founders of evolutionary physiology of the nervous system in the USSR, Leon Orbeli (1882-1959) is widely recognized for his scientific treatises (*Lectures on the Physiology of the Nervous System; Conditioned Reflexes in Dogs;* and others), and researches in the adaptational-trophical functions of the sympathetic nervous system and other problems of general physiology. In 1950, Orbeli was dismissed from all his leading positions for his reconciliatory attitude toward European and American theories and deviations from the teaching of Marx, Engels, and Pavlov. He was rehabilitated in 1955.⁴

A pioneer of jet aviation in the USSR and younger brother of the influential and durable Soviet diplomat Anastas Mikoyan (1895-1978), Artem Mikoyan (1905-1970) is the designer, with mathematician Mikhail Gurevich, of the famous MIG fighter aircraft—one of the first all-Russian jet fighters to go into service in Soviet squadrons. ⁵

Founder of the school of theoretical astrophysics in the Soviet Union, Victor Ambartsumian (also Hampartsoumian: b. 1908) is best known for developing a theory concerning the origin and evolution of stars and stellar systems, and for demonstrating the role of ultra-violet radiation. He has also studied the physical composition of the atmosphere and the shells of meteorites; radio signals coming from outside our galactic system of stars; and discovered new star clusters. Charles Whitney, Professor of Astronomy at Harvard University, concludes one of his texts by saying that if Ambartsumian is right, "astronomers stand at the brink of another revolution."

It was also Ambartsumian who organized the construction near Yerevan of the Byurakan Astronomical Observatory, now one of the most important observatories in the USSR. His other accomplishments include many papers and textbooks, one of which, *Theoretical Astrophysics* (1958), has gone through many editions and translations.

A riveting lecturer and a man of vast culture, Ambartsumian invariably attracts large audiences at international symposia and likes to enliven even his most abstrusely mathematical lectures with quotations from classic and contemporary poets.[6]

A pioneer in gerontology and director of the Geriatrics Institute of Bucharest (Rumania), Ana Aslan (Aslanian: b. 1897) is the discoverer of the "Aslan Method" based on novocaine and named "Gerovital" or "H-3"—a medication that is said to counter the degenerative processes associated with advancing age. She has treated some of the world's leading statesmen, financiers, and professional men.[7]

Among Armenian-American scientists, the following may be noted:

In mathematics (pure and applied): Vladimir Karapetoff (1876-1948), professor of electrical engineering, inventor of several electrical devices, poet, and author of many texts, including a 5-volume *Engineering Applications of Higher Mathematics* (1911-16).

Haroutiun Dadourian (1878-1974), professor of physics and mathematics in several American universities and author of such texts as *Analytical Mechanics* (1913), *Graphic Statics* (1919), *Introduction to Analytic Geometry and the Calculus* (1949), *How to*

Study—How to Solve (1957), and many other works on electrons, elasticity, radio-activity, sound ranging, X-rays, and relativity.

In medicine: Varastad Kazanjian (1897-1974), a pioneer in plastic surgery and co-author of the standard text on the subject, *Surgical Treatment of Facial Injuries* (1949).

John Sarkis Najarian (b. 1927), a transplant specialist and innovative surgeon of world renown, who developed a special serum that prevents the body's rejection of new organs.

Harry T. Arshak Seneca, surgeon, educator, and author of, among others, a 1180-page text titled *Biological Basis of Chemotherapy of Infections and Infestations* (1971).

Mueller M. De Van, inventor of the embrasure clasp: Hampar Kelikian, orthopedic surgeon, medical scholar, educator, and literary critic (see LITERATURE); John V. Basmadjian, professor of physical medicine and anatomy and author of numerous texts; and many, many others. [8]

[1] See Robert H. Hewsen, "Armenia's First Scientist," in *Ararat* (Spring 1974).

[2] See C. Burney and D. M. Lang, *The Peoples of the Hills: Ancient Ararat and Caucasus* (London, 1971). See also A. S. Ktsoyan, *Mekhitar Heratsi: XII Century Physician*, English translation by U. S. Derderian (Yerevan, 1969). Heratsi's *Relief Against Fevers* has been translated into several languages, including German by the medical historian Ernst Seidel (1850-1922), who is said to have studied Armenian for the sole purpose of translating Heratsi. His rendition, titled *Trost bei Fiebern*, with copious commentary, appeared in 1908 in Leipzig.

[3] See Vahram Torkomian, *Les manuscrits medicaux armeniens de la Bibliotheque Nationale de Paris* (Paris, 1925).

[4] Orbeli and many other Armenian scientists are discussed in *World Who's Who in Science: From Antiquity to the Present*, edited by Allen G. Debus (Chicago, 1968).

[5] See *Jane's All the World's Aircraft*, compiled and edited by Leonard Bridgman (London, 1957).

[6] See Charles Whitney, *The Discovery of Our Galaxy* (New York, 1971). For an excellent portrait of Ambartsumian, see Alla G. Massevitch's entry in the *Encyclopaedia Britannica: Macropaedia*, volume 1, page 656 (Chicago, 1974).

[7] For more on Ana Aslan and other Soviet-Armenian scientists, see *Who's Who in the Socialist Countries*, edited by Borys Lewytzkyj and Juliusz Stroynowski (Munich, 1978).

[8] These and many other scientists are discussed by Avedis Derounian, "The Professional Life," in *Ararat* (Winter 1977). In this same issue, see also my "Contributions to American Education."

Cuisine

Ancient observers like Xenophon and Plutarch agree that Armenia was rich in all kinds of produce. Plutarch calls Armenia "a land that abounded in all sorts of plenty." The Armenians had "all kinds of good food," writes Xenophon in his *Anabasis*. He mentions "meat, corn, old wines with a delicious bouquet, raisins, and all sorts of vegetables. . . and barley wine in great bowls." Xenophon's description of the barley wine (probably beer) is worth quoting: "The actual grains of barley floated on top of the bowls, level with the brim," he writes, "and in the bowls there were reeds of various sizes and without joints in them. When one was thirsty, one was meant to take a reed and suck the wine into one's mouth. It was a very strong wine, unless one mixed it with water, and, when one got used to it, it was a very pleasant drink." [1]

Armenian wines and brandies are widely recognized and acclaimed to this day. At the 1958 International Exhibition at Brussels, Armenian brandies took the first prize. One local brandy called "Dvin," was a favorite of Winston Churchill who first tasted it when his host, Josef Stalin, served it at the Yalta summit conference in 1945.[2] Others who have praised the variety and originality of Armenian cuisine: Lord Byron and Alexandre Dumas, and in our own day, Raymond Sokolov, Craig Claiborne[3] and Mimi Sheraton, who has written: "The Armenian style of cooking is, in general, richer and more luxurious than the leaner variations found in Middle Eastern countries, yet it is lighter and cleaner in flavor than the similar Greek cuisine."[4]

Shish Kebab (marinated lamb on a skewer with pieces of green pepper and onion and broiled until crispy brown) is one Armenian dish that has acquired universal popularity. Experts now agree that skewer cookery derives from a centuries-old Armenian custom of placing food on sticks and cooking it over open fires.[5]

The exact origins of certain Armenian dishes like *bulghur pilaf* (a traditional accompaniment to *shish kebab:* a type of risotto prepared with cracked wheat), *lahmajoon* (a pizza-like dish prepared with ground lamb or beef), *sarma* (rice rolled in grape leaves), *pakhlava* (flakey layer-pastry with walnuts), and *yoghurt (madzoon* in Armenian) are difficult to trace; but again it is generally agreed that Armenians were instrumental in introducing them to the West. It was an Armenian family by the name of Columbosians, for instance, that founded the first yoghurt dairy in the United States in 1931. The Columbosians, it is to be noted, are still in business and their product goes under the trade name Colombo.[6]

Among the uniquely Armenian dishes that are becoming better known are: *chee kufteh* (or *kheemah*), a steak tartare made with raw meat, cracked wheat, and kneaded with spices, and served as a first course; *herriseh*, a thick stew made with chicken or lamb, cooked with wheat for hours to a porridge consistency; *lavash*, lightly browned thin bread, rolled out in large circles, and eaten crisp or softened with a sprinkling of water; *tahn,* the Armenian version of buttermilk, made with equal parts of yoghurt and water and served ice-cold; and the Armenian Christmas pudding, *anooshaboor,* traditionally made with wheat, apricots, raisins, walnuts, pistachios, and almonds.[7]

[1] For more on the origins of the drinking straw see C. J. F. Dowsett, "A Detail in Xenophon," in *Ararat: A Decade of Armenian-American Writing*, edited by Jack Antreassian (New York, 1969).

[2] See George St. George, *Russia* (London, 1973).

[3] See Alexandre Dumas, *Adventures in the Caucasus*, translated by A. E. Murch (London, 1962); Craig Claiborne, *The New York Times International Cookbook* (New York, 1971).

[4] *The New York Times*, March 3, 1976.

[5] See *The American-International Encyclopedic Cookbook*, edited by Anne London (New York, 1972).

[6] See Sonia Uvezian, *The Book of Yoghurt* (San Francisco, 1978). Armenian Contributions to American cuisine are discussed by Peter Manuelian, "Armenian Cuisine: A Wayward Eater's Return," in *Ararat* (Winter 1977). One reason these and many other Armenian dishes have Turkish names is that Armenia was occupied by the Turks for nearly six centuries (see HISTORY), and, as a historian has remarked, "Now and then, here and there in inland Turkey, tongues were yanked out of the heads of persons who had spoken Armenian."

[7] The recipes of these and many other Armenian dishes are included in Sonia Uvezian, *The Cuisine of Armenia* (New York, 1974); Alice Antreassian, *Armenian Cooking Today* (New York, 1975); Rose Baboian, *The Art of Armenian Cooking* (New York, 1971); Rachel Hogrogian, *The Armenian Cookbook* (New York, 1971); George Mardikian, *Dinner at Omar Khayyam's* (Salt Lake City, 1969; originally published in 1944). In his memoirs, *Song of America* (New York, 1956), George Mardikian also discusses the historic background of a number of Armenian dishes; and Detroit AGBU Women, *Treasured Armenian Recipes* (Detroit, 1949). It is to be noted that these cookbooks are far from comprehensive. Sonia Uvezian's work, for instance, stresses West-Armenian cuisine—though in another book, *The Best Foods of Russia* (New York, 1976), she does include a handful of East-Armenian dishes.

National Characteristics

Life evolves by sensitiveness and awareness, by being exposed, not by being protected; by nakedness, not by strength; by smallness not by size. In a world dominated by monsters the future is given to a creature which has to spend its time taking notice of others and giving way to others.
                    Gerald Heard

The Armenian is an enigma that refuses to be solved.
                    Neshan Beshigtashlian

Resilient, adaptable, versatile, complex, even contradictory, the Armenian eludes categorization and definition.

In his *Anatomy of Exile: A Semantic and Historical Study* (1964), Paul Tabori calls Armenians "born murderees," but on the next page he changes his mind and calls *survival* "an Armenian talent par excellence."

In contrast to their neighbors the Georgians, the Armenians are "dour and dogmatic," says Laurens van der Post, echoing the words of W. E. D. Allen, an English diplomat and author of a *History of the Georgian People* (1932). "Armenians," van der Post goes on, "got themselves repeatedly massacred for their love and stubbornness of principles." He then proceeds to speak to Armenian humor and adaptability.

"Whatever are you going to do now, unfortunate man?" asks a missionary's wife to the Armenian hero of Arthur Koestler's *The Age of Longing,* shortly after the man barely escapes a massacre in which he loses his wife and six children. "I shall find another wife and have another six children," he replies. In that short sentence, Koestler has captured the Armenian spirit of steadfastness, ruthless will to exist, and primitive energy.

In his *Annals*, the Roman historian Tacitus (55-120 A.D.) calls Armenians *ambigua gens*, i. e. fickle and disloyal, perhaps because Armenians refused to submit to Rome.

In his *My Land, My People* (1979), Puzant Granian views the Armenian essentially as a poet and a mystic. His temperament is decidedly "mystical rather than analytical," he writes.

Osip Mandelstam, on the other hand, speaks of the Armenian's "inexplicable aversion to anything metaphysical," and his "splendid intimacy with the world of real things. . . ."

Being a more or less sexually inactive man himself, Anton Chekhov saw the Armenian as a passionate creature. "He was a very passionate man," he writes in a short story; "he was an Armenian" —as if one followed the other as night follows day. Elsewhere however, he spoke of the complex and contradictory aspect of the Armenian character. "In him alone," he writes in a letter speaking of the painter Aivazovsky, "there are combined a general, a bishop, an artist, a naive grandpa and an Othello. He is married to a very lovely young woman, whom he controls with an iron hand."

Like all people who work in an alien, challenging environment, Armenians are enterprising, industrious, intelligent. "One is immediately struck by the manifest intelligence and quick wittedness of the Armenians," writes Sir Fitzroy Maclean in his *To Caucasus: The End of All Earth* (1977).

Nothing escapes them. They have read one's thoughts almost before they have had time to take shape.

I know how dangerously unfashionable it is nowadays to suggest that any given race or nation possesses qualities or characteristics which others do not. But I just cannot help feeling whenever I am in Armenia that the Armenians are much, much cleverer and quicker than most other people. Whether you are talking to the aged Marshal Bagramian, to a parish priest, to the extremely alert young First Secretary of the Armenian Communist Party, to the head-waiter or to the clerk behind the reception desk in your hotel, you are struck again and again by that same penetrating, concentrated intelligence, gleaming in their dark eyes and reflected in the speed of their reactions.

Maclean goes on to call Armenians "tough, craggy and enduring."

Even the statues of Armenian national heroes [he writes], which adorn the parks and public squares, have a lapidary vigor which such monuments normally lack. Hewing stone, carving stone, building in stone, these are all Armenian trades, trades that well befit a people so tough, craggy and enduring, who possess, like the glittering black obsidian chips we found by the roadside on our way to Lake Sevan, an edge and a brilliance all their own.

Armenian business acumen has been noted by many observers. There is a saying in Italy: "It takes seven Genoese [the most cunning Italians] to fool a Jew, and seven Jews to fool an Armenian." (Armenians like to quip that where there are Armenians, Jews are superfluous.)

It has also been noted that Armenian business acumen is essentially a phenomenon of the diaspora. Until very recently, the dominant element in Trascaucasian Armenia was not urban but rural. The language of this region is rich with curses against money and those who coined it. In his *Wounds of Armenia*, the 19th-century novelist Khachatur Abovian (see LITERATURE) quotes several of them—"Money is rust and dirt in the hands; to taste it is like eating one's own flesh"; "Man must sell his soul in order to covet money." Writes August von Haxthausen, a German traveller and contemporary of Abovian: "As far as their character is concerned, one must distinguish sharply the merchants, particularly those living among other peoples, from the cultivators living in the land...."

"Behold the Armenian at work," writes Derenik Demirjian (see

LITERATURE) in a much quoted essay, "with a load on his back that is more like a mountain. Is he trying to make a living or kill himself?... Have you seen the miserable shack he calls his home? But walk through the countryside and you will see magnificent convents, stupendous towers, and delicately carved cross-stones.... Listen to him talk. He curses God and the Church constantly. But behold the magnificent cathedrals he has built...."[1]

According to the 20th-century satirist Neshan Beshigtashlian, the Armenian's ambivalent attitude towards God is reciprocated. Writes Beshigtashlian in his penetrating character study titled "The Armenian": "Even the Good Lord could not make up his mind what to make of the Armenian. First He made him an angel, then turned him into a devil, after which He changed His mind again. But the Armenian retained deep within him angelic as well as demonic traits." Beshigtashlian goes on to call the Armenian ("... his nose, a Mount Ararat; his speech, an earthquake...") "a Jew in the marketplace, a Byzantine in politics, a ruthless Kurd in his relations with his fellow men, a devil in public, but a veritable angel at home."

Passive victim, fierce warrior, pragmatic Sancho Panza, idealistic Don Quixote, introspective poet and mystic, stubborn farmer and builder, shrewd trader and daring adventurer, the Armenian continues to elude definitions perhaps because history, instead of allowing him to develop his temperament at leisure, has presented him with a long series of challenges forcing him to adapt or perish. Jose Ortega y Gasset once defined man with the following formula: I am myself plus my circumstances ("*Yo soy yo y mi circumstancia*"). To gain a more accurate insight of the Armenian temperament, perhaps we should modify this definition to: An Armenian is himself *minus* his circumstances. Because his circumstances have almost always been negative rather than positive factors in the development of his character. A significant portion of his energies has always gone into adapting himself to existing conditions.

This to some extent is true even today. Though recent rise in nationalist feeling, not only in Soviet Armenia but in the diaspora as well, has somewhat mitigated the fear of assimilation ("white massacre"), it remains nevertheless a real threat. "Like lumps of ice," Aram Haigaz has said, "Armenians in the diaspora will gradually melt away and flow into a sea of anonymity." Others have questioned this pessimistic prognosis. "Survival," Granian has said, "has always been dependent on creative minorities. Conditions, the environment, the times, the historic moment—they are all against us, granted. Those who take an active part in our national life constitute only a minority. True. But we have survived worst disasters in the past."

The future is not easy to predict—now more than ever because we are in the midst of a transition towards entirely new conditions and situations; and because, if anything, the Armenian is *unpredictable*. [2]

[1] Derenik Demirjian's essay, titled "The Armenian," has been translated into English by S. H. Varjabedian and included in his book *The Armenians: From Prehistoric Times to the Present* (Chicago, 1977).

[2] The rise of nationalist feeling in Soviet Armenia is discussed by Mary K. Matossian, "Armenia and the Armenians," in *Handbook of Major Soviet Nationalities*, edited by Zev Katz (New York, 1975). For an insightful essay on how others see us, see Leo Hamalian, "The Image of the Armenian in Fiction," in *Burn After Reading* (New York, 1978); see also my *Armenia Observed* (New York, 1980). Some of the social, cultural, and political problems and contradictions of the Armenian Diaspora are discussed in *La Struttura Negata: Cultura Armena nella Diaspora*, edited by Marc Nichanian and Remo Pomponio (Milan, 1979), a collection of essays written in English, Armenian, French, and Italian.

Index

Abdul-Hamid II, 20
Abeghian, Manoog, 43, 99, 100
Abgar, Amy, 142
Abicarius, Iskander, 124
Abicarius, John, 124
Abkar V the Black, 30
Abou Ala Al-Mahari, 92
Abovian, Khachatur, 58, 59-62, 71, 123, 127, 176
Acharian, see Ajarian
Adalian, Rouben, 130
Adamian, Bedros, 77
 see also Atamian
Adamic, Louis, 27.
Adamov, Arthur, 120-121, 130, 132

Adoian, Vosdanig (Arshile Gorky) 144, 149, 151, 154-155, 158, 166
Adonts, Nicholas (Nikoghayos Ter-Avedikian), 24, 99-100, 130
Aesop, 54
Aganoor, Vittoria (Aghanoorian), 123-124
Agathangelos, 50, 127
Aghababian, Sooren, 109-110
Aghajanian, Gregory Peter XV, cardinal, 34-35
Aghadjanova-Shutko, Nina, 160
Aghayan, Ghazaros, 61-62
Aghbalian, Nikol, 49, 50, 84, 99, 100, 126, 130

Aghbashian, H., 102
Aghishian, Noubar, 113
Aharonian, Avetis, 96
Aivazovsky, Ivan, 58, 149, 157, 175
Ajarian, Hrachya, 99
Ajemian, Anahid, 142
Ajemian, Haroutiun (Ariel), 150
Ajemian, K., 115
Ajemian, Maro, 142
Akhmatova, Anna, 85
Albertus Magnus, 56
Alchian, Armen, 118
Alemian, Manoug, 156
Alexander I, czar, 17
Alexander the Great, 9-10
Alexanian, Diran, 141, 143
Alishan, Leo, 25, 57-58, 71
Allen, W. E. D., 132, 175
Alp Arslan, 18
Ambartsumian, Victor, 168-169, 170
Amirian, Lemyel, 130
Amirkhanian, Nathan, 138
Amirtovlat Amassiatsi, 167, 168
Anania Shirakatsi (Ananias of Shirak), 126, 166-167
Ananian, Vakhtang, 106-107, 130
Ananikian, Mardiros, 24
Anderson, M. S., 25
Andonian, Aram, 26
Antoyan, Kero, 158
Antranik (Ozanian), general, 131, 151
Antreassian, Alice, 173
Antreassian, Antranig, 114, 131
Antreassian, Jack, 27, 128, 131, 173
Aprahamian, Felix, 141
Ara the Beautiful, 7, 24, 48, 166
Aragon, Louis, 92
Arakel Siunetsi, 56
Aram, king of Urartu, 7

Ardavast II, 46
Ardzruni dynasty, 16
Ardzruni, Tovma, 51
Argishti II, 9
Ariel, *see* Ajemian, Haroutiun
Aristakes Lastivertsi, 17, 51
Aristotle, 47, 166
Arlen, Michael (Dikran Kouyoumdjian), iii, 115-116
Arlen, Michael J., ii, iii, 26, 27, 116
Armen, Hrant, 24
Armen, Mkrtitch (Haroutiunian), 82, 89, 91-92
Armenian, Garo, 110, 115
Aroian, John, 26
Arout, Gabriel (Arouchian), 120, 122, 132
Aroutiunian, *see* Haroutiunian
Arpee, Leon, 35
Arpine (Aprahamian), 114
Arslan, Edoardo, 124
Arslan, Yervant, 124
Artinian, Artin, 120
Arzoomanian, Ralph, 132
Arzoomanian, Sevak, 110
Arzoomanian, Zaven, 126
Arzruni, Sahan, 139, 142
Asadourian, Hagop, 114
Ashot Bagratuni, *see* Bagratuni
Aslan, Ana (Aslanian), 168, 169, 170
Aslan, Gregoire, 162
Asoghik (Asolik), *see* Stepanos Taronetsi
Asratian, G., 156
Atamanov, Lev (Atamian), 160, 163
Atamian, Hagop, 42
Atamian, Sarkis, 27
Attarian, Karnig, 115
Attarian-Bryer, Mariam, 158
Augustine, St., 56

Avakian, Aram, 163
Avakian, Arra, 27
Avedikian, Gabriel, 57
Avedissian, Onnig, 157
  see also Avetissian
Avenati, Orietta, 25
Avetissian, Minas, 153, 154, 158
Ayvazian, Fred (Fred Levon, Kenneth Flagg), 132
Azarian, Levon, 156
Aznavour, Charles, 141-142, 143, 162, 164

Babajanian, Arno, 139, 142
Baboian, Rose, 173
Bach, J. S., 134, 141
Bagdassarian, Ross, 141
Bagdikian, Ben, 119
Baghdoian, H., 131
Bagramian, Ivan, marshal, 176
Bagratids, see Bagratuni
Bagratuni dynasty, 16-17, 51
Bagratuni, Ashot the Iron, 16, 51
Bagratuni, Arsen, poet, 57
Bagratuni, Sahak, governor, 48
Bagratuni, Sempat, prince, 16
Bagration, P. I., general, 17
Bakounts, Axel (Alexander Tevossian), 82, 83, 85, 87-89, 107, 110, 114, 131
Balakian, Anna, 118
Balakian, Nona, 118, 132
Balasamian, G., 163
Balasanian, Sergei, 142
Baldwin, Oliver, 22, 26
Balekdjian, Krikor, 25
Balmont, K. D., 72
Banker, Marie Sarrafian, 26
Barba, Harry, 132
Bardakjian, Kevork, 42, 127
Barkhudarian, P., 163
Barkhudarian, Sarkis, 138
Baronian, Hagop, 65-67, 69, 128

Baronian, S., 126
Barooshian, Martin, 158
Barsham, king of Assyria, 7
Bartholomew, apostle, 30
Bartholomew the Small, Dominican friar, 34
Basil I the Macedonian, 12-13
Basil II Bulgaroktonus, 16
Basmadjian, Garig, 132, 157
Basmadjian, John V., 170
Baudelaire, Charles-Pierre, 97
Baytarian, Hagop, 130
Beauvoir, Simone de, 46
Beckett, Samuel, 121
Bedikian, A., 127
Bedoukian, Kerop, 26
Bedoukian, Paul, 25
Bedronis, A. J., 24
Bedrossian, Vartkes, 108-109
  see also Petrossian
Beglarian, Grant, 139-140
Bek-Nazarov, Hamo (Hampartsoum Beknazarian), 159-160, 163
Beledian, Krikor, 115
Belinsky, V., 77
Bendiner, Elmer, 26
Benoist-Mechin, J., 148
Berberian, Ara, 143
Berberian, Cathy, 140
Berberian, Hampartsoum, 139
Berberian, Haroutiun, 110
Berberian, Onnig, 143
Berberian, Shahan, 143
Berberian, Vahe, 143
Berberova, Nina, 123
Bergson, Henri, 100
Beshigtashlian, Mkrtitch, 103
Beshigtashlian, Neshan, 101, 174, 177
Bezzerides, A. E., 132
Birkos, Alexander, 160, 163
Blok, Alexander, 92, 123

Boase, T. S. R., 25, 149
Boyadjian, Zabelle, 126
Boyajian, Aram, 163
Boyajian, Dickran, iii, 25
Bramante, D., 147
Braudel, Fernand, 75, 128
Broshian, Berj (Hovannes Der-Arakelian), 61
Brosset, M. F., 25, 126, 127
Bryce, James, 26
Bryusov, V., 72, 92, 103, 105
Buniat Sebastatsi, 168
Burney, Charles, 156, 167, 170
Byron, Lord, 40, 58, 72, 125, 172

Carducci, Giosue, 79
Carzou, Jean (Carnig Zouloumian), 122, 150-151, 158
Carzou, Jean-Marie, 25, 120, 122, 151
Carzou, Nane, 26, 151
Cavouk, Artin (Cavoukian), 155-156
Chahine, Edgar, 150, 157
Chamichian, Mikael, 57
Charanis, Peter, 24
Charents, Yeghishe (Soghomonian), 82, 83, 84-87, 89, 91, 96, 104, 105, 107, 110, 123, 152
Charkhoudian, N., 115
Chateaubriand, Francois-Rene, 57, 103
Chekhov, Anton, 76, 93, 94, 107, 121, 122, 149, 157, 175
Cher (Sarkissian), 141
Chernishevsky, N. G., 64
Chobanian, Arshak (Archag Tchobanian), 101, 103-104
Choisy, Francois, 145
Chookasian, Lili, 142
Chrakian, E. B., 129

Chukadjian, Tigran, 138
Churchill, Winston, 116, 155, 172
Cicero, 10
Claiborne, Craig, 172, 173
Cobb, Irwin, 115
Cocteau, Jean, 120, 162
Cone, Lawrence K., 157
Connors, Mike (Krikor Ohanian), 162
Constantine VII Porphyrogenitus, 13-14, 24
Constantine IX Monomachus, 17-18, 52
Constantine-Silvanus the Paulician, 33
Contenau, Georges, 24
Conybeare, F. C., 35, 126
Curcuas, John (Ohan Kourken), 11-12, 14

Dadourian, Haroutiun, 169
Dante Alighieri, 57, 87
Darbinian, M., 163
Darian, Zarzant, 108
Darius III the Great, 6, 9, 10
Dashtents, Khachik (Tonoyan), 75-76
Dasnabedian, Hratch, 25
David Anhaght (the Invincible), 50
David of Sassoun, epic hero, 44-46, 84, 126, 151
Davoyan, Razmik, 106
Davtian, Vahagn, 106
Debussy, Claude, 135
Dedeyan, Charles, 120, 122, 132
Defoe, Daniel, 76
DeMirjian, Arto, 155
DeMirjian, Arto Jr., 158
Demirjian, Derenik, 92-94, 110, 129-130, 176, 178
Demirjibashian, Yeghia, 64
Derderian, U. S., 170

Der Harootian, Khoren, 158
Der Hovanessian, Diana, 127, 128, 131, 132
Der Melkonian-Minassian, Chake, 126
Der Minassian, Rouben (Pasha), 131
Der Nersessian, Sirarpie, 24, 25, 28, 120, 126, 156-157
Derounian, Avedis, 170
De Van, Mueller M., 170
Dickens, Charles, 57, 61
Diehl, Charles, 15, 24
Digenis Akritas, epic hero, 12, 24
Dikijian, Armine, 142
Dikran, see Tigran
Dionysius Thrax, 50
Djivani (Serop Levonian), 74
Djughayetsi, Hovannes, 75
Dostoevsky, F., 67, 70, 93, 121, 122
Dournovo, Lydia, 157
Dovlatian, Funze, 163
Dowsett, C. J. F., 173
Driault, E., 25
Dulaurier, Jean-Paul E., 127
Dumas, Alexandre (fils), 69
Dumas, Alexandre (pere), 172, 173
Durant, Will, 7, 9, 12, 24
Durrell, Lawrence, 96, 130

Ehrenburg, Ilya, 92, 129
Ekmalian, Makar (Yegmalian), 138, 142
Eliot, Sir Charles, 29
Eliseus, see Yeghishe
Elliot, Lawrence, 35
Elliot, M. E., 26
Emin, Kevork (Karlen Muradian), 104
Emin, Mkrtitich Hovsep (Karapetian), 126

Eminescu, Mihai, 125, 133
Erimena, king of Urartu, 9
Erzinkian, Y., 163
Etmekjian, James, 132
Euclid, 47, 52
Euripides, 46
Eusebius of Caesaria, 30, 50
Evagrius Ponticus, 50
Eznik, see Yeznik

Faustus of Byzantium, see Paustos Piuzantatsi
Feydit, Frederic, 126
Fisher, Robert G., 27
Fitzgerald, F. Scott, 115
Floan, Howard, 132
Fodor, Eugene, 27
France, Anatole, 78, 103, 150
Francis, Arlene (Kazanjian), 162
Franzius, Enno, 24, 127
Frik, 73

Gaboudikian, Sylva, 41, 80, 104-105, 130
Galamian, Ivan, 141
Garabents, Hagop (Jack Karapetian), 110, 111-112
Garibaldi, Giuseppe, 64
Garitte, G., 127
Garo, John H. (Garoian), 155-156
Garsoian, Nina G., 25, 35, 128, 130
Garvarents, Georges, 141, 143
Gavoor, Rouben, 27
Gayane, St., 33
Genet, Jean, 121
Ghazamian, Matvey, 77
Ghazar Parbetsi (Lazarus of Pharpi), 48
Ghazikian, Arsen, 75, 124
Ghevont, Vartabed, 51
Gibbon, Edward, 13, 14, 24, 32, 35
Gibbons, H. A., 25
Gidney, James B., 26

Godel, Robert, 129
Godel, Vahe, 128-129
Godjamanian, Puzant, 158
Goethe, J. W. von, 57, 59, 72, 84, 87, 123
Gogol, N. V., 69, 93, 94, 121
Gombos, Karoly, 157
Gomidas, *see* Komitas
Goncharov, I. A., 121, 123
Goode, A., 127
Gorky, Arshile, *see* Adoian
Gorky, Maxim, 69, 72, 76, 78, 84, 121
Gosh, Mekhitar, 54, 127
Gramsci, Antonio, ii
Granian, Puzant (Chekidjian), ii, 27, 41, 112, 130, 131, 154, 175, 178
Gregoire, Henri, 13, 14, 15, 24
Gregorian, Rouben, 139
Gregory the Illuminator, St. (Grigor Loussavorich), 30, 33, 50
Gregory XIII, Pope, 18
Gregory, Charles, 132
Gregory Magistros, 51-52
Gregory, M. Marcar, 36
Grenville, J. A. S., 26
Greppin, J. A. C., 130
Grigor Loussavorich, *see* Gregory the Illuminator
Grigor Narekatsi (Gregory of Narek), 33, 52-53, 70, 86, 101, 105, 127
 see also Krikor
Grousset, Rene, 27
Gurdjian, Hagop, 151, 158
Guttmann, J., 25

Hagopian, Jacques, 98, 114
Hagopian, Richard, 132
Haig, Vahe (Tinchian), 114, 131
Haigaz, Aram (Chekemian), 114, 131, 177

Haigentz, M., 158
Haik, 3-4, 7, 48, 57
Hakhverdian, Levon, 110
Hamalian, Leo, 129, 131, 178
Hamalian, Linda, 27
Hamasdegh (Hampartsoum Kelenian), 114
Hamid, *see* Abdul-Hamid
Hampartsoumian, *see* Ambartsumian
Haroutiunian, Alexander, 139, 142
Haroutiunian, Haroutiun, 75-76,
Hartunian, Abraham H., 26
Harvey, John, 156
Hassun, Rizqallah, 124, 132
Haxthausen, August von, 127, 176
Haywood, John A., 132
Hazeltine, 13
Heine, Heinrich, 62, 72, 87
Hejinian, John, 132
Hemingway, Ernest, 115, 151, 155
Henry, Francoise, 156
Henry, Sheila, 27
Heraclius, emperor, 12, 50-51
Hermes Trismegistus, 50
Herodotus, 9
Herzen, A. I., 64
Hetum I, king of Cilicia, 18
Hewsen, Robert H., 170
Hogrogian, Rachel, 173
Holmes, E. G. A., 35
Homer, 48, 57, 59, 79, 111
Hoogasian-Villa, Susie, 127
Housepian, Marjorie, iii, 117, 132
Hovannes Otznetsi (John of Otzun), 33, 51
Hovannes Trashkhanakertsi, 51
Hovannes Tulkurantsi, 73, 128
Hovanesian, Edgar, 142

Hovannisian, Richard G., iv, 26
Hovhannes, Alan (Haroutiun Chakmakjian), 135-138, 142
Hovnatan, Naghash, 103
Hovsepian, Aramais, 26
Hripsime (Ripsimia), mother of Czar Samuel of Bulgaria, 16
Hripsime, St., 33
Huebschmann, H., 38, 99
Hugo, Victor, 76, 78, 79, 103, 120
Hussein, Fa'is El, 25
Hussey, J. M., 11, 24, 25

Ibraileanu, Garabed, 125, 133
Igitian, G., 158
Injikian, Aram, 110, 129
Ionesco, Eugene, 121
Iorga, N., 25
Ishak, Adib, 124
Ishkhan, Moushegh (Djenderedjian), 115, 130
Israelian, Margaret, 24
Israelian, Raphael, 152
Issahakian, Avedik, 62, 72, 78, 80, 86, 92-93, 103, 106, 110, 129
Issahakian, L., 163

Jacob of Tsurtavi, 31
Janashian, Mesrob, 57
Janjigian, Anahid, 158
Jansem (Jean Semerjian), 150, 157
Japhet, 3
Jason and the Argonauts, 5
John Chrysostom, St., 50
John of Kerna, 34
John I Tzimisces (Chemeskig), 12, 14, 54
Jude, apostle, 30
Justinian, emperor, 13, 15, 31

Kalpakian, Laura, 132

Kant, Immanuel, 79
Kaputikian, see Gaboudikian
Kara-Murza, Christopher, 138
Karamzin, N. M., 59
Karapetian, Jack, see Garabents
Karapetian, Tigran, 77
Karapetoff, Vladimir, 169
Karnusian, J., 27
Karsh, Yousuf, 155-156, 158
Katcha, Vahe (Katchadourian), 120, 122
Katchaturian, Armen, 155
  see also Khachaturian
Kavafian, Ani, 142
Kavafian, Ida, 142
Kayaloff, Jacques, 26
Kazanjian, Varastad, 170

Keghart, 115
Kelikian, Hampar, 110, 119, 130, 170
Kermian, M., 128
Kevorkian, Richard, 158
Kevorkov, S., 163
Keyishian, Harry, 116
Khachadourian, Sarkis, 150, 157
Khachadourian, Vava Sarkis, 158
Khachaturian, Aram 135-136, 138, 139, 142, 160
Khachaturian, Karen, 142
Khalapian, Zorair, 108
Khanjian, Aghassi, 91
Khantrouni, Dicran, 42
Khanzadian, Sero, 106, 107
Kherdian, David, 26, 132
Khorenatsi, see Movses Khorenatsi
Khosrov II Parvez, 51
Khrakhouni, Zareh (Arto Jumbashian), 115
Khrimian, Mkrtitch (Hairik), 58-59
Kirazian, Dikran, 130
Kochar, Yervant, 151

Kodjian, Varoujan, 142
Koestler, Arthur, 175
Komitas (Gomidas) Vartabed Kevorkian, 105, 135-137, 141, 142, 152
Koriun, 38, 42, 47
Kouchak, Nahapet, 73-74, 103, 128
Koushakdjian, Mardiros, 42
Kouyoumdjian, Dikran, *see* Arlen, Michael
Krautheimer, R., 148, 156
Krikor Datevatsi (Gregory of Datev), 56
Krikorian, Mesrob K., 25
Krum, Bulgarian khan, 15, 16
Ktsoyan, A. S., 170
Kudian, M., 126, 127, 128, 129, 131
Kulhanjian, G. A., 27
Kurkjian, H., 130
Kurkjian, Vahan, 28, 42

Laing, R. D., 120
Lamartine, Alphonse de, 103
Lang, D. M., 25, 27, 28, 35, 38, 133, 156, 167, 170
Langlois, Victor, 126, 127
Lanne, Peter, 25
Lastivertsi, *see* Aristakes
Lawrence, D. H., 116
Leart, M., 25
Lecapenus, *see* Romanus
Legrand, Michel, 141, 143
Lemerle, Paul, 15, 24, 147
Lenin, 61, 86
Leo II the Great, king of Cilicia, 18
Leo III the Isaurian, emperor, 12
Leo VI the Wise, emperor, 13
Leo VI de Lusignan, king of Armenia, 19
Leonardo da Vinci, 147
Leopardi, Giacomo, 57, 79
Lepsius, Johannes, 26

Lermontov, M. Y., 71, 72, 105
Leskov, N. S., 76
Limondjian, Hampartsoum, 138
Lindsay, Jack, 24, 53
Louis, Victor and Jennifer, 27
Lubin, Armen, *see* Shahnour
Lucullus, 10
Lukacz, Bela, 125
Lukacz, Denesh, 125
Lukacz, Georg, 125
Lukacz, Laszlo, 125
Lukacz, Mauritz, 124
Lukacz, Miklosz, 125
Luschan, Felix von, 6
Lynch, H. F. B., 25, 58

Maclean, Fitzroy, 175-176
Macler, F., 126, 127, 157
Maeterlinck, Maurice, 79
Mahakian, Charles, 27
Mahari, Gourgen (Ajemian), 82, 83-84, 110
Malcom, M. Vartan, 27
Malkasian, Stella, 42
Mamikonian, Hmayak, 31
Mamikonian, Shoushanik, St., 31
Mamikonian, Vahan, 31
Mamikonian, Vartan, St., 30-31, 33, 94, 137
Mamoulian, Rouben, 160-161, 163
Manandian, H. A., 24, 128
Mandalian, James, 131
Mandelstam, Osip, 29, 37, 40, 175
Mangurian, Siroon, 158
Mann, Thomas, 23
Manoogian, Haig, 163
Manoogian, Sarepig, 90
Mantaguni, Hovan, 47
Manuelian, P. M., 127, 128, 163, 173
Manuelian, Sooren, 114, 131
Manvell, R., iii

Mardikian, George, 173
Margossian, Marzbed, 127, 128, 131, 132
Marinetti, F. T., 96
Markarian, Maro, 105
Marr, Nikolai, 100
Martirossian, A., 163
Marx, Karl, 61, 90
Mashtots, Mesrob, St., 38-39, 42, 47, 48, 94, 105
Massehian, Hovannes, 75, 76
Matevossian, Grant, 106, 107-108, 130
Matossian, Mary K., 26, 36, 178
Matthew of Edessa, 16, 54, 127
Maupassant, Guy de, 120
Mavian, Salpi, 158
Mavian, Vahram, 115
Mayakovsky, V., 84, 86, 96

Mead, Margaret, 40
Medvedev, Roy, 129
Medzarents, Missak (Medzadourian), 70, 86, 97
Megrian, Leon, 128
Mehmed II, 29-30, 168
Meillet, Antoine, 38, 47, 99
Mekhitar Heratsi, 167, 170
Mekhitar, see Petrossian
Mekhitarists, 57-58
Melias, see Mleh
Melikian, Lucik, 132
Melikian, Mary, 158
Melkonian, Zareh, 42, 113
Mesrob, see Mashtots
Messiaen, Olivier, 122, 141
Metsop, Thomas, 54

Midas, king of Phrygia, 8
Mikhailov, N., 4, 27
Mikoyan, Anastas, 104, 168
Mikoyan, Artem, 168
Milton, John, 57
Minas Lutfi, 114
Mirzayan, Zorair, 115

Mirzoyan, Edward, 142
Mkrtitchian, Levon, 88, 114, 131
Mleh (Melias, Melik-al-Armeni), 12
Moliere, 65, 69
Montgomery, J. W., 24
Mooradian, Karlen, 158
Morgan, Jacques D., 28
Morgenthau, Henry, 25
Movses Khorenatsi, 3, 4, 7, 48-50, 100, 126, 130
Muradeli, Vano, 138-139
Muradian, Vazken, 139-140

Najarian, John Sarkis, 170
Najarian, Peter, 132
Nakian, Reuben, 151-152, 158
Nalbandian, Louise, 27, 131
Nalbandian, Mikael, 64, 101-102, 128
Nansen, Fridtjof, 21, 26
Narekatsi, see Grigor Narekatsi
Narses, general, 11
Nartuni, Shavarsh (Aivazian), 41, 100, 102-103
Natalie, Shahan, 114
Nazarian, Avedis, 139
Nazer, James, 25
Nerses Lambronatsi, 127
Nerses Shnorhali (the Gracious), St., 33, 53-54, 127, 137
Nersessian, Vrej, 142
Nersoyan, Hagop, 36
Neruda, Pablo, 92, 152, 158
Nicephorus II Phocas, 12, 14, 24, 98
Nichanian, Marc, 178
Nicholas I, czar, 149
Niebuhr, R., 118
Nietzsche, Friedrich, 64, 93, 122
Noah, 3
Nogales, Rafael de, 25
Noorigian, Peniamin, 78, 111, 131

Norehad, Bedros, 42, 128, 131
Novello, Adriano Alpago, 157

Obolensky, D., 35
Odian, Yervant, 66-69, 81, 128
Oganissian, G., 163
  see also Hovanesian
O'Hara, Frank, 152, 158
Orbeli, Leon, 168, 170
Orbelian, Stephen, 54
Orfalian, Kevork, 25
Ormanian, Malachia, 36
Oshagan, Hagop (Kufedjian), 79, 92, 98-99, 130
Oshagan, Vahe, 130, 131
Ostrogorsky, George, 14, 15, 24
Oton Matsaetsi, 148
Ottin, Merry, 11, 24

Papazian, K. S., 128
Papazian, Vahram, 77
Paradjanov, Sergei (Sarkis Paradjanian), 159-160, 163
Parlakian, Nishan, 128, 132
Parrot, Friedrich, 59, 127
Pasdermadjian, H., 27
Pasternak, Boris, 85, 104
Paulicians, 32-33, 35, 51
Paustos Piuzantatsi (Faustus of Byzantium), 48, 126
Payne, Elizabeth C., 26
Pel (Belus), 3-4
Pestalozzi, J. H., 60
Petronas, general, 11
Petrossian, Mekhitar, 57
  see also Bedrossian
Piotrovskii, B. B., 156
Plato, 7, 47, 52, 57, 166
Plutarch, 46, 171
Polo, Marco, 18
Porphyrius, 50
Post, Laurens van der, 175
Procopius, 11, 49
Prokhorov, A. M., 132, 142

Pushkin, Alexander, 62, 71, 72, 84, 105
Pushman, Hovsep, 150, 157

Rachmaninov, S., 123, 151
Raffi (Hagop Melik-Hagopian), 62-64, 96, 104
Raffi, Aram, 49, 53, 126
Rameses III, 6
Rapuni, Vahram, 54
Remarque, E. M., 84
Rivoira, G. T., 157
Rodin, Auguste, 151
Roebuck, Carl, 5, 24
Rolland, Romain, 135
Romanus I Lecapenus, 12, 14, 24
Rouben Pasha, see Der Minassian
Roucek, J. S., 27
Rousseau, Jean-Jacques, 60
Runciman, Steven, 12, 24, 35
Rusas I, 8, 9
Rusas II, 9, 166
Rusas III, 9
Russell, James, 128

Sahak, St., 47, 48
Sahakian, Arshak, 127
Sahian, Hamo, 105
Sakharov, Andrei, 26
Samsonian, Simon, 158
Samuel, Bulgarian czar, 15-16
Samuel of Ani, 54, 127
Sanjian, Avedis K., 126
Sapritch, Alice, 162, 164
Sarafian, K. A., 132
Sarafian, Nigoghos, 101
Sarafian, Richard, 163
Sarduri I, 8
Sarduri IV, 9
Sargon II, 8
Sarian, Armine M., 126, 130
Sarian, John, 142, 143
Sarian, Martiros, 85, 153, 158
Sarkis Pidzak, 149

Sarkissian, A. O., 25
Sarkissian, Karekin, 35, 36, 127
Sarkisyanz, Manuel, 26, 129
Saroukhan, Alexander, 128
Saroyan, Aram, 132
Saroyan, William, 76, 116-117, 131, 132
Sartre, Jean-Paul, 121
Sayat-Nova (Haroutiun Sayatian), 71, 73, 74, 86, 100, 105, 108, 128, 136, 139, 160
Sayce, A. H., 38
Schiller, F. von, 59, 62, 72
Schlumberger, G., 24
Schopenhauer, Arthur, 64, 93
Scott, George, 26
Sebeos, 50, 127
Seidel, Ernst, 170
Semiramis (Shamiram), 7-8, 24, 48, 166
Sempat Constable (Sparabed), 54, 127
Seneca, Harry T. Arshak, 170
Serebryakov, K., 123
Servantsediants, Karekin, 46, 59
Setian, Ralph, 131
Sevag, Baruir (Ghazarian), 105, 130
Sevag, Rouben (Chilingirian), 77, 80, 81-82
Shadoian, Jack, 163
Shaginian, Marietta, 123, 127
Shahnour, Shahan (Kerestedjian), 98, 100-102, 130
Shakespeare, William, 57, 62, 69, 71, 76-77, 90, 97, 163
Shalian, A. K., 126
Shalmaneser III, 7
Shamiram, see Semiramis
Shant, Levon (Seghbossian), 92, 98, 130
Sheraton, Mimi, 172
Shiraz, Hovannes, 106

Shirinian, Lorne, 132
Shirvanzadeh (Alexander Movsessian), 70-71, 79, 95, 103, 110, 114, 151, 159
Shoushanian, Vazken, 101
Siamanto (Adom Yarjanian), 77, 80-81, 110, 129
Siculus, Diodorus, 24
Sidal, Garabed, 114
Simeon the Paulician, 33
Simon, apostle, 30
Sinan, 148, 157
Slowacki, Juliusz, 133
Sluzkiewicz, E., 133
Snabian, Boghos, 115
Sokolov, Raymond, 172
Solzhenitsyn, A., 109, 114
Sourian, Peter, 132
Spendiarian, Alexander, 71, 136
Spengler, Oswald, 12
St. George, George, 27
Stalin, J., 22, 85, 92, 115, 139, 172
Stepanian, Angela, 108
Stepanos, Taronetsi (Stephen of Taron), *also called* Asolik (Asoghik), 16, 17, 51, 127
Stokowski, Leopold, 137
Stowe, Harriet Beecher, 94
Strabo, 38
Strzygowski, J., 144, 147, 152, 156
Suleiman the Magnificent, 148
Sundukian, Gabriel, 69, 159
Surmelian, Leon Z., 26, 98, 117, 126, 127, 132
Surmeyan, A., 126
Sutherland, James, 26
Svajian, Stephen, 28

Tabori, Paul, 174
Tacitus, 175
Tagore, R., 96

Tamanian, Alexander, 85, 152
Tamiroff, Akim, 162, 164
Tamrazian, Hrant, 110
Tarian, A., 115
Tashjian, James H., 27
Tashjian, Virginia, 127, 128
Tatikian, Shahen, 106, 107
Tavernier, Jean-Baptist, 128
Tchobanian, see Chobanian
Tcholakian, Arthur, 26, 155-156
Teilhard de Chardin, Pierre, iv
Tekeyan, Charles, 132
Tekeyan, Vahan, 76, 92, 96-98, 130
Tekian, V., 115
Telgadintsi (Hovannes Haroutiunian), 77-78, 90, 111
Ter-Ghewondian, Aram, 25
Ter-Mikaelian, Nerses, 142
Ternon, Yves, 25
Ter-Simonian, Drastamat, 82, 90-91
Tertullian, 30
Terzian, Alicia, 140
Thaddaeus, apostle, 30
Theodora, empress, 32
Theon of Alexandria, 50
Thomas Aquinas, St., 34, 56
Thomson, R. W., 42, 49, 126, 127
Thorossian, H., 28, 132
Thoreau, H. D., 109
Thureau-Dangin, F., 24
Tiglathpileser III, 8
Tigran II the Great, 10-11, 46, 145
Tigranian, Armen, 71, 138
Tikhonov, Nikolai, 92, 129
Timur (Tamerlane), 54, 56
Tiridates III, 30
  see also Trdat
Tiryakian, Edward, 118-119
Tjeknavorian, Loris, 139-140, 142

Tolegian, Aram, 126
Tolegian, Manuel, 158
Tololian, Kohar, 130
Tololian, Minas, 114
Tolstoy, Leo, 61, 62, 67, 71, 151
Topalian, Puzant, 101
Topchian, Edward, 71, 102
Toriguian, Shavarsh, 27
Torkomian, Vahram, 170
Toromanian, Toros, 152
Toros Roslin, 149, 157
Totovents, Vahan, 70, 76, 78, 82, 89-90, 110, 129
Toumanian, Hovannes, 71-72, 86, 94, 103, 110, 128, 136, 138, 160
Toumanoff, Cyril, 18, 25
Tourian, Bedros, 59, 69-70, 97, 103
Tournebize, F., 28
Toynbee, Arnold J., ii-iv, 4, 7, 13, 24, 25, 26, 145
Trdat, architect, 148
Turgenev, Ivan, 57, 76, 94
Turner, J. M. W., 149
Twain, Mark, 94
Tzimisces, see John Tzimisces

Unamuno, Miguel de, 96
Updike, John, 116
Utechin, S. V., 153, 158
Utudjian, Edouard, 157
Uvezian, Sonia, 173

Vahanian, Gabriel, 118
Vahe-Vahian (Sarkis Abdalian), 98, 115
Vakhtang I Gorgaslan, 31
Valery, Paul, 57
Varandyan, Emanuel, 132
Varjabedian, S. H., 178
Varoujan, Daniel (Cheboukiarian), 58, 77, 79-81, 86, 97, 98, 103, 129, 130

Vartan Aykegtsi, 54-55, 87
Vartan, Levon, 115
Vartan Mamikonian, see Mamikonian
Vartan the Great, historian, 54
Vartan, Sylvie, 141, 143
Vartan, Vartanig, 132
Varvarian, H. S., 128
Vazken, Georgian prince, 31
Veou, P. du, 25
Verhaeren, Emile, 84, 96, 103
Verneuil, Henri (Ashod Malakian), 160-162, 163-164
Vernier, D., 35
Virgil, 5, 57
Vorpuni, Zareh, 101
Vrampshapuh, king, 47

Walker, C., 27
Wellesz, Egon, 134, 142
Wells, H. G., 11, 76
Werfel, Franz, ii, 25, 131
Wertsman, V., 27
West, Rebecca, 115
Whitman, Walt, 84, 87
Wilde, Oscar, 78
Wortabed, John, 124

Xenophon, 171, 173
Xerxes, 9

Yacoubian, Adour, 42
Yaghjian, Edmund, 158
Yardumian, Richard, 139-140
Yeghenian, Aghavnie, 26
Yeghishe (Eliseus), 48, 58
Yegmalian, see Ekmalian
Yeretzian, Aram S., 27
Yeroukhan (Yervant Sermakeshkhanian), 77, 82, 129
Yessayan, Zabel, 82, 85, 89, 110
Yessenin, Sergei, 105
Yevtushenko, Y. A., 104
Yezdegird (Yazdgard), 31

Yeznik Goghpatsi (Eznik of Kolb), 47, 126
Zahrad (Zareh Yaldesjian), 115, 131
Zakaria Agouletsi, 75
Zakarian, Almast, 110
Zakarian, Zakar, 149
Zamkochian, Berj, 142
Zanazanian, Adrina, 158
Zarian, Gostan, iii-iv, 92, 95-96, 103, 130
Zarian, Rouben, 60, 90, 95, 128
Zaroukian, Antranik, 115, 131
Zartarian, Rouben, 77-79, 90, 95, 103, 129
Zeno of Citium, 50, 166
Zohrab, Krikor, 77, 81, 103, 129
Zola, Emile, 67
Zorian, Stepan, 92, 94-95, 110
Zweig, Stefan, 94